# GENDER AT WORK IN VICTORIAN CULTURE

*Personally, I have nothing against work, particularly when performed, quietly and unobtrusively, by someone else. I just don't happen to think it's an appropriate subject for an 'ethic'*

Barbara Ehrenreich

# Gender at Work in Victorian Culture

## Literature, Art and Masculinity

MARTIN A. DANAHAY
*Brock University, Canada*

ASHGATE

Published by
Ashgate Publishing Limited
Gower House
Croft Road
Aldershot
Hants GU11 3HR
England

Ashgate Publishing Company
Suite 420
101 Cherry Street
Burlington, VT 05401-4405
USA

Ashgate website: http://www.ashgate.com

**British Library Cataloguing in Publication Data**
Danahay, Martin A.
    Gender at work in Victorian culture.—(The nineteenth century series)
    1.English literature—19th century—History and criticism 2.Art, British—19th century
    3.Art, Victorian 4.Masculinity in literature 5.Masculinity in art 6.Sex role in literature
    7.Sex role in art 8.Work in literature 9.Work in art 10.Great Britain—civilization—19th century
    I.Title
    820.9'353'09034

**Library of Congress Cataloging-in-Publication Data**
Danahay, Martin A.
 Gender at work in Victorian culture / Martin A. Danahay.
    p. cm.—(The nineteenth century series)
 Includes index.
 ISBN 0-7546-5292-0 (alk. paper)
 1. English literature—19th century—History and criticism. 2. Working class in literature.
3. Literature and society—Great Britain—History—19th century. 4. Men—Employment—
Great Britain—History—19th century. 5. Division of labor—Great Britain—History—19th
century. 6. Working class—Great Britain—History—19th century. 7. Masculinity in
literature. 8. Sex role in literature. 9. Working class in art. 10. Work in literature. 11. Men
in literature. I. Title. II. Series: Nineteenth century (Aldershot, England)

PR468.L3D36 2005
820.9'3553—dc22

2005007232

ISBN-10: 0 7546 5292 0

Printed and bound in Great Britain by MPG Books Ltd, Bodmin, Cornwall

Arthur Munby and Ellen Grounds (1873)

# Contents

# List of Illustrations

*Frontispiece*  Arthur Munby and Ellen Grounds (1873)

Plate section is located between pages 84 and 85

# The Nineteenth Century Series
## General Editors' Preface

The aim of the series is to reflect, develop and extend the great burgeoning of interest in the nineteenth century that has been an inevitable feature of recent years, as that former epoch has come more sharply into focus as a locus for our understanding not only of the past but of the contours of our modernity. It centres primarily upon major authors and subjects within Romantic and Victorian literature. It also includes studies of other British writers and issues, where these are matters of current debate: for example, biography and autobiography, journalism, periodical literature, travel writing, book production, gender and non-canonical writing. We are dedicated principally to publishing original monographs and symposia; our policy is to embrace a broad scope in chronology, approach and range of concern, and both to recognize and cut innovatively across such parameters as those suggested by the designations 'Romantic' and 'Victorian'. We welcome new ideas and theories, while valuing traditional scholarship. It is hoped that the world which predates yet so forcibly predicts and engages our own will emerge in parts, in the wider sweep, and in the lively streams of disputation and change that are so manifest an aspect of its intellectual, artistic and social landscape.

Vincent Newey
Joanne Shattock
*University of Leicester*

# Acknowledgements

Writing this book has provided links, both real and virtual, to many people. At UT Arlington Johanna Smith was both an invaluable colleague and an eagle-eyed reader of an earlier version of this manuscript, while Kevin Gustafson was a congenial lunch companion when I took breaks. As I worked on various parts of the manuscript I posted sundry arcane and obscure queries to the VICTORIA listserv and benefited from the generosity of list members who were unstinting with their time and knowledge. The faculty at Haverford College, especially C. Stephen Finley, provided stimulating feedback on a lecture I gave on my Victorian work at their invitation. Ann Colley also through her encouraging remarks after a presentation of my ideas on Ruskin and digging at a conference in Texas helped motivate me to finish that part of the project.

I could not have written this book without the scholarly models provided by James Eli Adams, Joseph Kestner and Herbert Sussman. The following pages are studded with references to their work as I often agree, occasionally disagree, but always respect the achievements represented by their publications. These guys were collectively a tough act to follow.

Across the Atlantic, Trev Lynn Broughton is a kindred spirit toiling in the fields of masculinity and autobiography and I follow her parallel scholarship with great interest and benefit. In a different but related project on Victorian masculinity that indirectly helped clarify some of my ideas in the following pages, David Amigoni has been the very model of a good bloke. I'd also like to express my appreciation to Joanne Shattock and Vincent Newey for allowing my book to join the distinguished ranks of their Nineteenth Century Series and take its place alongside Andrew Dowling's monograph *Manliness and the Male Novelist in Victorian Literature*. Dowling's book on Victorian masculinity inspired me to submit my own manuscript to Ashgate, and I hope the series sees more titles in this area in the future.

Although I do not know who they are, I would also like to thank the anonymous reviewers of my initial manuscript who asked such probing questions and goaded me into explaining my analysis more fully. I have endeavored to answer the challenges of their queries as I revised the book for publication, and if there are any deficiencies in the following pages it is entirely due to my own inability to rise to the level of excellence that they demanded. I'm particularly grateful to them for having corrected my tendency to turn John Tosh (the eminent historian) into Peter Tosh (the reggae artist); although I'm a big reggae fan, the following pages owe very little to Peter Tosh and a great deal to John Tosh.

At Ashgate I was fortunate to find an encouraging editor in Ann Donahue whose enthusiasm for this book made many years of labor worthwhile. One of the nightmares of working on such a huge topic as Victorian concepts of work is the fear that it may never actually see the light of day, and her support of this project was for me a dream come true.

My parents Jeannette and Michael Maddocks have helped tremendously by writing cheques when recalcitrant British institutions refused to take my credit card, and by keeping me supplied with copies of the *Sunday Times* book review section.

My children Emily and Ian are quite rightly pretty indifferent to what I do when I'm not being their father, which is after all one of my most important roles. I would, however, like to thank Ian for saying with an aghast look when I told him how long it had taken to write the following pages 'you mean you've been working on it since before I was born?!' His amazement that anybody would be so foolhardy as to undertake writing a book for that amount of time was a salutary corrective to any remaining delusions of grandeur.

Finally I must acknowledge my partner in work and play, Debbie. Since we are both academics it is often difficult to separate work from leisure in what we do, but both areas of my life are enriched by her presence.

**Permissions to Reproduce Images**

I gratefully acknowledge permission from the following organizations to reproduce the images in this book:

Frontispiece, Figure 6 and Figure 7: The Master and Fellows of Trinity College, Cambridge

Figure 2: Christie's, New York

Figure 3: Wallington, The Trevelyan Collection (The National Trust), The National Trust Photographic Library

Figure 5: Manchester Art Gallery, Manchester City Council

Figure 8: Bodleian Library University of Oxford MS. Top Oxon d 496, fol. 8 (photo of undergraduates building a road)

Figure 9: The Harry Ransom Humanities Research Center, The University of Texas at Austin

Introduction

# Working Definitions

## Defining 'Men'

My title *Gender at Work in Victorian Culture* exploits the ambiguities of the phrase 'at work.' 'At work' denotes both the representation of work and the labor involved in the creation of these representations. The images and texts that I analyze reinforced Victorian ideologies of work yet also frequently contradicted the established division of labor along class and gender lines. I interrogate the gendered division of labor generally, but am primarily concerned in the following pages with the instabilities of masculine identity formation in relation to women. While all the men I analyze subscribed to the Victorian work ethic, they betray the difficulty of squaring their idealized image of masculine, self-disciplined labor with the anxieties about their class and gender position that beset them. The images and texts they created thus encoded the contradictions in the Victorian representation of work as a heroic, self-denying enterprise appropriate only for men in a society where women and the working classes performed a large part of the labor despite the 'separation of spheres' and the invisibility of menial tasks.[1]

The phrase 'at work' also for me conjures up images of roadside signs that I used to see as a child in England. These signs proclaimed 'Caution: Men at Work' and depicted a stylized image of a man with a shovel. This image emblematizes the way in which until recently 'men' and 'work' were so easily equated that they could unproblematically be represented by an image of masculine manual labor. According to this sign 'work' was something carried out by men with shovels, and was in some unexplained manner dangerous for others outside the category 'men.' The shovel was perhaps the most interesting aspect of the image, since the labor usually involved large machinery, but the sign implied that traditional manual labor was the most important symbol of the work. This visual image encapsulated the endurance of the representation of 'work' as an undertaking suitable only for men using their muscles. The shovel in this roadside image was the preeminent sign of muscular masculinity at work, as it is throughout this book.

I will therefore in this book examine the history of the construction of 'gender at work' as a literary and visual trope in the Victorian period and examine the ways in which 'men' and 'work' were used as virtual synonyms and the possibility of female labor excised. The equation of men and work was part of a redefinition of the division of labor in gender terms in the nineteenth century.

Sonya Rose has underscored how 'manliness' was emphasized in this period to exclude women from the category of 'work' and promote the image of the male as breadwinner (132–5).[2] The Victorian period registered the most extreme form of gender segregation yet seen in an industrialized nation. This gender segregation was articulated and reinforced by images and texts that either implicitly or explicitly argued that work was 'manly' and therefore inappropriate for women. Like R. W. Connell I see the definition of masculinity in terms of manual labor and male 'breadwinning' capacity as one of the key transformations in the shift from what he terms 'gentry masculinity' to 'hegemonic masculinity' in its industrial and urban forms (*Masculinities* 185–99).

The next two sections explain the theoretical parameters that govern my choice of subject matter in studying 'gender at work.' This theoretical introduction is in many ways an attempt to explain my multifaceted reaction to the photograph of Arthur Munby and Ellen Grounds that I have used as the frontispiece for this book. This multivocal photograph sums up for me the difficulty of the subject of 'gender at work,' especially the complex class and gender relations between a white-collar worker like Arthur Munby and the working-class woman with whom he is posing.

In this photograph Arthur Munby is standing next to his favorite Wigan 'pit brow girl,' Ellen Grounds. The 'worker' in the photograph is female, but is wearing conventionally masculine clothing. The gentleman posing next to her is not obviously a worker and stands in an ambiguous relationship to his model. Since Munby was a writer and intellectual he has no obvious symbol that would identify him as a 'worker.' Ellen Grounds, by contrast, displays her shovel as if it were a trophy, much like the cricket bat or oar to be found in photographs of Victorian gentleman athletes. Where the cricket bat or oar denoted leisure as well as masculine prowess, Grounds uses the shovel as a symbol of her labor. The image thus brings into focus the Victorian separation of work and leisure as well as codes of masculinity and femininity, and suggests that, despite Victorian ideologies that mandated their difference, their boundaries were permeable.

Munby's posture in this photograph provides a contrast with the arrangement of male bodies in the portraits examined by Louise Purbrick; in conventional Victorian formal portraits the male stance emphasized the power of the subject who faced the viewer surrounded by images that reinforced his social authority. Through dress and bodily posture the portraits represented male dominance of the public sphere of work and its separation from the private and feminine (91). Munby deviates from the conventional pose by standing sideways to the camera, while Grounds stands in the 'masculine' posture found in all the portraits. Also, by including the woman in the photograph Munby reinserts the feminine into the public sphere of male work, supposedly the province only of 'men in black' (Purbrick 93). This photograph encodes therefore contradictory codes of masculinity and femininity, and subverts the visual image of the 'man at work' in the formal portraits analyzed by Purbrick.

This book in its focus on men like Munby is an example of masculinity studies, which is itself indebted to feminism.[3] Masculinity as a term was not even available for analysis until feminist theory had denaturalized gender categories so that they no longer seemed natural, biological givens.[4] Thanks to feminist analysis, a category such as masculinity can be analyzed in social and cultural terms, and the changes in its use charted across history. Many feminists are still understandably uneasy about the very existence of masculinity studies, considering that most scholarly analysis was devoted entirely to a masculinist enterprise for decades anyway. To study men from this perspective can be seen as a retrograde activity.[5]

This study would certainly be retrograde if I were to assume that masculinity is a monolithic category. Rather than view 'men' as an unproblematic category I, like others in the field, approach masculinity as context-specific, mutable and constructed through representations. Such a formulation, however, remains maddeningly vague and the ambition of this book is to give concrete examples of such forces literally 'at work,' or encoded in the activity of representing labor by Victorian men.

I also define 'men' as a relational category that must be analyzed in combination with the term 'women.'[6] Thus the photograph of Arthur Munby and Ellen Grounds is fascinating because it has a man and woman posing in front of the camera, but their bodies and clothing raise subversive questions about masculinity, femininity and work in the Victorian period. The proximity of their bodies represents visually the interplay between the man as a 'gentleman,' marked by clothing and bodily posture, and the woman who would not under Victorian conventions be dressed as a female because of her trousers and shovel. The shovel in particular was often seen as a masculine tool, as it is in Ford Madox Brown's painting *Work*, for instance, and disrupts the identification of Ellen Grounds as feminine despite her being biologically a woman. Her 'masculinity' in this photograph represents visually the subversion of gender boundaries to be found in Munby's diary, and both the visual and textual representations of gender suggest that 'men' and 'women' were interdependent categories.

I would also characterize this book as part of a 'second wave' of masculinity studies. The 'first wave' was epitomized by excellent books by James Eli Adams and Joseph Kestner. These analyses used a typology approach, in which representative categories of masculinity were generated to bring together texts, in Adams' case 'dandies' and 'saints,' and in Kestner's types such as the knight in armor. Adams' incisive opening pages in *Dandies and Desert Saints*, which I wish I'd written myself, sketch much of the terrain that this book also covers. Adams announces his subject as the way in which the 'manliness of intellectual labor' was undercut by Victorian domestic ideology which implicitly feminized men's work (1–2). His analysis then departs from my own by emphasizing that he addresses 'affirmations of masculine identity' that attempted to compensate for the gendered contradictions in the subject positions of male Victorian intellectuals. Rather than examine the 'affirmative' masculine identities in the 'models' of 'the gentleman, the prophet, the dandy, the priest and the soldier' (Adams 2), I analyze the ideological contradictions in the masculine subject position as endemic to male identity itself. Under the rubric of 'the man at work' I analyze the ideological contradictions caused by the Victorian division of labor for the artist and writer.

My analysis is thus closer in spirit to Kaja Silverman's *Male Subjectivity at the Margins*. Silverman deploys a Freudian and Lacanian template to unpack the ideological contradictions in heteronormative masculine identity. Like Silverman I see masculine identity as undergirded by the mechanisms of splitting, projection and displacement. Unlike Silverman I locate the source of these ideological contradictions in the Protestant work ethic and the Victorian division of labor, not in Oedipal conflicts, castration anxiety or the construction of identity in Lacanian terms of the Imaginary and Symbolic. I argue throughout this analysis that the contradictions in Victorian male subjectivity were caused by an ideology that termed work as masculine and muscular; this caused particular problems for Victorian male intellectuals whose work could be viewed as feminine because it was often carried out in the domestic space and certainly did not involve muscles.

In addition to Adams and Kestner, I am indebted to Herbert Sussman's *Victorian Masculinities*. Sussman does not engage his subject through typology but through an analysis of ideological contradictions that he discerns to be a hallmark of Victorian masculinity. Sussman also begins to grapple with the issue of cross indexing Victorian painting and writing through such contradictions through a brief discussion of such images as Ford Madox Brown's *Work* (which is the subject of my fourth chapter). His book is therefore an important precedent for my own analysis, and I hope that the following pages expand and enrich the analysis that he inaugurated in *Victorian Masculinities*.

The foremost contribution of this book, therefore, is to extend this kind of ideological analysis of masculinity to a greater range of visual images and texts. I interrogate the ideologies of work in terms of class and gender encoded in paintings and photography as well as written material.[7] It is in some ways much easier to interrogate visual images such as the photograph of Munby and Grounds in terms of gender identification than literary texts. Some excellent analyses of masculinity in terms of clothing have been published, most notably John Harvey's *Men in Black* and David Kuchta's *The Three Piece Suit*. *Men in Black* charts how a veritable uniform of black clothing for men was created in the nineteenth century, and *The Three Piece Suit* examines class relations through the adoption of an aristocratic form of dress by middle-class men.[8] Examining written texts for such signifiers of gender is more problematic because, just as men and women can 'pass' for another gender if suitably disguised, in language a man can 'write as' a woman or a woman write a book under a male pseudonym. I am particularly interested in the following pages in cases where men identified imaginatively with and 'wrote as' people of a different gender or class and attempted to transcend what were in the Victorian period held to be immutable biological and social markers.

I analyze men whose work placed them in Victorian terms symbolically close to the feminine, but their intellectual labor was also class specific. For this reason I don't examine milliners, cooks or other workers whose physical labor was potentially feminized but who were considered of a lower class than male intellectuals. I could indeed have included such men but this would have been a different book as a result, much closer in spirit to such studies as E. P. Thompson's *The Making of the English Working Class* or Regenia Gagnier's *Subjectivities* in focusing more on working-class culture as represented by the working classes themselves.[9] While my analysis is similar to such recent studies of male subjectivity as those by Arlene Young and Jim Hammerton, who examine the subject position of lower-middle-class men, I examine a higher social class.[10]

I do not examine how the working classes represented themselves, but how they were represented by men from a class position that would have been considered 'above' them in Victorian terms. The men in this study are of high social status and would have been recognized from their clothing and language as having privileged backgrounds; they would have considered themselves 'gentlemen.'[11] As Karen Volland Waters remarks, 'if a man could appear to attain prosperity without resorting to manual labor, he might be considered a gentleman' (17); this opposition between the gentleman who does not resort to manual labor and the representation of labor via images of the working classes points to one of the schisms in Victorian middle-class masculinity that I chart in the following pages. While a gentleman's identity was often defined in opposition to the working classes, manual labor was also represented as the preeminent symbol of manly industry, which created a contradiction between the representation of 'manliness' and the subject position of the male artist or writer.

My interest in this area is similar to Patricia E. Johnson's in *Hidden Hands*. Where she approaches the topic from the vantage point of working-class women, I approach work from the perspective of middle-class men. In an excellent passage in her Introduction, Johnson discusses the relationship between gender and class ideologies in the Victorian period that demonstrate 'the masculine bias in the construct of the Victorian working class and the middle-class bias in its construct of femininity' (8).[12] The men I analyze in this book are caught between a masculinity that they represent in working-class terms, and a middle-class identity that is implicitly feminized. Contradictory codes of class and gender thus create ideological conflicts within Victorian masculinity.

I do not completely jettison the category 'men' in my analysis of Victorian masculinities. The problem with rejecting 'men' as a category can be seen in John Stoltenberg's *Refusing to be a Man*. Stoltenberg is not rejecting his masculinity totally but rather trying to reject those aspects of masculinity that oppress women. His book is a guilt-ridden exploration of the many injustices perpetrated under the rubric 'men.' He cannot, however, simply reject his ascribed social identity no matter how much he dislikes it, and his revulsion at oppression leads him to ignore the positive social uses of a term like 'men.' The problem is not in the term itself but in the ways in which it is used.

Given that masculinity operates in a wider cultural environment, the crucial question becomes whether or not representations of men are repressive or empowering. I pose this question rather than reject the category 'men' outright. Different deployments of the label 'men' need to be analyzed in terms of their 'cultural work,' or their ideological import, rather than simply negated as Stoltenberg does in 'refusing' to be a man. While all the men in this study would have professed themselves to be defenders of women, the effect of their representations was often unintentionally to make women's lives more difficult. The effect of their representations was determined by the wider culture and they could not, just as Stoltenberg cannot, simply 'refuse to be a man.'

Problematic uses of the category 'men' are often referred to as 'hegemonic masculinity.' This term is used by authors such as Michael Kimmel and R. W. Connell to denote a dominant form of masculinity against which other ways of behaving are considered deviant or inferior. I would qualify this use of masculinity by pointing out that Antonio Gramsci, from whose thought the term 'hegemony' derives, did not see 'hegemony' as something only imposed from without but also as a way of thinking and behaving that was internalized by the subject.[13] Stoltenberg objects to a 'hegemonic masculinity' that is used to oppress women because he is afraid he has internalized it as part of his identity. To 'refuse to be a man' is to reject 'hegemonic masculinity' in both these senses, but I would argue that it is impossible to escape being interpellated by gender identity within a social context and that it behooves men to discriminate between repressive and enabling forms of masculinity.[14]

The impossibility of refusing one's gender identity was even more evident in the Victorian period than it is now. The idea of 'refusing to be a man' would be unthinkable in Victorian terms. Even the most subversive sexual dissident analyzed in these pages, Arthur Munby, is recognizably a man in his photographs and would have identified himself as masculine. Rather than reject masculinity and recognize himself as a 'feminine man' (a contradiction in terms in Victorian culture) he played out his resistance to masculinity through an imaginative identification with women like Grounds, who dressed like a man and carried out physical labor.[15] Within the cultural field of Victorian gender identities being a dandy was about as close as any man could come to rejecting his masculinity.[16]

I often make generalizations in the following pages about 'Victorian' men. Like the category 'men,' the term 'Victorian' can be called into question. There are obvious questions about when to begin the 'Victorian' period; in 1832 with the First Reform Bill, in 1837 with Victoria's ascension to the throne, or at a point where Britain ceased to be an agricultural and became an industrialized and urban society. My own study begins in the 1840s when, I would argue, the effects of industrialization on the gender and class definitions of work began to be felt most strongly. Like Rose, I believe that gender relations were transformed by industrialization and see the 1840s as a crucial moment in the creation of gendered ideologies of work. This was the period in which 'male unionists…began to argue that women's hours and jobs ought to be restricted' (Rose 57) and marks the beginning of a sustained effort that lasted up until the 1880s to define 'work' as appropriate solely for men and to restrict the possibilities of women's employment. In the 1880s the New Woman and new technologies challenged this assertion of masculine prerogative at work. New technologies of writing helped subvert the gendered definition of 'man's work' and provoked a crisis of male self-definition that is visible in many late Victorian texts, especially in the novels of George Gissing.

Male Victorian identity was modeled on the Protestant work ethic. Max Weber in *The Protestant Ethic and the Spirit of Capitalism* summarizes this ethos: guided by John Calvin's teaching, the 'work ethic' assumed that all people, especially men, were constrained to labor by the will of God, and that thrift and sobriety were necessary for salvation.[17] These ideals find their expression in the Victorian period in an emphasis upon self-discipline, self-denial and hard work. During the Victorian period 'everyone proclaimed that man was created to work' and so the refusal or inability to work was castigated and seen as 'a moral and social sin' (Houghton 189). The compulsion to labor was thus made an integral part of normative masculinity.

Weber suggests that the virtues inculcated by the Protestant work ethic were best suited to the 'clerk, labourer, or domestic worker' (139) which leaves open the question of how these values would relate to intellectual occupations.[18] The problem posed for such intellectual workers is that 'inactive contemplation' is valueless in this schema of physical labor; the work ethic was enforced through 'passionate preaching of hard continuous bodily or mental labour' (158), but it is of course easier to measure physical activity than contemplative studies that may look 'inactive' on the physical level. This was an especially important problem because 'idleness' was seen as inviting the influence of Satan and the flesh (Weber 157; Houghton 245). Mental labor was not obviously a form of exertion in the same way as physical toil, and could thus be seen as idleness. Idleness, it was believed, would lead to sin and should be repudiated through self-disciplined physical exertion.

The imperative to work was thus a counter to the threat of sexuality. Weber does not comment on the gender basis of this doctrine, but, as we shall see, while work was seen as antidote to temptation for men, it was viewed as having the opposite effect on women. For women to work was often represented as releasing a dangerous sexuality rather than repressing sexual desire. Therefore, while it was appropriate for men to work, for women it was seen as an inappropriate libidinal activity.

The obligation to work was most often expressed in the Victorian terms as a 'duty.' William Wordsworth summed up this concept in his 'Ode to Duty,' a poem that navigates a complex path between a divine imperative and a self-imposed discipline.[19] The poem begins by invoking duty as 'Stern Daughter of the Voice of God' (line 1) but this disciplinary force is tempered by an appeal to 'freedom.' By the middle of the poem Wordsworth argues that 'my submissiveness was choice' (line 45) so that even though he will be Duty's 'bondsman' his self-discipline is freely chosen. The poem carries out in microcosm the redefinition of duty from a divine edict into an appeal to a 'spirit of self-sacrifice' (line 62) that esteems self-denial and self-restraint above all else. It encapsulates within one poem the translation of the Protestant work ethic from a divine edict into a self-imposed discipline.

Wordsworth's poetry was widely influential in the Victorian period, and lines from the 'Ode to Duty' in particular were reproduced in Elizabeth Gaskell's *Ruth*, which Stephen Gill characterizes as 'a novel about Duty' (143).[20] While *Ruth* definitely does explore ideas of duty and self-sacrifice it is also a novel about women's work. Disturbingly, the heroine of the novel dies as a result of her labors as a nurse, and so joins the gallery of expiring women workers that I discuss in Chapter 2. Rather than a male Bildungsroman in which the protagonist finds a vocation, the novel reinforces the idea that work is at some level fatal for women. Where work countered sin for men, in Gaskell's schema it redeems the woman through death. As we shall see in Chapter 2, Gaskell is in this narrative participating in a literary and visual tradition that equated women, work and death.

Perhaps the most important distinction between the original 'Protestant work ethic' and its Victorian version is the internalization of the compulsion to work as a mark of masculine morality.[21] Where originally work may have been a necessity for all people, in the Victorian period it was seen primarily as a masculine duty. Whereas early in the century Thomas Carlyle specifically invoked God as the origin of the compulsion to work, by the 1880s the compulsion to work was described as a moral issue and a question of masculine character. The drive to work became less a divine order than a discipline that originated within the subject. Following the model of the internalization of discipline proposed by Norbert Elias in *The Civilizing Process*, the compulsion to work in the Victorian period was increasingly represented as a natural masculine desire to labor as part of a healthy psyche. This emphasis is made explicit in a letter by the Rev. R. Shilleto to the Headmaster of Harrow quoted by David Newsome:

> Do, my dear Montagu, throw into your Sixth Form your own love of work. Make them feel the manliness, the health, the duty…of work. (Newsome 195)

Education, as an essential part of the civilizing process, is here represented as reinforcing work as integral to masculine health.[22] To embody masculinity most successfully, the Headmaster is exhorted to inculcate an internalized 'love of work' that will presumably last well beyond the Sixth Form and shape the adult character of his pupils. Work and manliness are assumed to be equivalent terms in this list, which represents work as 'healthy' for both body and mind.[23]

There is continuity from Thomas Carlyle through to George Gissing that marks them as Victorian men in their belief that work was a necessity for a healthy male identity. Often these same men found it difficult to live up to the Victorian ideal of the diligent 'man at work,' who sacrificed his desires and practiced self-denial and self-control, and some rebelled overtly against its constraints. Nonetheless, they are all marked as Victorian men in the terms of my study through their belief in the centrality of work for manliness and the need to repress desire in favor of sustained, self-denying labor.

So integral was the idea of working for masculine identity that even a radical figure like William Morris could not imagine a world in which men chose not to work. Instead in *News from Nowhere* he imagines a world in which work has become pleasure and every man (though not necessarily every woman) works voluntarily. This is obviously a Utopian solution to the perennial problem of the existence of dirty, unpleasant or even dangerous jobs. Far from rejecting work as a category, Morris makes the internalization of the work ethic even more pervasive so that people labor not from economic necessity but because of enjoyment. This is the most extreme example of the internalization of the work ethic and the way in which it replaced the compulsion to toil as an economic necessity with a self-imposed duty in Victorian texts. While Morris wanted to escape the existence of oppression, as a product of Victorian culture he could not reject the definition of work in terms of masculine self-discipline.

## Culture at Work

The unifying term in my title is 'culture.'[24] The term plays a crucial role in bringing together 'men' and 'work.' All the men I analyze in this book produce 'culture' as part of their work, and these days would be labeled as working in the 'culture industry.' 'Culture industry' is another term, like 'feminine men,' that would make no sense in the Victorian context. 'Industry' in the Victorian context refers to the creation of material goods, as well as to a host of ideals connected with work, but not to books and paintings. These were not 'industrial' products but part of 'culture' in the Arnoldian sense of a high culture that represents the highest aspirations of a society. All the men in this book are involved in creating high culture, and would see themselves as distinct from working-class men who produced material goods.

I use 'culture' in a way that aligns me with cultural studies, but there is a crucial ambiguity in the term that informs my choice of subject in this book. Raymond Williams charted the shift in meaning of 'culture' in *Culture and Society*, noting how it was increasingly used to refer to a 'way of life' rather than 'high culture.' While cultural studies dismiss the distinction between 'high' and 'low' culture, the residual meaning of the term 'culture' as referring to works of high social status remains. I am interested in this book in men who were artists and intellectuals and would consider themselves 'cultured' in the Arnoldian sense, which would set them apart socially from the working classes. Often this distinction was more imaginary than real, but it was a powerful dividing line nonetheless.

The subjects of my book, particularly John Ruskin and William Morris, used the category of 'work' to try to cross class boundaries and express their support for the working classes. Arnold, by contrast, used 'culture' as a unifying principle in much the same way to oppose the forces of 'mechanization' and Philistinism (Arnold 96–7). However, the class politics of Arnoldian culture were quite different from theirs, and his concept of culture was articulated in opposition to the 'anarchy' of working-class radicalism. Arnold's class politics provide a useful corrective to the rosy use of 'culture' as a universal glue to bind together different social groups. Ruskin, for instance, had to admit that his attempt to write to 'the labourers of England' in *Fors Clavigera* was failing, although he hoped that over time his message would be appreciated (*Fors* II 121). Like the Ferry Hincksey road project that I discuss in Chapter 6, Ruskin in his writing and utopian projects found that Victorian class difference could not be erased so easily. Even though Arnold would have argued that culture as 'perfection' transcended class positions, he was under no illusions that his evangelical attempts to reform Victorian society through a secular religion would be welcomed by the middle or working classes. His recognition of Victorian class politics is therefore a useful corrective both to contemporary celebrations of 'culture' as a universal panacea and to the tendency of the Victorian intellectuals that I analyze to forget the differences between themselves and their working-class subjects. When they celebrated 'work' writers from Carlyle to Ruskin would forget the differences between their labors and the kind of toil expected by the working class subjects that they represented in texts and images.

The subjects of my book are therefore all implicated in Arnoldian 'high' culture even when they celebrate working-class labor.[25] Arthur Munby, for instance, although he worked in an undemanding clerical position, had aspirations to be a poet. He felt his taste for images of working-class women simply marked him as ahead of his time, and that people in the future would be able to appreciate the aesthetic qualities of women like Ellen Grounds. The writers and artists in this book quite obviously aspired to a position in high culture, although they often sought to make cultural artifacts either more accessible to the working classes, or to embody the working classes in print or oil paint. While I use the term 'culture' to denote a shared set of beliefs about how the world is organized, I am also still incorporating a residual sense of the word as referring to creative artifacts that have a high social status. This interest in 'culture' as Arnold would have understood it is what sets this book apart from an art historical, social historical or sociological analysis and guides my choice of subject matter.

All the men studied in this book possessed what in contemporary terms would be called 'cultural capital.' Quite often this 'cultural capital' was at odds with their actual financial resources, as it was for Ford Madox Brown for instance. Brown worked in oil painting, which had high social status, but was frequently under pressure to earn money as quickly as possible to support his household. He had great difficulty defining his own social standing because of this status incongruity. While aware of this incongruity, Brown did not express it directly but instead represented it through his paintings of working-class men. His attempt to elevate working-class navvies to noble heroes is an imaginative compensation for the uncertainties of his own position as a man who aspired to the status of a 'gentleman' but had to work for a living.

I must confess that I am myself a victim of many of the ideologies of work that I analyze in this book, especially as a salaried professional who carries out what is often unpaid overtime. The boundaries of my 'work' are extremely blurred, as they are for many of the men I study, and it is frequently unclear whether I am working or at leisure. Many people would consider reading a Victorian novel a leisure activity, although of course for me it is work. My work also often puts me, like the subjects of my book, in situations that place me symbolically close to what is thought of still, despite decades of feminist analysis, as 'women's work.'

For instance, I would in the past quite frequently take care of my preschool children in public during the day, and feel some anxiety because I might be perceived as somehow less than masculine because I was not 'at work.' Did people think, I wondered, that I was unemployed? Or a male nanny? Was I perceived as just 'babysitting' even though I was as much a parent as my wife? Such thoughts would make me angry as I experienced the unspoken social pressure on me to conform to models of masculinity, especially the role of the breadwinner. I was on a personal level experiencing both the 'substantial changes in the division of labour' that MacInnes describes in *The End of Masculinity* (1–2), but also the pressure of social expectations that lagged far behind such structural changes. This personal experience has provided much of the impetus for this analysis.

This book also continues an analysis of masculinity inaugurated with my first book. For the cover of *A Community of One* I used a painting of Charles Reade in his study and analyzed it in terms of the effaced female presence in the room. Trev Lynn Broughton has since extended this analysis to consider the status of men in their studies as part of her ongoing examination of Victorian masculinity.[26] I have developed my own analysis in another direction and would now view that image as one of a man at work, with all the inherent contradictions of male intellectual labor in the Victorian domestic context.

Writing this book has often led to an amusing (for me at any rate) response when people have asked me what I am researching; I would tell them that I was 'working on work' and then marvel at the incredible complexity generated by the ideological contradictions in this apparently innocuous phrase. To even answer the question I would have to consider what was meant by 'work' and then deal with the self-consciousness of studying what one is doing whilst engaged in writing. There is a less amusing side to 'working on work' in that it is a frustratingly slippery category. Writing this book has often felt like trying to map the contours of a blob that changed shape every time that I thought I had its boundaries fixed. My problem is akin to that sketched by Connell in his essay on 'Intellectuals and Intellectual Work' where he tries to dispel the mystification of writing as work whilst saying that 'in writing this paper I am doing a job of work' (*Which Way is Up?* 238). The tautology 'job of work' shows how such discussions of writing as work can seem like an exercise in repetition of categories.[27]

I sometimes wish that I was not so interested in the word 'work.' As I shall explain in the next section, it is a complex term and it was ubiquitous in the Victorian period. Setting aside the Victorian period for a moment, the term 'work' was also invoked frequently where I lived in Texas while writing this book, and is still a problematic term. Texas is a 'right to work' state. The phrase sounds vaguely empowering and good for workers until you realize what it really means. My wages were much lower than colleagues in other states because 'right to work' legislation is really aimed at weakening unions. In fact, if I were to have gone on strike for more pay I could have been summarily fired; so a 'right to work' statute in Texas meant that I lost the right to refuse to work.

This is just one example, and a particularly glaring one, of how the word 'work' can be used for hegemonic purposes. Much more subtle are the ways in which people are encouraged to identify themselves in terms of their work and to pass judgment on those who do not work. Weber, in an overly pessimistic conclusion to *The Protestant Ethic and the Spirit of Capitalism*, refers to 'the cage' of a soulless, mechanized approach to life that he sees as the legacy of the work ethic (181–3). This conclusion ignores the widespread desire for meaningful activity that leads people to labor whether they are paid to do so or not. I would not myself feel comfortable if I did not work, but analyzing the effect of a term like 'work' in the context of Victorian culture helps show the ways in which the term continues to have disturbing implications. 'Work' can be an oppressive term, especially if one is a worker caught within its many contradictions. 'Work' is often used as a stick with which to beat the lower classes, both in the Victorian period and today. It is also a term, however, that many people, including myself, have internalized and we must live with its ideological contradictions. The men in this book represented these contradictions in their writing and painting. The chief difficulty for all of them, as for me, was in defining the term 'work.'

**Defining 'Work'**

Work is a term that can encompass the whole range of human activities, and is a complex signifier that shifts with context.[28] Anything can at some point be considered 'work' if it results in payment or is carried out at the behest of somebody else. The most obvious example of this is child care. An adult attending to the needs of a child can have a range of possible meanings, from a parent caring for a child, to a casual babysitter looking after a child for a short term while the parents are away, to a teacher supervising children for large parts of a day on behalf of the State. These activities in themselves could provide the basis for an entire book as they bring into consideration the history of the family, the relationship between children and labor, and the creation of a national system of compulsory education. In the Victorian period it would have been especially difficult to recognize any of these activities as work if they were carried out by women, because work was defined as the prerogative of masculinity.[29]

Work was the foundation of male identity in the Victorian period, but as an unstable marker it proved an insecure basis on which to build subjectivity.[30] Many studies have addressed the ways in which the Victorian attempt to construct women's identity on the work/woman axis was riddled with contradictions and fissures.[31] The most striking example of this is sewing, which was an occupation that cut across class and gender lines. The ubiquity of sewing made it possible for male authors and artists like Thomas Hood and Richard Redgrave to create images with broad popular appeal. However, such images also elided the distinction between the 'lady' and the working woman, or even worse the 'fallen' woman and thus drew upon problematic Victorian gender ideologies.[32]

Equally, male attempts to represent work as rough, ennobling labor foundered on the class distinctions between 'brain work' and what they represented as 'real' work. While male intellectuals might romanticize working-class labor, their own work had little in common with the manual labor they idealized. They thus subverted their own social position while advocating the primacy of manual labor.

What counts as 'work' shifts across histories and cultures.[33] While it may be argued that this is true for any word (as a glance at the *Oxford English Dictionary* will reveal) some words are more important than others. The word for 'turnip,' for example, means a different vegetable in England and Scotland, but apart from a culinary surprise for tourists the difference has little ideological import.[34] The term 'work,' on the other hand, was used from such radically different perspectives in the Victorian period that it is vital to map the ideological implications in the deployment of the term. Not only did the word mean radically different things to different people, but it also underwent significant changes in reference. In the Victorian period the term 'work' was redefined in terms of gender.[35]

In brief, certain forms of labor in this period were defined as inappropriate for women and thus gendered male. While women continued to work in many occupations, such as mining for example, the assumption was articulated from the 1840s onward that these forms of labor were appropriate only for men. The redefinition of occupations and the Chartist call for 'universal manhood suffrage' are part of a gender conflict in this period in which male dominance was asserted at the expense of the woman worker (Johnson *Hidden Hands* 10). While there has been much excellent work on how this process affected women and separated them from the masculine world of 'work,' more attention needs to be paid to how these changes affected men.

In particular, the subject of this book is men whose labor placed them in close proximity to 'women's work.' This was often represented through an imagery of hands; a writer's hands would be soft and not calloused, whereas the men they idealized would have rough and dirty skin. Their intellectual labor was thus not immediately or obviously 'masculine' and as a result they faced difficulties in representing what they did as manly work. Just as women's bodies were 'unstable' so were men's when it came to representing work; men's hands, if uncalloused and clean, could appear dangerously close to a woman's hand rather than a worker's hand.[36]

Arthur Munby is again a crucial reference point in this regard. One of the photographs in the Munby collection is of a pair of hands. There is some ambiguity as to whose hands are being shown; they could be Hannah Cullwick's, although the body behind the hands, which is blurred and indistinct, seems to be muscular. The muscles and the calluses on the hand would seem to mark them as masculine. However, while muscles are thought of as a sign of masculinity, Cullwick herself was very proud of her own muscles and her strength. The ambiguities of Munby's photograph of hands destabilize visually, as his diaries do in writing, the boundaries between masculine and feminine, and women's work and man's work. This is a territory that Munby mapped extensively and which makes his diaries a unique contribution to the interrogation of Victorian class and gender ideologies expressed through the body, especially the hands. As he noted frequently, his hands compared to Hannah Cullwick's seemed the more 'feminine.'

Many of the men in this study idealized working-class manual labor as a compensation for their own class and gender anxieties, such as in Ford Madox Brown's painting *Work*. The muscular working-class figures in the center of the canvas implicitly define work as manual labor. This is obviously an idealization since working-class men were not high in social status in the Victorian period and Brown has to explain why he is turning the 'English navvy' into a heroic figure in his canvas. He was not alone in making working-class men into heroes; Dickens carried out a similar process in *Hard Times*. This idealization of the working classes reverses the usual narrative of middle-class influence over the working classes.

As Ruth Danon has argued in the context of the novel, in the newly industrialized society of nineteenth-century England, the working classes provided English middle-class novelists with their most powerful heuristic in understanding what she terms 'the myth of vocation' (3). Danon makes a persuasive case for the symbolic importance of the working classes in the Victorian novel, but in this study I will focus on the ideological contradictions that such a romanticization of working-class labor produced in male intellectual discourse rather than the 'myth of vocation' favored by the middle classes.[37] In this book I examine intellectuals whose subject position was contradictory because, while at one level they subscribed to conventional Victorian ideologies concerning the class and gender status of work, at another level their own experience did not fit the prevailing ideology.

In contemporary theoretical terms these male intellectuals were aligned more closely with the 'feminine' subject than the 'masculine' subject. All these men idealized women in part as compensation as an antidote to their own anxieties about their subject positions. The most extreme example of this is Arthur Munby who, thanks to his own radically unstable masculinity, idealized working-class women and their labors. The proximity of intellectual labor to domestic work is what caused many male intellectuals particular anxiety.

The Victorian division between the home and work that came with industrialization was the source of the problem for intellectuals. Their work frequently placed them in the domestic sphere. As Arlene Young has argued, 'the counterpart of the domestic woman was the new bourgeois gentleman' (5), but Young does not go on to suggest the anxiety that the proximity of the 'domestic' and masculinity would provoke. Men who would combine daily domestic tasks such as balancing the family accounts and managing servants were implicitly eroding the boundary between masculine work and domesticity. Writing or painting were 'work' while the other activities were not according to conventional ideology because they were domestic and associated with women. Yet all men recognized that at some level all these activities could be thought of as 'work' and that the boundaries between work and domestic labor were for them blurred and unstable.

Given the increasing separation of work and home in the Victorian period as industrialization created more and more factories and offices, the home became associated with relaxation and leisure, not with work. Men found at home during the day were assumed to be out of place, their natural environment being defined as the public sphere. This ideology is analyzed most cogently by Florence Nightingale in *Cassandra*:

> If one calls upon a friend in London and sees her son in the drawing-room, it strikes one as odd to find a young man sitting idling in his mother's drawing-room in the morning. For men, who are seen much in those haunts, there is no end of the epithets we have; 'knights of the carpet', 'drawing-room heroes', 'ladies' men'. But suppose we were to see a number of men in the morning sitting round a table in the drawing-room, looking at prints, doing worsted work, and reading little books, how we should laugh! A member of the House of Commons was once known to do worsted work. Of another man was said, 'His only fault is that he is too good; he drives out with his mother every day in the carriage, and if he is asked anywhere he answers that he must dine with his mother, but, if she can spare him, he will come in to tea, and he does not come.' (Nightingale 23)

The pejorative terms 'knight of the carpet' and 'drawing-room heroes' show how being in the domestic sphere emasculated Victorian men. 'Knights' and 'heroes' should be out in the meads slaying dragons and rescuing damozels, not having tea with the ladies.[38] This was the kind of ideal reinforced by Ruskin in 'Of Queen's Gardens' when discussing the obedience of the 'young knight' to his lady (*Sesame* 96). Of course, Victorian middle- and upper-class men were not out slaying dragons when they were not at home, and were just as likely to be dining in their clubs as performing heroic acts. Such constructions as 'knights of the carpet' invert the image of 'Captains of Industry' found in Carlyle that I will discuss in the next chapter; one powerful strain of Victorian 'hegemonic masculinity' represented men as aggressive and military figures who would rather wield a sword than hold a cup of tea.[39] 'Physical prowess and readiness for combat' were defined as essential qualities of 'manliness' in this period (Tosh 111) and this kind of masculinity appealed not only to Thomas Carlyle but also to Samuel Smiles who admired the way in which 'tailors, shoemakers, mechanics, weavers and ploughmen' could be turned into disciplined military units (Briggs 127–8). For this reason, men who would rather do worsted work or take a drive with their mother were 'ladies' men,' not in the sense that they were veritable Casanovas but in the sense that their preference made them appendages to 'ladies' rather than autonomous and aggressive males.

Nightingale's comments underscore the vexed position of men working at home. A man at home during the day would be viewed as a potential 'knight of the carpet' even if he had a legitimate reason for being there. It is for this reason that the men in this book show a profound interest in and sympathy for women's work such as sewing or housekeeping. They themselves occupied a fraught position as 'home workers' and were sensitive in ways that other men were not to the gender implications of 'work.' A few were also equally aware of the class issues involved in the valuation of work, and recognized not only that the activities of genteel ladies could be considered work, but also that many working-class women labored in occupations that were conventionally defined as the prerogative of men.

Texts like Isabella Beeton's *Book of Household Management* represent the domestic sphere as governed by and populated by women. While industrialization is usually thought of in terms of discipline in factories, it also created a subjective compartmentalization for men and women through work. E. P. Thompson linked the notion of clock time to the Protestant work ethic in the creation of an industrialized sense of time that can also be found in the Victorian home in 'Time, Work-Discipline and Industrial Capitalism.'[40] The internalized discipline of work meant making sure that one was not at home during conventional 'working' hours, which obviously presents a problem if one works at home. Increasingly domestic servants were the only ones who officially 'worked' in the home and according to Beeton they were supposed to be invisible.

John Tosh in *A Man's Place* argues initially that masculinity and domesticity were not as opposed as our received image of the Victorian period would suggest and that 'the domestic sphere...is integral to masculinity' (4). Through careful historical analysis of individual cases, he is able to show how Victorian men in private negotiated the contradictions between masculinity and domesticity, particularly in the context of marriage. Subsequent pages of his book, however, only serve to underscore the separation of home from work in the Victorian period and its troubling consequences for men. He documents the Victorian 'polarization of values' in the home and notes that if the household's function was domestic (rather than involved in production) 'then anyone employed in business was out of place there' (18), which is precisely the contradiction that Nightingale describes. Victorian middle-class culture, Tosh suggests, was 'constructed around a heavily polarized understanding of gender' that was more extreme in the Victorian period than before or since (46). Tosh's use of 'polarized' underscores the radical separation of men from women, and the home from work in the Victorian period and contradicts his assertion that masculinity and domesticity were not necessarily opposed.

Perhaps the most compelling quotation in Tosh's book that registers most profoundly the separation of work from the domestic comes from *Mark Rutherford's Deliverance*. Tosh quotes the narrator saying that 'I cut off my office life....from my home life so completely that I was two selves' (140). A similar case is to be found in Alton Locke who when at work started to use his imagination and 'began to live two lives' thanks to his temporary escapes from his labors (Kingsley *Alton Locke* 80). These are examples of the 'divided men' who permeate Victorian fiction, and in this case the internal division arises directly out of the conflict between the competing demands of masculinity in the public sphere and the private 'domestic affections.'

As Tosh says, Victorian gender ideology was riddled with contradictions that individuals negotiated with more or less success. Tosh identifies the key difference between my analysis and his when he admits that the 'popular image of Victorian domesticity is almost entirely focused on women and children' because 'so much contemporary imagery was tilted that way' (48). My examples are drawn primarily from such popular imagery. I therefore deal in this analysis with images that register strongly this extreme polarization of work and the domestic sphere, and I am interested in what Tosh briefly refers to as the way in which 'men...were the invisible subject directing attention to women as object' (45). I suggest that men represented the ideological contradictions in their own subject positions by using women as 'objects' who expressed contradictions for 'men at work' in the domestic sphere. Because many of the images that I analyze were meant for popular consumption, they subscribe to the polarization of values that Tosh describes in *A Man's Place*.

Just as Victorian domesticity was riddled with contradictions, so was the ideology of work. The work ethic, says Tosh, 'exacted a heavy price in alienation'

(30). Once again, this is a useful corrective to Victorian ideology in that it reminds us that work, even for a middle-class Victorian man, was often alienating and demoralizing. However, Victorian popular images of work do not acknowledge this alienating aspect, and instead emphasize self-discipline and self-denial as the only path to individual self fulfillment. This is particularly true, as we shall see, of Thomas Carlyle's representations of work.

Work was a key tool of self-discipline for Victorian men. As one of the primary attributes of masculinity, the rejection of idleness in favor of work as 'industry' was the central topic for two figures most closely associated with the work ethic in the Victorian period, Thomas Carlyle and Samuel Smiles. The 'industrialization' of masculinity and its separation from the domestic is codified most obviously in their texts. Their beliefs are usually described in terms of the Victorian 'Gospel of Work,' which is the subject of my first chapter.

## Notes

1.  Unfortunately Tim Barringer's *Men at Work: Art and Labour in Victorian Britain* was published while this book was in production, and I was thus unable to incorporate references to his study. His book is, however, a fascinating art historical analysis of industrialization and labor in Victorian Britain that covers similar ground to my own from a very different perspective.
2.  Arata has also exploited the connotations of the phrase 'men at work' in his chapter 'Men at Work: From Heroic Friendship to Male Romance,' which examines the homoerotics of late Victorian imperialism (79–104).
3.  My reading of 'masculinities' as socially constructed codes is indebted to feminist theory, especially Butler, Silverman, Moi and Segal.
4.  In my own particular field of masculinity studies, the Victorian period, Eve Kosofsky Sedgwick's *Between Men* was a pioneering text in its argument that 'masculinity' and male biological sex were not necessarily coterminous, and masculinity and femininity were 'independently variable' and not polar opposites.
5.  For a succinct account of the history of relations between feminism and masculinity studies, and a very perceptive account of the continuing tensions between the two, see Judith Kegan Gardner's introduction to *Masculinity Studies and Feminist Theory* (1–29).
6   In their introduction to *Manful Assertions*, Roper and Tosh call for such a relational approach to gender (11–13).
7.  In theoretical terms this approach has been exemplified most obviously by R. W. Connell whose books such as *Which Way is up?* and *Masculinities* carefully triangulate masculinity, gender and class formation.
8.  John Berger's essay 'The Suit and the Photograph' has become a classic analysis of the relationship between class and clothing in this area.
9.  Regenia Gagnier in a particularly interesting discussion of the class politics of literary aesthetics has wrestled with the difficulty of including working-class texts in an analysis

of 'high' culture artifacts in Chapter 4 'Working-Class Autobiography, Subjectivity and Value' of *Subjectivities* (138–70).

10. See A. James Hammerton 'Men as well as Clerks:' Normative Masculinity and the English Lower Middle-Class, 1870–1920' and Arlene Young's *Culture, Class and Gender in the Victorian Novel*. Robbins in *The Servant's Hand* starts his study with Arthur J. Munby, and charts the ways in which the presence of the working-class touch is effaced in the Victorian novel; see especially 1–3 and 20–23 on Munby.

11. There have been a number of excellent recent analyses of the status of the 'gentleman' in the Victorian period; see Trev Lynn Broughton *Men of Letters, Writing Lives*; Mark Girouard *The Return to Camelot*; Ellen Moers *The Dandy: Brummell to Beerbohm*; David Castronovo *The English Gentleman*; David Rosen *The Changing Fictions of Masculinity*; J. A. Mangan and James Walvin *Manliness and Morality: Middle-Class Masculinity in Britain and America, 1800-1940*. Catherine Robson in the Introduction to *Men in Wonderland: The Lost Girlhood of the Victorian Gentleman* says that she uses the term 'gentleman...to indicate that the principal subjects of this study are of the well-to-do classes' (9) but admits in an endnote that she is sidestepping the issue of how to define 'men' (200). Martin Wiener has studied this relationship in his chapter on 'Middle-Class Men and Gentry Values' in *English Culture and the Decline of the Industrial Spirit* (30–40), which deals with many of the same writers as are found in the following pages.

12. Newman in his definition of the gentleman in *The Idea of a University* shows some of this implicit femininity within class codes when he uses terms like 'tender,' 'gentle,' 'patient' and 'forbearing' could all be applied to women as much as men. His ideal gentleman is marked by a reticence and concern for others that makes him sound closer to Florence Nightingale than models of aggressive masculinity.

13. See Raymond Williams *Marxism and Literature*. As Williams says, 'hegemony...does not just passively exist as a form of dominance. It has continually to be renewed, recreated, and modified.' (9).

14. I derive the term 'interpellation' from the work of Louis Althusser; the term refers to the idea that the individual is framed by powers such as the State and education that 'call into being' subjectivity.

15. It is, of course, only recently that such a formulation has become possible in literary theory; see Judith Halberstam *Female Masculinity* and Jean Bobby Noble *Masculinities Without men?: Female Masculinity in Twentieth-Century Fictions.*

16. See James Eli Adams' excellent analysis of the dandy figure in this regard, especially Carlyle's anxieties about the 'Dandiacal Body' (21–26).

17. Houghton sees a similar emphasis on work as 'an absolute necessity' in the 'business society' of the Victorian period (189).

18. These remarks occur in the chapter on 'Methodism' which is the closest of the doctrines surveyed by Weber to the ethos of Victorian England. Tosh argues that whilst Methodism is usually associated with the laboring classes, its influences spread to the 'upper ranks' as well (35).

19. Matthew Arnold selected the 'Ode to Duty' for his edition of Wordsworth's poetry indicating its resonance in the Victorian period; see Appendix 'Arnold's Selections from Wordsworth's Poems' in *The Complete Works of Matthew Arnold* (IX: 319).

20. My thanks to Peter O'Neill for suggesting the Gill book as a reference for Wordsworth's reception in the Victorian period.

21. Wordsworth's emphasis on 'submissiveness' corroborates Adams' and Sussman's definitions of Victorian masculinity in terms of self regulation. Adams contrasts masculine 'self-mastery' with feminine 'self-denial' in *Dandies and Desert Saints* (9).

22. The connection between manliness and the civilizing process is made even more evident by later references to 'self-government' in Newsome's chapter on 'Godliness and Manliness' (196–7).

23. Bruce Haley's *The Healthy Body and Victorian Culture* explores the connection between spiritual and physical healthiness in the Victorian period. As Haley notes, the Victorians even managed 'to make play into work' through an emphasis on physical activity as a duty (258).

24. Christopher Lane has assailed the use of 'culture' as a determining category (specifically in the analysis of male desire, xi–xiii) but his analysis is actually more nuanced than his introduction would suggest; he still uses the term 'culture' throughout his book in ways that show it operating as a unifying (but not a determining) term.

25. The same class conflict is present also when men like Walter Sickert paint images of working-class leisure activities such as music hall; see my 'Sexuality and the Representation of the Working-class Child's Body in Music Hall.'

26. See especially her article 'Studying the Study: Gender and the Scene of Authorship in the Writings of Leslie Stephen, Margaret Oliphant and Anne Thackeray Ritchie.'

27. Like Connell, I am pleased by Bertrand Russel's definition of work as 'of two kinds: first altering the position of matter at or near the earth's surface relative to other such matter; second telling other people to do so' (238); this is in essence a summary of Brown's painting on the subject of 'work.'

28. As a human activity that involves the body, the term 'work' is as 'unstable' as the representation of sexuality in the Victorian discourse examined by Jill L. Matus in *Unstable Bodies* (and Matus is of course indebted to the theories of Judith Butler on sex/gender and representation). Adams in *Dandies and Desert Saints* has characterized masculine identity itself as a 'complex and unstable construction' (3). However, while work is an 'unstable' and socially constructed term I do not, like Elaine Scarry feel that it 'resists representation' as she argues in *Resisting Representation* (65) but rather that it is overdetermined by conflicting discourses of class and gender.

29. Helena Michie has noted the way in which women's work was made invisible in novels like *Jane Eyre* and *Little Dorrit*; as I will show, the difficulty in representing work was not confined to female protagonists but also affects male artists (*Flesh Made Word* 30–58).

30. Rose in *Limited Livelihoods* has suggested that it is important that analysis be focused on 'men's work as having something to do with men as men' (3) if we are to understand the social basis of gender.

31. Butler argues that 'discursive routes like being a good mother, a fit worker' are performative and not the stable subjectivities posited by ideology (145).

32. See Anderson and Nead on the rhetoric of 'fallenness.'

33. See the history of work sketched in Anthony's *Ideology of Work* and Donkin on new forms of work.

34. What the Scots call a 'turnip' the English would call a 'swede' and Americans a 'rutabaga.'

35. McClelland identifies the Victorian discourse of work as a complex linguistic field informed by 'Protestantism, Romantic critiques of industrialism, and hard-faced utilitarian notions of what it was to be human, or more particularly, a man' (184).

36. Patrick Joyce has emphasized the importance of recognizing factors such as gender and class in the labor process as well as the need for greater attention to issues of consciousness in labor history (6). I hope that this analysis fulfills in part what Joyce had in mind.

37. Danon here draws on the previous work of Thompson, Briggs and Hobsbawm on the symbolic and actual roles of the working classes in Victorian Britain.

38. See Kestner's analysis of the heroic knightly figure in this context (92–140). The insistence on metaphors of war to describe Victorian men corroborates Pierre Bourdieu's contention that 'male privilege is also a trap...in the permanent tension...imposed on every man by the duty to assert his manliness in all circumstances' (*Domination* 50) so that men must not allow themselves to be tainted by the feminine or the domestic.

39. I am of course not denying that many Victorian men dissented from this form of 'hegemonic masculinity,' most notably John Ruskin in his aversion to war and destruction, and John Henry Newman who promoted self-discipline over aggression. For an alternative masculine tradition see David Newsome's *Godliness and Good Learning* and Claudia Nelson's *Boys Will Be Girls: The Feminine Ethic and British Children's Fiction, 1857-1917*.

40. Tosh has pointed out that in some Victorian homes the routine was made to 'conform to a punctuality hardly less strict than the shop floor' (47).

# Chapter 1

# Victorian Work and Industry

## The Gospel of Work

The 'Gospel of Work' is now used as shorthand to characterize the dominant attitude toward labor in the Victorian period; while not all Victorian men would have assented to its doctrines, it sums up the mixture of self-discipline and piety that constituted a broad middle-class consensus in the period. Thomas Carlyle is the author most often credited with articulating the early Victorian version of the doctrine, and Samuel Smiles for spreading it worldwide; indeed, Asa Briggs asserts that Smiles' *Self-Help* was spread around the globe 'as efficiently and fervently as any of the great nineteenth-century missionary enterprises' (118). As Briggs's formulation implies, the 'gospel of work' espoused by writers like Carlyle and Smiles can be likened to a religion. It preached that all human beings were put on this earth to accomplish one supreme task, that of work.

The conventional view of the 'Gospel of Work' defines it as part of a rejection of the cultural and social authority of the ruling aristocratic classes in favor of an emergent middle class agenda. The 'Gospel of Work' implied that the upper classes were indolent and that their parasitical position in the economy should be supplanted by self-disciplined, hard-working 'Captains of Industry' to use Carlyle's famous term. Middle-class criticism of the upper classes, such as those found in Carlyle's attacks on 'dilettantism' for example, asserted the moral superiority of the middle classes.

However, the situation for Victorians writers such as Carlyle was much more complex than this thumbnail summary of the historical context would imply. Firstly, the middle classes did not reject the upper classes as a model completely and actually assimilated much of the ethos of the class they attacked. David Kuchta's *The Three-Piece Suit and Modern Masculinity* shows through an analysis of clothing how middle-class men adapted to an aristocratic style of dress; the same process occurred throughout middle-class culture. Also, as Adams suggests in *Dandies and Desert Saints*, writers like Carlyle had 'internalized the aristocratic contempt of the professional writer's lack of independence' (28) which undermined his attacks on aristocratic idleness.

Secondly, the writers who attacked the upper classes also idealized the working classes. Others have studied the vexed relations between the middle classes and the aristocracy and the attempts by the new industrial elite to assimilate into aristocratic ranks.[2] My interest in this book is the uneasy class position of writers who professed admiration for the 'Gospel of Work' but chose the working classes as their ideal rather than the middle classes. If the symbolic heart of work lies in manual labor then the intellectual is marginal to the industry of Victorian society.

Work in this period was linked closely to religion and was the most frequently used term in the Victorian lexicon after God (Houghton 243). This is made explicit by Thomas Carlyle in *Past and Present* when describing 'Happy Work:'

> All work, even cotton-spinning, is noble; work is alone noble: be that here said and asserted once more. And in like manner, too all dignity is painful; a life of ease is not for any man, nor for any god. (Carlyle *Past* 149)

Carlyle, with his love of absolutes, terms all work 'noble' and presents it as a moral imperative. Indeed, even more than a moral it is a divine imperative, for even God has to work. The middle classes, according to Carlyle, are on a mission from God. He makes this explicit in Chapter 11 when he says that 'there is a perennial nobleness, and even sacredness, in work' (Carlyle *Past* 190). There is no room for idleness on earth or in heaven. Carlyle is not saying, though, that work is pleasurable or joyful. The term 'noble' very quickly shades into the term 'painful,' implying that work involves pain and suffering, even though it ennobles. As Haley says of Carlyle's thought on this topic 'without pain there is no life,' so that this is the normal human condition as far as he is concerned (77).

Carlyle is a looming presence in this study. A wide range of authors used Carlyle as a touchstone in their own representations of work. Ford Madox Brown included Carlyle in his painting *Work*, and Carlyle is cited by novelists either directly or indirectly in their fiction. Even when their message would seem to be antithetical to Carlyle's, as in Kingsley's *Alton Locke* for example, Carlyle is still cited with reverence as an authority.[3] David Amigoni has argued, Socialists 'were able selectively to appropriate and mobilize discourse from Carlyle's contradictory rhetoric' and read him as a radical writer (72). He is thus a central figure in defining the Victorian 'Gospel of Work' for writers from across the political spectrum.

Kingsley's *Alton Locke* conforms to some of the same masculine dynamics found in Carlyle's definition of work. Adams suggests that Locke achieves manhood in the surrender of 'all the markers of normative manhood' to the figure of an upper-class woman (145). The text enacts the subordination of the working-class male to an aristocratic, feminine image and, like Gissing's later *New Grub Street*, shows the writer ultimately as an emasculated failure. While Kingsley's politics were very different from Carlyle's his text subscribes to a vision of masculinity that Adams refers to as potentially masochistic (147). *Alton Locke* therefore does not represent an alternative to the Carlylean doctrine of 'the

Gospel of Work' but rather a continuation of the definition of labor as painful, masculine renunciation.

Carlyle's view of work arises from a long religious tradition that represented it as punishment for sin, especially the sin of Adam and Eve that led to the expulsion from the Garden of Eden.[4] Carlyle is scathing in the pages that follow his definition of work about the 'atheism' that defines happiness as an important consideration in work. For Carlyle work is the antithesis of happiness because it is by its very nature difficult, painful and arduous. If work were enjoyable it would not be an adequate punishment for Original Sin. For this reason he sees the attempt to sever work and suffering as an attack not only on religion but the very idea of God and therefore as 'atheism.'

Carlyle makes a gesture toward real work in mentioning cotton spinning, but his use of the term 'work' is meant to be transcendent. It would be useless to ask 'so what is work?' in this context because it would be like asking 'what is God?' God is everything and to begin to answer that question you would have to go back to the book of Genesis and move forward to the present. John Stuart Mill argued that Carlyle 'revolves in an eternal circle round the idea of work' as if it were an end in itself; he was right, because for Carlyle it *was* an eternal circle and an end itself (Mill 90). Similarly, for Carlyle to answer the question 'what is work?' would involve trying to untangle the eternal circle of God.

John Stuart Mill attacks Carlyle's 'Gospel of Work' as 'cant' and tackles the definition of toil in concrete terms. He is clearly exasperated by Carlisle's equation of work with God, and offers instead a Utilitarian definition of 'useful' work (90). It would seem that Mill offers a clear alternative to Carlyle's 'Gospel of Work' but in fact he ends up affirming some of the same contradictions to be found in his adversary's text:

> I do not include under the name labour such work, if work it be called, as is done by writers and afforders of 'guidance,' an occupation which, let alone the vanity of the thing, cannot be called by the same name with real labour, the exhausting, stupefying toil of any kinds of agricultural and manufacturing labourers. (Mill 91)

Mill's point here is to underscore the contrast between the people who Carlyle attacks, who carried out backbreaking labor in sugar plantations for instance, and his own relatively comfortable experience. In racial and class terms this is a cogent critique. However, it also makes all writing not 'work' and inferior as an example of effort and toil in comparison to manual labor. In this Mill, like other Victorian intellectuals, denigrates writing as not being 'real' work.

Unlike Mill, Carlyle operated within a conventional Christian distinction between soul and body, and equated the soul with work and the body with suspect physical appetites. He berated his contemporaries for being overly focused on bodily matters at the expense of the spiritual. In other words, they should be thinking about 'higher' things like the soul and work, but focus instead on the body. Work is in Carlyle an antidote to the body and sin which is why he often makes the initially puzzling assertion that hungry people should not focus on the body so much but should be concerned with higher spiritual issues, including work. Carlyle in general is revolted by the body and employs repression and imaginative compensation to transcend embodiment.

Fred Kaplan in a very perceptive biography of Carlyle collects many of his criticisms of his own body as well as society as a body. Kaplan argues in his biography that Carlyle 'felt degraded by his "misfunctioning bowels,"' for which he took pills and castor oil (63). Sussman has noted the same 'dis-ease' that Carlyle felt toward the male body, although he does not make the connection directly to Carlyle's 'misfunctioning' bowels.[5] Kaplan at one point refers to Carlyle's 'angry dialogue' with Victorian society that had 'been deeply internalized' and ascribes this to Carlyle's vision of 'the world as an extension of self rather than self as an extension of the world' (403). Carlyle expressed his anger in a generally violent and hostile denunciation of his society, but this anger was a redirected form of the aggression that originated in his ambivalence toward his own body. As Sussman notes, 'Carlyle's language consistently conflates the physical and the psychological' and the boundaries between his own body and his image of the social were amorphous (19).

Haley in his analysis of the healthy body has underscored the way in which Carlyle equated bodily sickness and introspection so that 'self-sentience, dispute and deliberation are always signs of ill-health' (73). In Victorian society according to Carlyle 'all seems diseased self-consciousness...everything lies impotent, lamed, its force turned inwards' (Haley 76). The antidote to this was 'putting mind and body in motion' above all in 'action–religious action' (Haley 78). However, the highest form of action was not praying or acts of charity as this formulation might suggest, but work as a cure for the disease of introspection. Work for Carlyle was an ideal that banished disease and doubt simultaneously, at least on the ideal level. In practice Carlyle lamented in a letter that 'Writing is a dreadful Labour, yet not so dreadful as Idleness.'[6] In letters he could express the alienation of intellectual labor that is repressed in his published texts. He uses the dread term 'idleness,' which connotes sinful doubts and desires, to goad himself to work.

Carlyle stresses self-denying masculinity in his writings on work as a way of overcoming embodiment. While Victorian culture generally stressed self-denial and abstinence as virtues, Carlyle takes these virtues to a disturbing extreme. His system is founded on a revulsion against literal embodiment which leads him to turn work into a religious and transcendent imperative that escapes the sins of the flesh. Carlyle's criticism of Victorian society is therefore based not on an indictment of social organization as is that of Marx or Engels but on a denial of the male body.[7] This connection becomes explicit when a typical Carlyle rant about the Corn Laws veers into Mammonism, and then from there to the body. Carlyle says that Mammonism 'is not the essence of his or my station' but 'the adsciticious excrescence of it; the gross, terrene embodiment of it' (*Past* 201). Money and Mammonism for Carlyle reinstate the material conditions of existence, especially the body, which for him is connected with embodiment as a pathological or diseased condition. Carlyle would much rather see work in transcendent and God-like terms rather than in terms of the organization of Victorian society and as connected with the human body.

Carlyle makes a crucial transition into a definition of masculinity as work as he rejects the claims of the 'stomach' which leads the discussion away from the demand of the body for food to the 'duty' of all men to work:

> The only happiness a brave man ever troubled himself with asking about was, happiness to get his work done. Not 'I can't eat!' but 'I can't work!' that was the burden of all wise complaining among men. It is, after all, the one unhappiness of a man, that he cannot work; that he cannot get his destiny as a man fulfilled. (Carlyle *Past* 152)

Carlyle is not using 'man' here as a synonym for 'human' but rather for 'male.' Men have only one mission in life and that is to work. Carlyle makes the rather absurd assertion that somebody should not complain that they have no food, but that they have no work. In an increasingly complex industrialized society like Victorian England, unemployment was becoming a structural constant in the economy. Especially during economic downturns of the 1840s, large numbers of men could not find work. If they could not find work they could not eat, but simply enjoining them to work glossed over the problem of unemployment as an economic constant. Carlyle, working on an abstract, spiritual plane, is not interested in whether or not somebody does not have food because there are not enough jobs available. It is the destiny of man to work, and if man is not working he is not fulfilling his destiny. There is no room for the word 'unemployment' in Carlyle's doctrine.

To not work is to leave the category of 'man.' In other words if you are not working you are not masculine. This formulation haunts the texts in this study, because the situation is far more complex than Carlyle in his aphoristic, polemical style allows. The difficulty for the men in this study lay not in the fact that they could not get work, for most of them are members of the upper classes or at least comfortably middle class, but that what they did was not necessarily recognized as work. Many forms of work were not 'manly' and so it was impossible for some men to feel that they were fulfilling their masculine destiny in Carlyle's terms. They therefore felt less than men and in compensation romanticized other forms of labor undertaken by women and the working classes.

The conventional view of a Victorian male as a powerful, active subject depended upon the rejection of self-doubt. Ruskin in 'Of Queens' Gardens' defined the Victorian male as 'active, progressive' and 'eminently the doer,' not as idle or introspective (*Sesame* 99). Tendencies to idleness or introspection had to be sublimated and were expressed in terms of a rejection of anathematized feelings of inadequacy and impotence projected onto a gender, class or racial other. In the context of Carlyle, Sussman has noted that 'Carlyle clearly transfers his own revulsion at the male body to the female' in *Past and Present* and represents his anxieties about his own body in the form of a female other (21). This is, however, only one example of such transference in *Past and Present*.

In Carlyle's schema, the antithesis of work is 'idleness.'[8] In this category Carlyle includes not only those things that are not 'manly' but also those that are not English and not white. The term idleness is used in the most disturbing way in his 'Occasional Discourse on the Nigger Question' (1830) where it is deployed both as a gendered and racial category. Carlyle creates in this essay the fantasy of a West Indian man who does not need to work because he can live on gathering pumpkins for half an hour a day instead of working in the sugar cane plantations. Carlyle reaches a hysterical point of indignation as he contrasts this figment of his imagination with the situation of the English working classes, especially the male worker:

> An idle White gentleman is not pleasant to me; though I confess the real work for him is not easy to find, in these our epochs; and perhaps he is seeking, poor soul, and may find at last. But what say you to an idle Black gentleman, with his rum-bottle in his hand...no breeches on his body, pumpkin at his discretion, and the fruitfulest region on earth going back to jungle around him? (Carlyle 'Occasional Discourse' 300–1)

The 'jungle' that Carlyle refers to in *Past and Present* as the opposite of order and work is given a more concrete location here. Carlyle connects the jungle, racial stereotypes and a fear of the body in this passage. The 'chaos' referred to previously is the repressed desires that are sublimated into labor; the idle body is a sensual and pleasure-seeking threat to male labor, while work is equated with a masculine, white, self-denying subject who represses the body in favor of toil. The West Indian man Carlyle is represented by Carlyle as indulging the senses in his drinking, sexuality and primitiveness, symbolized by his lack of breeches. Carlyle is fairly light on the white 'gentleman' idler in contrast to the fear and loathing expressed in his portrayal of West Indian subjects newly emancipated from slavery. As Rachwal says, 'blacks are idle while the English are temporarily indolent' underscoring the racial uses of terms related to work (51).[9]

Rather than the idle aristocracy at this point in *Past and Present*, his target here is the 'pretty man' of the Caribbean who, in Carlyle's tropical fantasy, has only to lie in a hammock all day and eat pumpkins ('Occasional Discourse' 302). Obviously calling the Caribbean male 'pretty' feminizes him, and indicates that racial and gender categories are both implicated in Carlyle's tropical fantasy. For Carlyle the British creation of a plantation system in the Caribbean has rescued the area from swamps and pestilence and introduced an era of God-like work. The

Caribbean was an area of 'waste and putrefaction' before the empire, the invocation of waste recalling Carlyle's representation of the body as 'excrescence' above and his linking of 'idleness' and 'putrefaction' in *Past and Present* (190). This is simply an imperial version of his attempt to escape from embodiment and find refuge in an idealized image of work and the transformation of nature through human labor. In Carlyle's idealized empire, the divine interference of British work has banished the demon idleness and the threat of 'terrene' embodiment.

Carlyle's depiction of the West Indies is part of a wider colonial and imperialist use of the category of 'work' in Victorian discourse. As Michael Hechter has argued, British imperial attitudes were initially formulated as part of the subjugation of Ireland, Scotland and Wales. This same process can be seen in the discourse on work:

> The English people are naturally industrious – they prefer a life of honest labour to one of idleness...Now all the Celtic tribes, famous everywhere for their indolence and fickleness as the Celts everywhere are, the Irish are admitted to be the most fickle. They will not work if they can exist without it. (quoted in Curtis 'Echoes of the Past' 179)

'Work' could be used as a category to define national and racial identity was well as masculine identity as this quotation shows. The Irish are stigmatized by ascribing 'idleness' to them in contrast to the biologically 'naturally industrious' English. This is the discourse on which Carlyle is drawing in the 'Nigger Question' which explicitly racializes work. In this later and unappealing Carlyle, the exhortations to find fulfillment in work are replaced by an undisguised use of colonial and military power. The diatribes against trying to find 'happiness' rather than working have been replaced by direct threats that if inducing somebody to work is not effective, then they must be compelled to work, or 'forced into holy labor' (Rachwal 52). Carlyle's promise to coerce West Indians into working would be palatable to British industrialists, as their resistance to the Ten Hours Bill showed. Carlyle's prescription for Demerera would also be well received in England by factory owners who would like to enforce industrial attitudes to time, as E. P. Thompson has argued in the context of the conflict over 'St. Monday.' In both cases 'work' is used as a category to refashion workers into the image of Carlyle's prescriptions on self-discipline and suffering in the 'Gospel of Work.'

While Carlyle shows the fusion of religion, masculinity and imperialism in the 'Gospel of Work,' the text that can claim the title as the Bible of Work is of course Samuel Smiles' *Self-Help*. In *Self-Help* Smiles sings the praises of a male life structured on the imperative to work. Smiles invokes the Biblical aspect of his project in his introduction to *Self-Help*:

> Biographies of great, but especially of good men, are nevertheless most instructive and useful, as helps, guides, and incentives to others. Some of the best are almost

equivalent to gospels—teaching high living, high thinking, and energetic action for their own and the world's good. The valuable examples which they furnish of the power of self-help, of patient purpose, resolute working, and steadfast integrity, issuing in the formation of truly noble and manly character, exhibit in language not to be misunderstood, what it is in the power of each to accomplish for himself; and eloquently illustrate the efficacy of self-respect and self-reliance in enabling men of even the humblest rank to work out for themselves an honourable competency and a solid reputation. (Smiles *Self-Help* 9–10)

Smiles lays out the *modus operandi* of *Self-Help* here, which is primarily a collection of narratives of 'great' men's lives and numerous quotations from various authorities. His biographies exemplify the kind of 'heroic labor' called for in more abstract terms in Carlyle. Reading such a text can be a frustrating experience because Smiles eschews definition of his categories and expects the narratives he presents to 'speak' for themselves. He engages in very little analysis but relies instead on his examples to act as templates for his readers. He does, however, show some of his preconceptions in his vocabulary. He expects his texts, for example, to teach the formation of a 'manly character.' This emphasis on manliness is carried over into later works such as *Life and Labour*:

The life of a man in this world is for the most part a life of work. In the case of ordinary men, work may be regarded as their normal condition. Every man worth calling a man should be willing and able to work. The honest working man finds work necessary for his sustenance, but it is equally necessary for men of all conditions and in every relationship of life. (Smiles *Life* 1)

The proposition that 'every man worth calling a man should be willing and able to work' makes the terms 'man' and 'work' into synonyms; take away work and you negate masculinity altogether. If you do not work you cannot be called a man, according to Smiles so that 'work' is the basic building block of masculine identity. Part of the problem with this gospel of work is already implicit in the next sentence, however; there may be those who do not need to work because they are wealthy. Smiles' definition of manliness fits the middle and working classes who have no choice but to work; economic necessity ensures that they are pious in their observance of the doctrine of work. Smiles believes, however, that members of the upper classes should work also if they wish to be included under the rubric 'man.'

Immediately the class basis of Smiles' position causes him problems, even before the gendered assumptions about work interfere. Presumably most of the activities of the aristocracy from Smiles' perspective would fall under the category of 'leisure' rather than 'work.' Leisure activities for Smiles are not a crucial part of the definition of manliness; indeed, as we shall see, leisure places the person, whether biologically male or female, closest to the gendered category woman, not man. The aristocracy therefore is potentially dangerously effeminate or decadent, terms that seem often interchangeable in Victorian invective against the upper classes. Part of being a Victorian man seems to entail making sure you can never be mistaken for an idle woman.

If you prove you are a man by working then the aristocrat is in a dangerously ambiguous position. In *Self-Help* Smiles sees the aristocracy as close to 'idleness' and therefore 'unmanliness,' and hopes that the wealthy will be led by their consciences to work:

> Yet the rich man, inspired by a right spirit, will spurn idleness as unmanly; and if he bethink himself of the responsibilities which attach to the possession of wealth and property he will feel even a higher call to work than men of humbler lot. This, however, must be admitted to be by no means the practice of life. (Smiles *Self-Help* 436)

A real man in Smiles' schema will reject the 'unmanly' fate of having no work even if it is not an economic necessity for him to toil. The aristocratic man will reject the feminine implicit in idleness and identify himself wholly with the masculine worker. This is of course the ideal rather than actual Victorian conduct and Smiles is aware that very few aristocratic men live up to his fantasy. The final admission shows that the wealthy fall far short from Smiles' ideal. Smiles really wishes to do away with the category of 'rich' or 'aristocratic' in a classless meritocracy based on work rather than the status of being a 'gentleman:'

> Riches and rank have no necessary connexion with genuine gentlemanly qualities. The poor man may be a true gentleman,—in spirit and in daily life. He may be honest, truthful, upright, polite, temperate, courageous, self-respecting, and self-helping,—that is, be a true gentleman. The poor man with a rich spirit is in all ways superior to the rich man with a poor spirit. (Smiles *Self-Help* 560)

Smiles in his 'Gospel of Work' applies a religious vocabulary to class distinctions; 'rich' and 'poor' in this quotation shift from references to money to spiritual propriety. The quotation suggests that the term 'gentleman' is not linked to pounds per annum but to the amount of spiritual worth possessed by a man in an effort to separate social status from capital. Smiles had faith that all men of worth were 'gentleman' and could identify each other immediately, but this was based 'not on observation but on a rooted belief in a moral code' (Briggs 135). It was, in other words, an expression of his beliefs rather than based on how Victorian society actually operated. Smiles tried to avoid class-based difficulties by broadening the definition of the term 'gentleman' to include both the upper and working classes and assert that 'the true gentleman is of no rank or class' (*Self-Help* 25). Unfortunately, this is suspiciously like trying to have your cake and eat it too because the term 'gentleman' cannot be so neatly severed from its class connotations.

Ruskin, as we shall see, carries out a similar sleight of hand in *The Crown of Wild Olive* when he initially introduces cricket as an example of 'play' versus 'work,' but then differentiates cricket from pure idleness and implies that even cricketers are workers and thus closer to the working classes than the 'idle,' who he dismisses out of hand (*Crown* XI 7). The working classes are, it appears, honorary cricketers and thus gentlemen. As Ruskin says, in his utopia 'we shall all be workers in one way or another; and this much at least of the distinction between 'upper' and 'lower' shall be forgotten' (*Crown* XI 8). Class distinctions will be eradicated by work according to both Smiles and Ruskin.

This is on the face of it a patently absurd assertion. One could not be a 'gentleman' in the Victorian period without a certain level of education and income that marked one as belonging to a certain class. What Smiles attempts to do here, just as Ruskin does in *The Crown of Wild Olive* (and even more disastrously in the Hincksey Road project, as we shall see) is link the term 'gentleman' to work and create a sort of nobility of labor, or in Carlylean terms an 'Aristocracy of Labour.' Those who work are automatically 'gentlemen,' and since all men must by definition be willing and able to work, it follows that all men, no matter what their class, can be 'gentlemen of work' rather than the usual 'gentlemen of leisure.' These men form a class based on work who know each other by sight because, says Smiles, 'gentlemen at once identify each other. They look each other in the eye and grip each other's hands. They know each other instinctively' (Smiles *Self-Help* 33). Any class markers are conveniently transcended by this knowledge that bypasses the usual conscious processes of thought. Smiles reaches a rather startling climax in his description of true breeding with a final swerve into gender relations with the assertion that 'the lady is but a counterpart of the gentleman' (*Self-Help* 37). Work can therefore also magically cross gender boundaries also.

Work is therefore a transcendent category in both Carlyle and Smiles. For Carlyle work allows men to escape sin and the body and enter a higher spiritual plane. For Smiles work allows men to escape class distinctions and enter a realm where all are equal. In neither case is work a concrete activity. The discourse of both writers operates at a level of ideal that has no reference to everyday reality. For both men work is part of a religious doctrine that expresses hopes for spiritual redemption. The contradictions between the elevated ideal and the reality of working-class labor in Victorian England are not acknowledged because their discourse is concerned with transcending the quotidian.

'Work' therefore functions explicitly as a religious category in Carlyle and Smiles, bearing out Briggs' assertion that this was a 'missionary enterprise.' The 'crisis of faith' in the Victorian period provoked the creation of many alternatives to belief in God. Matthew Arnold famously for tried to provide one in literature in 'The Study of Poetry.' Work ranks alongside literature as a candidate to replace God. As a transcendent category, work has much more in common with a divine being than with the actual activities of real men. For Carlyle in his most exalted mood, God actually becomes a worker:

Giant LABOUR, truest emblem there is of God the World-Worker. (Carlyle *Past* 165)

Carlyle makes God into a Worker. This is, however, not God as an author or artist but God as a practical maker of things. As Ulrich points out, Carlyle makes God the 'stabilizing force of a meaningful system of representation' that will combat the disconnection of sign from signifier in Victorian England (92). However, Work as God does not solve the problem of the disconnection between sign and signifier; what Carlyle does, in effect, is turn manual labor into a form of religious worship. Carlyle may indeed wish to combat the 'alienated commodification of labor' (Ulrich 93) in the Victorian period, but he does so by romanticizing those most alienated by their work, the working classes. God is a 'World-Worker' rather than a 'worker of the world' but this still raises manual labor to the top of the symbolic hierarchy, whereas in reality the working classes were the most exploited. God is supposed to be above class and gender divisions, but Carlyle's deity is a working-class laborer, as well as being a man.

Engels, who shared Carlyle's aims, criticized his use of religious vocabulary, and this passage shows most clearly where Engels and Carlyle diverged. While recognizing alienation on one level, Carlyle magically transforms Work into God. As Sharon Aronofsky Weltman has shown, Carlyle's God in *Sartor Resartus* is a masculine force who controls a female Chaos (91); in other words, Carlyle's God if analyzed betrays a definite gender politics. English men in creating sugar plantations in the West Indies are making themselves in God's image and bringing a female chaos under control through work. For this reason the supposedly idle Caribbean 'pretty man' is a threat to both to Victorian masculinity and the godliness of work.

This is also not God the Scribe. While the 'man of letters' does represent a form of 'heroic masculinity' for Carlyle in *On Heroes and Hero Worship*, as Carol Christ has argued he does not make God a writer ('Hero as Man of Letters' 21). Carlyle emphasizes that he values most 'Practical Material Work' and the 'grim inarticulate veracity of the English people' who make things and not words (*Past* 164).[10] He extols the virtues of 'the strong inarticulate men and workers' (Carlyle *Past* 19) and clearly favors the strong, silent types over voluble writers. His ideal of work is therefore, as it is for most intellectuals in this study, a romanticized image of working-class labor, especially work that involves muscles and material objects. This idealized image of the worker represents a peculiar imaginative compensation for both the effects of industrial labor on the working classes and the status of intellectual labor in a society that values things over words.

While Ulrich's analysis of Carlyle's 'reinscription of labor into the heart of the social and individual body' (105) is certainly accurate in terms of its account of the logic of Carlyle's argument, it fails to account for the class system in which the text is embedded. Ulrich is correct that Carlyle wishes to create a new

'Chivalry of Labor' that would overcome class differences in industrializing England, but like Ruskin's later schemes and William Morris's utopian vision, this substitutes fantasy for actual social relations. Marx criticized German philosophers for such fantasies in *The German Ideology* and the same critique can be leveled at Carlyle. As Marx and Engels realized, Carlyle mounted a sophisticated critique of commodification in his attack on the 'cash nexus,' but he idealized work rather than suggesting remedies in terms of social organization.

Carlyle recognized the social crisis caused by industrialization, but his romanticization of masculine work created a new set of problems for the writers who came after him. His response to work was to make it into a transcendent signifier, whereas other writers redefined work as oppression. He could not recognize what Marx came to term 'alienated labor,' that is work in which the subject's own labor is turned into a force that oppresses him. In the context of industrializing Britain Carlyle espoused a heroic, masculine ideal of work that made him unsympathetic to any calls for direct intervention from the working classes.

Marx and Engels are obviously the figures from this period who articulated the connections between labor, industrialization and capital. Rather than see work as a transcendent signifier, they emphasized the way in which labor was converted into capital in a system that depended upon the exploitation of the working classes. However, as we shall see, they were also not immune from the ideal of the 'man at work,' advocating the liberation of the working classes, yet still subscribing to a model of productive masculinity that in the final analysis had much in common with Carlyle's position.

### Work as Oppression: Before and after Engels and Marx

After the publication of Marx and Engels' *Manifesto of the Communist Party* in 1848 the idea of work, especially by the working classes, has been linked to exploitation in a capitalist and industrialized system. The *Manifesto* defined the 'proletariat' as 'a class of laborers, who live only so long as they find work' and who were slaves to capital (61–2). Engels also referred to workers under capitalism as 'slaves' earlier in his *The Condition of the Working Class in England* (1845). However, even before Marx, work was seen as a form of oppression, and this oppression was accepted as a natural fact in the division of labor along class lines. This idea can be found in texts from the Classical period on the order of society:

> What are called the mechanical arts carry a social stigma and are rightly
> dishonored in cities. For these arts can damage the bodies of those who work at
> them or who act as overseers, by compelling them to a sedentary and to an indoor
> life, and in some cases, to spend a whole day by the fire. This physical

degeneration results also in a deterioration of the soul. (Xenophon quoted in Donkin 27)

While it is difficult to make comparisons across histories and cultures, this quotation is striking both for its similarities and differences from Victorian ideals of work. Xenophon's text is the product of an aristocratic perspective whereas the texts in this study are a product of the increasing ascendancy of the middle classes. In this passage the higher moral status of those who do not work is assumed as part of the social fabric.[11] The aristocracy in Carlyle and Smiles, by contrast, is criticized as an effete and leisured class. Ironically, lost in their outlook is Xenophon's clear-sighted recognition of the bodily toll of manual labor which is largely effaced in the writers considered in this study (with John Ruskin being a notable exception). Oscar Wilde in 'Soul of Man under Socialism' skewered the 'nonsense that is being written and talked nowadays about the dignity of manual labour. There is nothing necessarily dignified about manual labour at all, and most of it is absolutely degrading' (25–6). Wilde also, in contrast to the other writers in this study, terms artists 'real men' (5) and criticizes the notion of a 'duty' to work (6).[12] These are, however, simply typical Wilde witticisms, turning Victorian values on their head. It is also especially ironic that Wilde should say this, because he was a participant in the Ruskin Hincksey road building project that I discuss in Chapter 4, which was an attempt to restore the dignity of manual labor. Aside from Wilde's witticisms, for a thoroughgoing critique of the idealization of work in the Victorian period, one must turn to Marx and Engels.

Marx and Engels represented work as oppression and were explicit about the toll of this labor on the working classes. Rather than see work as a product of sin as in the gospel of work, they saw its pernicious effects as the byproduct of an exploitative social system. Where Smiles tried to transcend class, they saw the class system as intimately connected to the system of production. Nevertheless Engels, at least initially, was sympathetic to Carlyle's critique of British society.

Engels was sympathetic to Carlyle's critique of the 'cash nexus' because he shared his antipathy to commodification. Engels quotes Carlyle approvingly in several places, especially in regard to his portrayal of the 'money-greed' of the English bourgeoisie (*Condition* 34, 176, 180). Engels was particularly impressed by Carlyle's famous statement that 'cash payment is the only nexus between man and man' which seemed to him to accord with his own and Marx's critique of the way in which commodification was undermining community in industrializing nations (*Condition* 314). For both writers the redefinition of human relationships in economic terms was one of the most disturbing aspects of English industrialization and urbanization.

In later editions of *The Condition of the Working Classes In England* Engels recanted his support for Carlyle saying that the 'half-German Englishman, Thomas Carlyle' has become 'an out-and-out reactionary' whose 'righteous wrath against the Philistines turned into sullen Philistine grumbling at the tide of history and cast him ashore' (298). Although Engels tried later to distance himself from his sympathetic reading of Carlyle's prose, there remains a bedrock assumption in both writers that work is masculine. In the 'Preface to the English Edition' Engels praises the 'great Trades Unions' forming in England:

> They are the organizations of those trades in which the labour of *grown up men* (Engels' italics) predominates or is alone applicable. Here the competition neither of women nor children nor of machinery has so far weakened their organized strength. (Engels *Condition* 321)

Both Carlyle and Engels see work as an exclusively masculine enterprise.[13] As we shall see, in the 1840s there was a large-scale movement toward defining work as inimical to women and children. While it is obvious that children should not be employed in factories or mines (although the category of 'child' was itself extremely fluid, as various reports and hearings showed) it is not so self-evident that women should be excluded from all occupations. Engels' insistence here on 'grown up' men and their strength is striking because he acknowledges that women and children are not just threats to earnings for men, but threats to their very masculinity. They must avoid being infantilized or feminized lest they lose their masculine strength.

Machines are also a symbolic threat as much as an economic one to organizations of working men. The supervision of machines depended less and less on muscular strength and more and more on dexterity and attentiveness. Engels makes this explicit when he notes that, thanks to mechanization, 'real work' has been transformed from 'the work of full-grown men' into 'mere supervision which a feeble woman or even a child can do quite as well' (147). Masculine muscles were rendered irrelevant by mechanization, which threatened to make men the equivalents of women and children. The mechanization of work in Engels' view represented a threat to masculinity itself.

This threat to masculinity impresses Engels most forcefully when he relates the story from a letter he received about a Lancashire worker who was compelled to stay home while his wife worked. Engels twice describes the man as crying as he talks to the friend who finds him sitting at home by the fire mending his wife's stockings instead of working in the factory. Where Florence Nightingale above saw the gendered division of labor as artificial, at this point Engels fully identifies with an ideal of work as the province of 'full-grown men' and can only react with horror and outrage at this inversion of the natural order. For Engels the family is 'turned upside down' and men are 'condemned to domestic occupations' (154). His ideal is the 'man at work' not the man at home.

To be fair to Engels, he does see the situation as largely the product of a distorted social system in which both men and women are exploited:

Can anyone imagine a more insane state of things than that described in this letter? And yet this condition, which unsexes the man and takes from the woman all womanliness without being able to bestow upon the man true womanliness or the woman true manliness—this condition which degrades, in the most shameful way, both sexes...is the last result of our much-praised civilization. (Engels *Condition* 155)

Unfortunately, Engels does not elaborate on what a man who finds 'true womanliness' or a woman who finds 'true manliness' might look like. His comments on manliness and womanliness do show that he recognizes, like Nightingale, that these are social categories that are not anchored in biology. In his remarks in this context on the basis of the bourgeois family in property, there are signs of his later work on property, women and marriage (156). Engels recognizes the slippage of gender categories to a certain extent, but he is still bound by the discipline of a gendered division of labor that ascribes factory work to 'manliness' and domestic work to 'womanliness.' This is not to say that Engels is some nineteenth-century Judith Butler; the terms 'man' and 'woman' are not performative as they are for Butler in *Gender Trouble*, but rather have a material reality. It is possible to be a 'true' man or woman, but not a hybrid that would combine manliness or womanliness. A title like Judith Halberstam's *Female Masculinity* would be meaningless for Engels.

This is most evident in the way that he complains that factory work destroys the family by depriving the children of their mother (177). Engels, like many Victorian commentators after him, implicitly makes the man an invisible father who can be absent from the family with no damage to the children.[14] It is not just that Engels defines women as mothers above all else, but also that he marginalizes the father as a force in the family completely. A man who finds 'true womanliness' presumably would be able to fulfill some of the family functions ascribed to a 'mother' but Engels does not seriously entertain this idea. The image of a man at home mending his wife's stockings and looking after the children is 'insane,' and while he may blame oppressive social organization, it is far from clear if the utopian social system that he envisages would change gender roles. The aporia here is similar to that found in William Morris's utopia in *News from Nowhere* in which women *choose* to stay home even though theoretically all occupations are open to them.

Like many of the bourgeois Victorians of whom he is so critical, Engels also links working in the factory with an excessive sexuality, and with prostitution. Engels criticizes the 'bad' and 'filthy' language in the factories, linking it to the pernicious effects of big cities (181). He quotes a man saying that 'most of the prostitutes of the town had their employment in the mills to thank for their present situation.' This is a common narrative in Victorian fiction; in Elizabeth Gaskell's *Mary Barton* for example Mary's aunt goes from working into a factory to prostitution. The money she earned as a single woman working in the factory is seen as the cause of her downfall. As many feminist scholars have documented, the linkage of women, work and money inevitable raised the specter of prostitution.

Where Carlyle advocates a spiritual antidote to the ills he sees in English society by turning work into a divine imperative, Engels sees the antidote to work as oppression as lying in free choice. He asserts that:

> Another source of demoralization among the workers is their being condemned to work. As voluntary, productive activity is the highest enjoyment known to us, so is compulsory toil the most cruel, degrading punishment. Nothing is more terrible than being constrained to do some one thing every day from morning until night against one's will....Why does he work? For love of work? From a natural impulse? Not at all! He works for money, for a thing which has nothing whatsoever to do with the work.. The division of labour has multiplied the brutalizing influences of forced work. (Engels *Condition* 129)

Carlyle's response to this passage would be that work was not meant to be 'happy' but inevitably entailed suffering; he would not see men as being 'condemned to work' but coerced to do so for their own good. For Engels it is the new forms of social and industrial organization, especially the division of labor, that create oppressive forms of work and forced labor. Carlyle, however, does not attempt to reach the level of specificity that Engels aspires to in his analysis of work. Where Carlyle gestures toward forms of work like spinning, Engels gives examples culled from contemporary British newspapers:

> In November, 1843, a man died at Leicester, who had been dismissed two days before from the workhouse at Coventry....The man George Robson, had a wound upon the shoulder, the treatment of which was wholly neglected; he was set to work at the pump, using the sound arm; was given only the usual workhouse fare, which he was utterly unable to digest by reason of the unhealed wound and his general debility....Two days later he died at Leicester. (Engels *Condition* 293)

Engels gives an example and an extended narrative to illuminate the problems of those forced to work when they were unable. The story stands as an almost perfect counterpoint to the Carlyle statements quoted above that men should not complain about not being able to eat but not being able to work. In the Victorian schema there was little differentiation between 'those who would not work' and those unable to work because of physical difficulty. Engels shows a man rather than a woman dying as a result of his labors, which is a very rare narrative in Victorian representations of work. Carlyle and Engels both give exemplary narratives, one set intended to reinforce the nobility of work, the other to underscore the inhumanity of British social organization.

While Engels' approach is obviously anecdotal here, it is also close to that of Smiles, the foremost advocate of work. Smiles gives biographies and stories of successful workers. Engels gives a story of a worker dying because of lack of food and being forced to work while sick. The content is radically different but the format is the same. Engels sees clearly that the organization of work in the division of labor, and the definition of work in terms of money alone, have contributed to the 'de-spiritualization' of work and its redefinition in the nineteenth century.[15]

At the other end of scale from Engels is Goldwyn Smith who in 1859 saw the division of labor as part of God's plan working for greatest good

> The laws of the production and the distribution of wealth are...the most beautiful and wonderful of the natural laws of God, and through their wonderful wisdom they, like the other laws of nature which science explores, are not without a poetry of their own. Silently, surely, without any man's taking thought, if human folly will only refrain from hindering them they gather, store, dispense, husband, if need be against scarcity, the wealth of the great community of nations. (quoted in Donkin 135)

Smith is like Carlyle and Smiles in his connection of work and God, but he is also not that far from Engels. While Engels and Smith have diametrically opposed views of the division of labor they both agree on the importance of 'the laws of production.' Engels may have a very different model of production in mind from Smith, who sees it in terms of money and wealth, but both agree that work is an essential human activity and that it must be 'productive.' This emphasis upon 'production' however leads to theoretical problems in the work of Marx and Engels and problems in identity formation for men.

**Work and Production**

Masculinity and industry are primary concepts in the Victorian 'Gospel of Work.' To be a man is to be industrious. As Ruskin said in *The Crown of Wild Olive* his ideal was an 'industrious man' (*Crown* XI: 17) and he abjured idleness. The contemporary word for 'industry' would be 'productivity' and it carried a similar weight in the Victorian period as today. To be a successful man is to be a productive man and to be a successful society is to have a large (and ever expanding) Gross Domestic Product. The individual male is remade in the image of social production and the imperative to work combines economics and morality. Similarly, industriousness in the Victorian period combined connotations of individual effort and industrial production.

The word 'industry' itself shifted in meaning from the seventeenth century when it meant the application of skill to work, to the early Victorian sense in which it came to mean simply hard work undertaken assiduously and for an extended time. Carlyle's *Past and Present* (1843) participates in the older pre-nineteenth-century meaning of the word as 'skilled work' and its new meaning of 'hard work.' The term 'industry' is important in Carlyle for its connotations of hard work, self-sacrifice and diligence. While Carlyle's use of 'Captains of Industry' is usually thought of as drawing upon the definition of the term as 'systematic work or labour' and 'a branch of productive labor,'[16] it actually has more reference to an internalized sense of duty that compels 'leaders of industry' to work very hard even when they don't have to; it refers to a sense of inner compulsion to work that is also encoded in John Ruskin's motto 'Work' and inscribed in the references to toil on the frame of Ford Madox Brown's painting *Work* that extol labor as a redemptive activity.[17]

I am not claiming here that other commentators have misread Carlyle but rather that the word 'industry' in its Victorian incarnation contained within it multiple and conflicting meanings and that it is important to stress the historically specific connotations of the term. The dates and citations for 'industry' given in the *Oxford English Dictionary* suggest a gradual redefinition of the word throughout the nineteenth century from hard work to particular forms of manufacture or production, or essentially the equivalent of 'business.' When Carlyle and other Victorian commentators used 'industry' it frequently meant not just 'business' as it came to be defined in the twentieth century, but hard physical labor undertaken as a form of manly duty. The sense in which we now understand 'Captains of Industry' as the equivalent of Chief Executive Officer narrows its focus too much and eradicates the sense of masculine self-discipline encoded within the term in its Victorian usage. This is made explicit by Smiles in *Self-Help* when he defines 'industry' as a national character trait:

> The career of industry which the nation has pursued, has also proved its best education. As steady application to work is the healthiest training for every individual, so it is the best discipline of the state. Honourable industry travels the same road with duty...Labour is not only a necessity and a duty, but a blessing; only the idler feels it to be a curse. (Smiles *Self-Help* 58–9)

Smiles does not just mean 'industrialization' when he invokes industry, but rather a long self-discipline expressed through work. Work is both a 'duty' and 'healthy' and provides 'discipline' at the individual and state levels. Work therefore entails self-discipline in the subject and the State, and in this is close to the Foucault term 'governmentality,' meaning the government of self and others. Inevitably the 'idler' is invoked as the nightmare figure against whom 'Captains of Industry' must fight both internally and externally in order to remain industrious and productive.

For Carlyle therefore a 'Captain of Industry' was not just somebody who ran an organization but a dutiful man who had internalized a sense of discipline akin to that found in the army. The connecting term between Carlyle's use of industry and the present use is 'production.' Carlyle emphasizes that the 'productive' man avoids sloth and idleness. However, not all forms of 'productive' work were equal, and some forms of labor could seem perilously close to idleness.

As Deirdre David has pointed out, the Victorian middle classes tended to view intellectual labor as 'unprofitably utilized leisure' and valorized only 'useful' work (quoted in Clarke 39). Adams has also noted how an increasingly utilitarian Victorian society viewed the literary world as 'a realm of unprofitable, and thus unmanly, intellectual exchange' which underscores the connection between productivity and masculinity (28). This view is also found in Hipployte Taine, who complained that in 1860s England 'there is nothing beyond work conscientiously done, useful production, and a secure and convenient comfort in one's home' (quoted in Tosh 123); while Tosh emphasizes the 'home' part of this remark, I would underline the consequences of the emphasis upon work and 'useful production.' This emphasis upon useful work assigns intellectual labor to the category of leisure, and 'unproductive' leisure at that, making it doubly contemptible. Intellectual labor from this perspective can appear quite useless and would not fit under the rubric of 'industry;' 'Captains of Industry' in other words were not intellectuals but hard workers.

Clarke, quoting G. M. Young, says that in the Victorian period 'there had been a feminizing of intellectual work and a consequent...loss of virility' (39).[18] This devaluing of intellectual labor was a consequence of the raising of the materially productive male 'industry' to the pinnacle of the economic hierarchy. This hierarchy was internalized by male intellectuals themselves, who as a consequence devalued their own labor. While Carlyle would have overtly repudiated the devaluation of intellectual labor, his commitment to a productive masculinity, with productive labor understood as manly and muscular, subverted his own position as a writer and intellectual. As we have seen, both Mill and Carlyle subvert writing as labor in this way even though they were at opposite ends of the political spectrum.

The epitome of the male writer as 'producer' was Anthony Trollope. In his most astute chapter, Andrew Dowling analyzes Trollope's *Autobiography* in terms of work, showing how Trollope deliberately made writing into a trade (88) and denigrated men who did not force themselves to write as 'unmanly' (91). While Dowling says that Trollope was deliberately mounting a critique of the Romantic artist, it would be equally true to say that he was deliberately constructing himself as the 'productive man' rather than the conventional 'unmanly' and unproductive writer. In this he follows a similar path to James Thomson in Linda M. Austin's account of the way in which the poet viewed writing as 'mental exertion' and thus as a form of labor (71).[19] Trollope, like Thomson, turns words into things by comparing himself to a shoe or candle maker, and goes to great length to prove his 'industry' compared to other writers. He feminizes his rivals by questioning their manliness and asserts his own virility by claiming he produces words that are just like things; this is what makes writing into 'industry' and thus manly.

'Industry' was a term that cut across political divisions in the Victorian period. Marx and Engels share with Carlyle a view of masculinity as 'industry.'

They do not want to redefine masculinity in terms other than labor, but rather wish to refashion social conditions so that a man's productive potential can be expressed more fully. Marx and Engels want to change the relations of production, but not escape from production. The 'industrious' man is as much at the heart of their hopes for the future as it is for Thomas Carlyle. Thus Engels can deplore the demasculinization of work as one of its most pernicious side effects, rather than question the conjunction of work and masculinity itself.

The emphasis on 'industry' as production skewed Victorian values in favor of material products and visible signs of industrial production. This is epitomized by the photograph of Isambard Kingdom Brunel, standing in front of the chains of the Great Eastern, which is frequently invoked in representations of Victorian industrialization.[20] (Figure 1). The photograph is a visual embodiment of Smile's *Self-Help* and his *Lives of the Engineers*, representing a heroic, individual man standing in front of his greatest material achievement.

Lost in this celebration of the power of the single male linked to the visual embodiment of his industry is the 'brain work' represented in the John Callcott Horsley portrait of Brunel at his desk, and the social cost for the laborers involved in the construction of the ship. The chains in front of which he is standing whipped out of control shortly after the photograph was taken and killed a worker; rumor also had it that two skeletons of workers were found in the hull of the ship when it was demolished. The people who actually created the ship are not in this photograph; instead we have a single male, his class status indicated by his clothing and cigar, standing in front of a massive industrial project that the photograph implies belongs to him alone. As in the formal portraits analyzed by Purbrick; his stance and setting reinforce his social authority and his connection to the world of masculine industry.

The image of Brunel participates in what Keith McClelland has termed, drawing on Raymond Williams, the isolation of the image of the 'man at work.' In the context of shipbuilding, McClelland analyzes the way in which the shipbuilders, the very people who helped construct the Great Eastern, increasingly internalized a definition of the 'man at work' that disempowered them. Partly this was due to mechanization, which separated 'mental' versus 'manual' labor. Overall, however, these men worked harder because they internalized a model of 'production' that even the leaders of the union accepted, as the comments of John Burnett, quoted by McClelland, show:

> Political economy defines labour as the voluntary exertion of mental or bodily faculties for the purposes of production, or as the action of the human frame directed to the manufacture of useful articles. (McClelland 188)

This definition, as McClelland points out, excluded the previously articulated rhetoric of exploitation. The worker has become in this formulation a single, autonomous unit who is defined entirely by his position in the production process and his worth defined solely in terms of 'the manufacture of useful articles.' The result of this was to impose harder work and longer hours for shipbuilders and to set limits on the way in which the image of the 'working man' could be challenged that lasted well into the twentieth century (McClelland 209). This exploitation is also excluded in the image of Brunel as the single productive 'brain worker' who has produced the giant chains behind him.

The Victorian male, especially in the middle classes, remade himself in the image of production and free trade. Middle-class ideology fused free trade and masculinity and 'naturalized a cultural construction of masculinity by embedding it deep within the language of capital' (Kuchta 160). The languages of capital and masculinity fuse in the ideal of 'productivity' that was seen in opposition to the feminine and 'useless' consumption. This opposition was worked out at the level of language and the body, in words and through clothing which was uniformly self-repressive. Brunel's clothing itself marks him as a member of a managerial and business class. Brunel is a 'man in black' straight out of John Harvey's analysis of Victorian male clothing in *Men in Black*.[21] He is a photographic version of Carlyle's 'Captain of Industry' with the weight of the giant chains behind him attesting to his prowess and productivity.

The 'industry' of the Victorian period was therefore imagined in terms of single, heroic men and large industrial projects that led to 'the manufacture of useful articles.'[22] This is encoded even in Marx's formulation that history is only 'the production by men of their material life' (*Writings* 60). Jean Baudrillard claims in *The Mirror of Production* that in Marx's writing 'the liberation of productive forces is confused with the liberation of man' and so Marx's approach is indistinguishable from that of conventional Political Economy (21). There is a bias in Marx, as there is in the thinking of Carlyle, toward 'the definition of labor power as the source of 'concrete' social wealth' (Baudrillard 25). Work in Marx as for other thinkers in the nineteenth century becomes the basis for all definitions of human value. Marx's schema raises the working classes to the apex of a hierarchy of value, but does not question the value of this hierarchy founded in the idealization of work as material production. Ideas and intellectual production, ironically, have little place in the philosophy of one of the nineteenth century's foremost philosophical critics of capitalism; Marx privileges, as does Carlyle, the production of material goods.[23]

In the context of Ruskin's thought, P. D. Anthony has argued that 'capitalists and communists agree about the absolute importance of *homo faber*' (*Labour* 166). Expressed in less theoretical terms than Baudrillard's, Anthony's argument nonetheless makes the same point that there is much agreement between Marx and Political Economy when it comes to the importance of manly 'production' in both systems of thought. I would add that both philosophies enshrine the 'man at work' as the basic productive unit of their systems and thereby codify masculinity as self-imposed labor in the ideal of the 'man at work' as the symbol of their systems of thought.

The same aporia is to be found in the thought of William Morris who approached most closely a Marxist critique of Victorian social conditions. While Morris mounts a cogent critique of the position of the working classes in such lectures as 'Useful Work vs. Useful Toil' the word that recurs throughout his text is 'production.' Morris does not criticize the compulsion to 'produce,' but rather intensifies it into a self-imposed desire to work rather than something imposed from outside.

This approach to work may arise because, as Alasdair Clayre argues, 'Marx and Morris were both writers...in their own lives they gave a very high place to work and most of their own "play"...was integrated with their work' (122). Clayre astutely contrasts the intellectual's approach to work with the value placed on 'play' by 'people who worked with their hands' underscoring their respective class positions. For Morris and Marx, then, the boundary between 'work' and 'play' can disappear in a magical transformation; because they have internalized the work ethic, both Marx and Morris can redefine work as an internalized compulsion.[24] Both writers accept 'production' as the basis of masculinity because of their own ease in turning 'work' into 'play' in their utopian visions.

The same procedure is carried out in *News from Nowhere* where the abolition of private property leads to the abolition of law and the imposition of the new commandment that 'thou shalt work in order to live happily.' Since work is happiness, it does not need to be imposed by violence (Morris *News* 81). All work in the utopia is pleasurable and undertaken voluntarily (Morris *News* 92). Like Engels, Morris believes that making work voluntary will cure the problem of exploitation, but does not question the conjunction of productivity with the definition of being a man, which places work at the heart of masculinity.

It should not be surprising that Morris has this aporia in his thinking, because even Marx had difficulty mounting a critique of work that did not privilege material production. As heirs to the Victorian division of labor, we still struggle with the contradictions inherent in the injunction to be 'productive' workers when many activities are not considered productive and are not paid and are thus 'unproductive.' Many tasks that people (especially women) carry out are vital to the reproduction of social conditions, but do not receive any symbolic or actual capital in return. Much of the work of society therefore goes unremarked and unrewarded.

Baudrillard's critique of Marx is at its most powerful when he condemns the overdetermination of the worker in terms of production. For Baudrillard, Marx does not assail the fundamental importance of production for the worker, but instead turns it into the essential characteristic of his identity. The worker in Marx is masculine and cannot escape definition in terms of his labor power:

> Marxism...assists the cunning of capital. It convinces men that they are alienated by the sale of their labor power, thus censoring the much more radical hypothesis

that they might be alienated as labor power, as the 'inalienable' power of creating value by their labor. (Baudrillard 31)

If Baudrillard is correct in his criticism of 'labor power' in Marx's thought, and I believe that he is, then idleness would be an anathematized category for Marx as much as for the English writers in this study. Clayre inadvertently reinforces this claim when he terms 'man's' 'life-activity' in Marx's thought as 'the act of production' (49); this statement underscores the identification between masculinity and production as the ultimate value for Marx. The antithesis of the productive male worker in Victorian Britain is, as James Eli Adams has argued, the dandy, a figure who called into question the very definition of masculinity. I would add to the threat posed by the dandy as analyzed by Adams the representation of an 'idle' man who does not produce, but consumes and displays his leisure through his clothing. The dandy, with his mixture of masculine and feminine markers and his rejection of 'labor power,' would be as threatening a figure for Marx as he was for Carlyle because he was unproductive.

The Victorian definition of work as masculine, therefore, trapped men into a relentless life of labor that could not accommodate idleness or pleasure.[25] Idleness and pleasure could not, however, be banished simply by proclaiming the industrious male to be the epitome of virtue. The forces of pleasure, represented most powerfully by sexuality, reasserted themselves at the margins of representations of sweaty, muscled labor as the ultimate in masculine productivity and troubled the serene assertion of Victorian masculine values. The chapters in this book excavate the signs of the troubling eruptions of the excluded forces of sexuality and pleasure as they disturbed the stability of Victorian masculine identity. Men's bodies at work are 'unstable' because like women's bodies they are subject to desire. The Victorian discourse on work is intertwined with the Victorian discourse on sexuality no matter how much authors like Carlyle may have wished to banish it to the margins, or at least to the tropics. The history of work in the Victorian period is, therefore, the history of the attempt to define work as masculine and the male body as productive and free from the threats of the feminine, idleness and sexuality. The first stage of this definition of work as masculine was symbolically to separate women from work, as we shall see in the next chapter.

## Notes

1.  Houghton's *The Victorian Frame of Mind* makes this argument, as does F. M. L Thompson in *The Rise of Respectable Society: a Social History of Victorian Britain, 1830–1900* whereas Martin Wiener's *English Culture and the Decline of the Industrial Spirit 1850–1980* makes the case for the continuity of aristocratic ideals which, he argues, contributed to English industrial decline. Wiener asserts that 'the zeal for work,

inventiveness, material production and money making gave way within the capitalist class to the more aristocratic interests of cultivated style, the pursuits of leisure, and political service' (13). From this perspective there was no rupture between middle-class and aristocratic values.

2. See for instance Thompson and Wiener.

3. David Alderson argues that Kinglsey is not in fact as radical as he appears and finds the intersection between Kingsley and Carlyle in 'Christian Manliness;' see also Donald Hall on 'muscular Christianity.'

4. See Anthony *The Ideology of Work* on the history of work for an account of this Christian tradition.

5. Sussman notes perceptively that for Carlyle 'sickness is associated with a slackening of psychic control' as it was for the Victorians generally (23).

6. Carlyle, quoted in Kaplan (151–2).

7. Adams has an intriguing discussion of the Victorian male body in the context of Walter Pater in *Dandies and Desert Saints*.

8. The contradictions in Carlyle's positions have been characterized by Norma Clarke (echoing Wordsworth) as 'strenuous idleness;' 'strenuous' denotes a male world of validation through hard work and 'idleness' a female world of leisure' (25–43).

9. Simon Gikandi's extended analysis of the way in which English plantations were dependent on West Indian labor for profit whilst representing its workers as 'idle' is particularly relevant here, as is J. M. Coetzee's analysis of the function of 'idleness' as a racial category in the apartheid system. Catherine Hall also analyzes the connection between Carlyle's racial attitudes and the idea that white males should be 'master' in the domestic sphere as well as in the West Indies (273).

10. Michele Cohen locates the origin of the idea of the English as a people of few words in the eighteenth century, when it became 'emblematic of English masculinity' in opposition to French talkativeness (3).

11. Dupré and Gagnier find a similar clear-sighted distinction between use value and exchange value in Aristotle (553).

12. Wilde also defines work as 'activity of any kind' (10).

13. This is not to deny that Engels was not sensitive to the exploitation of women, but he saw this exploitation in the context of marriage and the family in *The Origin of the Family, Private Property, and the State*.

14. On the subject of the marginalization of the father figure in the Victorian family see Claudia Nelson's *Invisible Men*.

15. George Friedmann notes that a French industrial sociologist described the 'despiritualization' of work (137).

16. I am drawing upon the Oxford English Dictionary online (http://dictionary.oed.com) in citing these definitions.

17. Linda M. Austin has analyzed the 'futile asceticism' that James Thomson found in this motto against which he championed 'indolence' (69).

18. Such judgments are obviously relative; from the point of view of women writers such as Margaret Oliphant Victorian intellectual life was a club dominated by the 'manly pen' (Shattock 170–71).

19. Austin in an echo of my own focus on 'production' says that Thomson was 'attuned to signs of production-based discourse' and valued poets such as Browning as masculine workers as a consequence (76).

20. This photograph has become a free-floating image of Victorian work 'detached from the historical circumstances of its making,' as has Smiles' *Self-Help* (McLaurin 34).
21. See also Moers on the dandy as a rebellion against 'men in black.'
22. Of course, Ruskin and Morris attempted to challenge a definition of 'useful' that operated primarily as 'profitable' rather than having any real sense of utility for peoples' lives.
23. Raymond Williams has provided a cogent critique of this tendency in Marxist thought in his essay on 'base' versus 'superstructure.'
24. Christopher Shaw, by contrast, argues that 'Marx rejected the idea that work could become play; Morris did not,' (24).
25. As has been recognized from Marx and Morris through to E. P. Thompson, the Victorian definition of 'work' brought into being the category of 'leisure' at the same time, and led eventually to the creation of a 'leisure industry.'

# Chapter 2

# Gendering Work in the 1840s

**Richard Redgrave and Thomas Hood**

Richard Redgrave and Thomas Hood's representations of women at work mark a crucial stage in the Victorian redefinition of 'work' as masculine and as fatal for women. Both men were deeply sympathetic to the plight of women employed in 'piece work' and dramatized their long hours and economic exploitation. However, their representations were produced in the context of legislation that reinforced the gendered 'separation of spheres' in the Victorian period. While the Victorian 'separation of spheres' is well understood and widely studied, I focus in this chapter on the well-meaning efforts of such men who wished to protect women, but unwittingly helped to separate the terms 'woman' and 'work' in ways that they did not foresee. Their representations mark the beginning of a process that was not reversed until the 1880s.

Richard Redgrave provides a classic example of how a male artist's or writer's sympathies can lead to a form of representation that has the opposite effect from its intended consequences. Redgrave professed deep sympathy with the working classes and with impoverished women who were forced by circumstances to toil in poverty and hunger. His most famous paintings such as *The Sempstress* (1844) (Figure 2) and *The Poor Teacher* (1843) concern lonely and isolated women carrying out work under difficult circumstances. [1] They represent women in desperate situations, cut off from all social support and dying of poverty, hunger and overwork.

Redgrave in his painting *The Sempstress* and Thomas Hood in his poem 'The Song of the Shirt' (1843) represent an important phase in the creation of the Victorian 'man at work.' Their immensely popular images suggested that to enter the 'cash nexus' of waged work was fatal for women, and thus only men should undertake waged labor. This is not to suggest that they knowingly entered some vast male conspiracy to exclude women from working, but rather that their images coincided with a cultural shift in the representation of the division of labor along gender lines. Both Redgrave and Hood were committed to social reform and deeply moved by the lot of women trapped in low-paying, exploitative labor. Their images of working women, however, inadvertently cemented the tie between 'men' and 'work' that became a hallmark of Victorian gender ideology.

Redgrave saw himself as attuned to the working classes, having worked in his father's business alongside working-class men. Redgrave claimed in his memoir that his experiences had given him 'a genuine acquaintance with the feelings and modes of thinking of the working classes, with a power of talking to them in harmony with their own prejudices' (16) and his depiction of the seamstress is part of this sympathy for the working classes. Redgrave's words above have often been quoted, but not the rest of the sentence that goes on to say that his experiences gave him 'a real knowledge of several trades practiced in the manufactory.' He thus claimed not only to have an innate sympathy for the working classes, but also an intimate knowledge of industrial labor. While a painting like *The Sempstress* shows Redgrave's sympathy for the working classes, it does not show his knowledge of manufacturing.

    In fact, his paintings focus on a form of production, that of piecework, which is at the opposite end of the scale from the new industrial forms of manufacture which were increasingly concentrated in large factories. In this his representational strategy is similar to that of Henry Mayhew and John Thomson who Thomas Prasch has argued 'focused on static forms of labor, largely unchanged by the forces of industrial society' (180). The piecework that Redgrave portrays is individual and carried on in homes. Where the new industries collected large numbers of people together into one building and fostered the kind of class consciousness that Marx and Engels believed would lead to social change, piecework isolated individuals in domestic spaces. It was 'home' work rather than organized industrial labor such as that depicted in William Bell Scott's *Iron and Coal* (Figure 3). Rather than use his personal knowledge of manufacturing to represent industrial labor, Redgrave instead focuses on women workers whose labor is carried out in a domestic setting. Redgrave's first-hand experience of industrial production did show itself in his later efforts to bridge the gap between art and industrial design, as in his design work for the Great Exhibition for example (Casteras and Parkinson 5), but his knowledge of manufacturing does not appear in his paintings of women workers.

    Rather than express solely his sympathy with the working classes, his paintings instead represent work as a lethal threat to women.[2] Partly his fusion of women, working and death was the result of seeing his sister die after leaving home to be a governess. His sister Jane, he said 'pined over the duties of a governess away from home, caught typhoid fever, and was brought back to die among us' (Redgrave 26). Redgrave seems to feel that being a governess was responsible for his sister's death and may well have led to his opposition to women working. This belief accounts partly for the inclusion of references to death in 'The Poor Teacher,' who is shown reading a black-edged letter with sad tidings from home. However, Redgrave was not the only one to depict women dying thanks to their work, and in his representation is reacting to a wider cultural anxiety about women and work.[3]

    Quite apart from his autobiographical connection to this painting, Redgrave himself as a Victorian paterfamilias may have felt the position of governess as a rebuke to his own status. Like the seamstress, the governess would present an implicit appeal to imagine the woman as a metaphorical 'sister' for whom the man should be able to provide. The governess provides material evidence that the patriarchal system, in the sense of a society ordered and governed by wise male figures, could break down and thrust them into working in such conditions. Redgrave himself would of course feel this rebuke more powerfully than most because of the death of his own sister.

As Lynn Alexander points out, the seamstress when represented in both art and fiction was turned into a symbol, and the actual conditions of millinery workers themselves were overwhelmed by the representation.[4] The image represented by both Redgrave and Hood 'runs contrary to most parliamentary accounts of the time' because in fact most needlewomen 'gathered in someone's room for company' or were located in millinery houses (2). Redgrave and Hood focused, by contrast, on solitary figures rather than women gathered together in social groups. Redgrave's 1840s image contrasts with Frank Holl's later *The Song of the Shirt* (1875) which shows women sewing in a group. Holl continues the use of a domestic setting and that of death in that the women shown are in mourning, but sewing is seen as a more social act. Similarly in *Alton Locke* Kingsley describes a scene in which a small family worked and later invokes Hood's 'Song of the Shirt' (89, 93). Alexander traces the influences of Redgrave's painting and Hood's poem on the visual iconography of the seamstress throughout the century; John Everett Millais' *Stitch! Stitch! Stitch!* (1876) invoked the connotations of the lonely, starving seamstress while the woman depicted seems more winsome than distraught. The title itself, however, was enough to conjure up the associations of exploitation and death suggested by *The Sempstress*.

The painting's iconography too had personal resonance for Redgrave; as it includes such conventional tropes as the guttering candle and an open window representing the seamstress's imminent death, but these were powerful personal symbols for Redgrave also. In the memoir edited by his son, Redgrave recounts sitting with his mother watching a guttering candle that his mother had indicated would be an omen as to whether she would recover from her illness (10). The candle went out, and his mother later died. The candle in the painting for Redgrave invokes his own feelings of helplessness at witnessing his mother's death. Combined with the loss of his sister, the death of women close to him accounts for some of his evangelical zeal in crusading against piecework and going out to service. The images of working women thus had powerful personal resonance for Redgrave as a symbol of personal loss as well as a depiction of the plight of the poor. This emotional attachment seems to have helped Redgrave capture the pathos of the situation for Victorian men generally.

Redgrave's painting thus achieved widespread recognition because both its subject matter and its strong emotional appeal to men as protectors of women struck a chord among Victorian men. The painting represents a 'distressed needlewoman' in need of the intervention of a male family member in her plight. This is the same appeal made in Thomas Hood's 'Song of the Shirt' in its refrain:

O Men, with Sisters dear!
O Men! with Mothers and Wives!
It's not linen you're wearing out
But human creatures' lives! (Hood 28)

Hood's poem makes all women into members of the family, linked to men
as sisters, mothers or wives; his lines make explicit the implicit appeal to men as
heads of families encoded in Redgrave's painting. This appeal automatically makes
all women dependents who should not work, and all men into their guardians. This
construction of the man as protector of women was in the back of the mind of the
artist P. F. Poole when he wrote to Redgrave about *The Sempstress* saying that it
made him think of his own sisters and want to 'wage war against current social
arrangements, and make us go shirtless to our graves' (Redgrave 45). Picking up
on the correlation between shirts and death, the male writer links his resistance to
family obligations, just as Hood links the need of men to react as 'brothers' and
'fathers' to the image. While it does evoke a desire for social change, the focus of
the letter is on men and their wearing of shirts, not on the economic conditions that
created sweated labor in the first place. Redgrave's painting, like Hood's poem,
evokes a visceral but extremely personal response from male viewers that is
expressed in the context of the women depicted as potential members of their
family.

This male reaction is also provoked by the emphasis on the shirt as an
article of clothing. If the seamstress were sewing a dress then the exploitation
might be regarded as a problem solely between women. The shirt, as Edelstein
remarks, distinguishes the seamstress from lace making or sewing associated with
leisure and makes it clear that she is working (204); but the most important aspect
is the gender associations of the clothing. The emphasis on the shirt as an article of
men's clothing invokes the kind of reaction quoted above to mobilize male
passions against oppression. The symbolism of the shirt implicates men in the
woman's work and makes them directly responsible for her situation.

The popularity of the image and the poem resulted therefore from male
guilt. The Redgrave painting and the Hood poem make men directly responsible
for 'wearing out' women like their mothers and sisters through overwork. Of
course, women did perform a great deal of labor for men in the household, as
books like Langland's *Nobody's Angels* make clear. Rather than acknowledge the
female labor that made their own comfortable existences possible, however, men
externalized guilt and their own dependency onto figures of 'distresses
needlewomen' who could act as surrogates for their own mother and sisters. Rather
than worry about the female members of their own households working too hard,
they could wax indignant about the condition of women separated from their
families and thus from the domestic sphere. The domestic sphere could thus be
preserved as a haven and the evils of piecework blamed for the woman's death. A
similar appeal is encoded in *The Poor Teacher* who is 'left, when worn out with

her day's work, to muse over and long for home and happiness' (Casteras and Parkinson 113); the implicit appeal is to reincorporate the lonely working woman back into the family and rescue her from work defined as drudgery.

Both Redgrave and Poole focus on the single figure of the seamstress and her status as a potential family member. Alexander points out that the iconography established by Redgrave and those that followed him 'remained focused on the seamstress herself, never growing to envelop the laboring classes generally' (68). Redgrave's imagery was translated into identification between men as protectors of women as individuals rather than sympathy for the working classes as a whole. Its net effect was to suggest that men should protect women from work rather than to mobilize feelings on behalf of the working classes as a whole.

The images also helped indirectly bolster the image of the 'man at work.' In her analysis of industrial disputes Rose has documented the ways in which factory reforms and legal reforms helped reinforce the 'definition of what it was to be a man' which was threatened when women entered the workforce (127). Women working were a direct threat to masculine identity founded on a gender ideology that mandated that 'men were to be breadwinners; women were to take care of day-to-day affairs of their households and remain economically dependent on men' (Rose 127). Male trade unionists would work to exclude women from factories, whilst allowing other men to compete for business, underscoring that gender and not economics was at the heart of their opposition to female labor. The figure of the dying seamstress helped reinforce the message that women should not be working, and implicitly reaffirmed that men alone were breadwinners and protectors of dependent women. Where work was fatal for women it reaffirmed masculine identity in the ways represented by Carlyle and Smiles.

The seamstress was a universal figure in that all women were taught to sew regardless of social class and this made it easy for men to identify with the symbol of the needleworker (Alexander 9). A 'distressed needlewoman' could thus become a symbol of women from all ranks of life, regardless of class differences. An *Art-Union* reviewer claimed that the subject of the painting 'is not a low-born drudge' (quoted in Alexander 61) even though there is little in the painting to indicate the woman's class status. Presumably she is supposed to be working class but some of the objects point to a higher social status, such as the clock behind her; such a clock would require a higher amount of capital than was usually associated with 'distressed needlewomen.'

Similarly, the seamstress is clean (Edelstein 204) and neat (Edelstein 196), reinforcing a middle-class ideology that correlated notions of cleanliness and order as attributes of good character. These markers of middle-class femininity are, as Hood makes clear in his poem, threatened by the woman's proximity to work. The net effect is, as a reviewer in the *Athenaeum* says, to make the painting 'too sentimental' so that it only reaches a 'a sort of theatrical and elegant sorrow' (Quoted in Edelstein 197). While it is a tear jerker, the painting presents a 'genteel' poverty that subverts Redgrave's desire to dramatize the plight of working-class women, turning them instead symbolically into members of middle-class families. While Redgrave may have asserted his desire to support the working classes, his painting was therefore widely interpreted as showing the suffering of a middle-class woman who has lost her class status. Like the governess, the seamstress in Redgrave's painting came to represent anxieties about loss of middle-class status, and the incongruity of 'ladies' being compelled to work. Middle-class outrage could be mobilized, it seems, if the subject was made acceptable in some way for the viewer or reader in class terms.

Both the power and the weakness of Redgrave's paintings and Hood's poems come from the very personal relationship between work and production enabled by focusing on the single figure of the woman.[5] Increasingly in the nineteenth century the relationship between work and production was occluded as machinery took over the process of production. Rather than labor resulting directly in the production of one piece of clothing, as in the example of the woman making the shirt, the model in the textile industry was of one person running many looms or other machines that produced textiles *en masse*. It was becoming increasingly difficult to represent the relationship between the worker and his or her production, as John Ruskin lamented, and as Karl Marx diagnosed in his analysis of 'commodity fetishism.' In his image of Medieval craftsmanship Ruskin was appealing to exactly the same method of production as Redgrave and Hood; the intimate relationship between manual labor and its product. Marx, of course, gives the most powerful analysis of this relationship in his remarks on the 'alienation' of the laborer in an industrial capitalist system. Marx talked about the products of labor as an 'alien' force that oppressed the worker, Redgrave and Hood on the other hand see the problem in terms of individuals and families, in a characteristic Victorian translation of social policy into a question of family relations.[6]

Hood's poem strikes the contemporary reader as melodramatic, and thus falls within the category defined by Elaine Hadley in *Melodramatic Tactics* as organizing an appeal to the emotions for political ends.[7] However, while Hood's poem has definite designs on its reader's emotions and seems to be advocating some kind of action, it does not call for social reform so much as the rescue of individual women. Like the Victorian social reform novel generally, the poem translates social oppression into individual suffering, but where the novel or the melodrama would populate the page or the stage with multiple characters, Hood's poem is a universe of one. While the social problem is clear, its representation is severed from any suggestion of political reform in favor of individual salvation.

Hood added a stanza to 'The Song of the Shirt' that directly invoked the threat of industrialization when he distinguished the seamstress from the machinery that was being used to produce textiles in industrializing Britain:

> Work, Work, work,
> Like the Engine that works by steam!
> A mere machine of iron and wood

That toils for Mammon's sake –
Without a brain to ponder and craze
Or a heart to feel – and break! (Hood 30)

The seamstress is not a machine, but she is in competition with machines. Hood represents the seamstress in terms of 'heart' or women's supposed more highly developed emotional susceptibility as a counter to the heartless machine.[8] As Lloyd N. Jeffrey remarks of this simile, its effect 'might be vitiated...as we make the more apposite comparison between the machine and the wretched factory worker of the period' (134). From Jeffrey's perspective this stanza is flawed because it detracts from the focus on the figure of the seamstress by introducing machinery and industrialization. Jeffrey's discomfort with the stanza is prompted by the recognition that the poem, like Redgrave's painting, derives its power by excluding the possible social references to industrialization and the mechanization of labor; it celebrates a form of feminine manual labor rather than mechanized work in a factory.

Both Redgrave and Hood are thus representing a form of manual labor in their respective media. This form of labor, since it involved manual dexterity rather than muscle power, could be defined as a 'women's work.' Neither Redgrave nor Hood would have considered showing one of Arthur Munby's beloved pit brow girls, for example, as an image of women's work (Figure 7). The labor is itself gender appropriate and the woman involved can become an object of sympathy. This form of labor would also be perfectly acceptable if it were carried out in the domestic setting and on behalf of the family because it would not be 'work.'

What makes this act of sewing 'work' is its status as labor carried out for money on behalf of people outside of the family. It is the intervention of money and market relations that marks what these women are doing as 'work,' not the labor of sewing itself. Hood's brief reference to Mammon acknowledges the intervention of market relations in the definition of the woman in the poem, but this is an uncharacteristic moment since the presence of the 'cash nexus' is usually obscured by the domestic setting. Redgrave's painting and Hood's poem therefore resist the intervention of market relations in the representation of women's work. It is the idea of 'women outside the protection of home, family and religion...who risked seduction' that evokes the male instinct to protect these women and remove them from the 'cash nexus' (Nead 318).

The intervention of market relations in the domestic sphere is represented in both Redgrave and Hood as the advent of death. In Hood's poem the shirt becomes a shroud that the woman is making for herself. These lines are very close to Percy Bysshe Shelley's 'Men of England' in which the workers of England are represented as digging their own graves:

With plough and spade and hoe and loom,
Trace your grave, and build your tomb,

And weave your winding-sheet, till fair
England be your sepulchre! (Shelley 573)


However, where Shelley is very explicit about class exploitation in his
poem, and calls for a revolution to overturn the contemporary social order, Hood
never looks beyond the immediate. He appeals to the 'rich' to 'hear' his message,
but does not ascribe blame or call for any particular action. He does use a
vocabulary very close to Engels describing industrial workers when he describes
the woman as a 'slave,' but does not see her working conditions as arising from a
particular social order. It is as if 'work' in his poem were an independent natural
force that was an inevitable part of human lives like the Spring to which he appeals
at another part of the poem. The concept of work has been naturalized as a part of
human identity rather than being represented as an external compulsion. There is
no sense within the poem that the woman's living conditions and work are
produced by the upheavals of the industrial revolution that made her form of labor
increasingly marginalized and in competition with mechanized forms of
production.

Hood's frame of reference is not a social theory like that of Engels, or a
revolutionary ethos of like that of Shelley, but a Christian framework in which
ideas of sin and redemption are implicitly operative. When Hood compares the
woman to a 'slave' he has recourse immediately to the familiar bugbear of the
'barbarous Turk' who enslaves his women because he has no 'soul.' The woman's
situation is an affront to Christian values therefore, not a subject of social theory.
The woman is not doing 'Christian work' in her labor and this makes civilized
British men dangerously close to barbarous Turks who would supposedly enslave
women in ways that would be unthinkable in a Christian nation. The focus of
outrage is primarily a question of the ethical treatment of women, and the cause of
the working conditions and inadequate pay for her work are subsumed under a
general masculine and Christian defense of women's virtue.

The power of the redemptive frame of reference can be seen in the use of
work in Elizabeth Gaskell's *Ruth*, which is critical of the connection of 'fallen
women' and work. Gaskell has Ruth redeem herself though her labors as a nurse,
in an implicit argument that work could provide the same spiritual benefits for
women as well as men. However, Gaskell has Ruth die at the end of the novel.
While Gaskell uses work to 'expose the arbitrary fictions and the role playing of
gender identity' (Masters 36) she reinforces the idea that work is fatal for women.
Many readers were distressed that Gaskell had Ruth die at the end of the novel, but
the ending is testament to the power of the narrative created in the 1840s that work
was fatal for women.

In the final analysis Hood's poem is not really about working conditions
at all, but the definition of women's identity in relationship to men's work. Like
Redgrave's painting, while it appeals at a surface level for intervention in working

conditions, it actually announces as its theme from the outset the proper definition of 'woman:'

> With fingers weary and worn
> With eyelids heavy and red
> A woman sat, in unwomanly rags,
> Plying her needle and thread. (Hood 30)

The poem presents an immediate fissure between woman/unwomanly in terms of clothing. The woman's 'rags' make her not a woman, and she is wearing rags because of her working conditions. The conventional gloss of the lines would be that the clothes she is wearing make her 'unwomanly' because they are unsuitably dirty and full of holes. However, the clothing here creates a schism between woman/unwomanly that goes more deeply into gender identity by suggesting that work has somehow defeminized her. Her work of course is also involved in the system of clothing, and the implication of the poem finally is that if the woman were not working she would not be in rags and not in danger of death. The solution implicitly to the problem is to restore the woman to the category of the feminine by separating her from the category of 'work.' Because work is masculine, to carry out such labor puts the woman in the category of the 'unwomanly' and in danger of death. Removing work would remove the fissure within the category 'woman.'

'The Song of the Shirt' follows Carlyle's *Sartor Resartus* in making identity and clothing synonymous. The opening lines of the poem attest to the power of clothing to make a person a 'woman' and also the power of death to liberate the women from 'unfeminine' conditions. This same constellation of associations is to be found in the 'Bridge of Sighs,' Hood's poem on the dead body of a prostitute who has fallen into a life of sin:

> Look at her garments,
> Clinging like cerements,
> Whilst the wave constantly,
> Drips from her clothing. (Hood 204)

The seamstress and the prostitute are linked by the symbolism of clothing. For Hood the prostitute's clothing makes her a powerful figure of transgressive sexuality where instead of selling a commodity like shirts she is selling her own body. Clothing marks a symbolic connection between the seamstress and the prostitute in terms of the cleansing effect of death in that they are both released from sin by death; thus Hood writes of the prostitute:

> Touch her not scornfully,
> Think of her mournfully,
> Gently and humanly,

> Not of the stains of her,
> All that remains of her,
> Now is pure womanly. (Hood 204–205)

Death restores the prostitute to the category of 'woman' just as death will release the seamstress from her 'unwomanly' rags.[9] The common denominator in both these cases is that of sin; death washes away the 'stain' of sexuality and of work. The refrain of 'The Song of the Shirt' is 'Work, work, work' but this is 'work' understood as a Christian conception of labor as punishment for the sins of Adam and Eve, as it was by Carlyle in the 'Gospel of Work.' In many ways the only possible antidote for the condition of both the seamstress and the prostitute is death because they are experiencing the prevailing human condition after the Fall. Death releases them from their fallen state. The clothing represents sin, but this sin and this clothing will be cast off after death and the soul will rise cleansed and pure after the body, like a garment, has been cast off.

This is the same kind of impetus as shown in the 1842 *Report of the Commission on Mines*. Mining was dirty, dangerous work for children and adults, but the *Report* returns obsessively to the danger to young girls in the work environment:

> In the West Riding it appears, girls are almost universally employed as trappers and hurriers, in common with boys. The girls are of all ages, from seven to twenty-one. They commonly work quite naked down to the waist, and are dressed – as far as they are dressed at all – in a loose pair of trowsers. These are seldom whole on either sex. (*Report* 25)

The outrage expressed here is similar to that documented by Catherine Robson in *Men in Wonderland* in connection with inquiries into factory work (61). Robson's analysis is chiefly concerned with how male preconceptions with the image of the 'ideal girl' were mapped onto the real children in front of the Commission that produced the report. Her analysis of the interaction between Richard Henry Horne and one unsuspecting little girl is particularly compelling in its interpretation of the apparently bizarre questions that were posed (63–5). Robson does not comment on the sexual revulsion that is expressed in the *Report* in connection with work. Sexuality is used in the report to exclude both children and women from the workplace.

Robson charts the same kind of ideological approach to the representation of girls as is evident in the representation of women. While the invocations of sexuality may seem odd to us now, within the context of the 1840s such references introduced sin as a direct result of women working. Keeping women out of the workplace would therefore be seen as protecting their virtue. The sordid and unhealthy conditions were perceived not primarily as a threat to bodily health but as a threat to moral virtue. There was persistent anxiety that women dressing in men's clothing and performing 'men's work' would lead to promiscuity. Where work was seen as an antidote to sin in men, it was represented as leading to excessive sexuality in women.

Just as Hood's seamstress is dressed in unwomanly rags, these female mine workers are dressed, or not dressed, in unwomanly trousers. Some of these 'girls' would also seem to qualify as working women if they are as old as 21. The report is outraged by the possibility of the lack of clothing leading to sex. The report stated that there was 'nothing more disgustingly indecent or revolting than these girls at work. No brothel can beat it' *(Report* 24). Despite the fact that they are dirty and dressed in trousers, these women are still connected with prostitution.

This eroticization of women's labor is often thought of as peculiar to Arthur Munby, who collected images of women wearing mining clothes. The men quoted in the *Report* consistently term women dressing as men as 'disgusting' and would view images like the Wigan 'pit brow girls' (who are clearly women rather than 'girls') as sexual threats. Such women subvert both sex and gender in their work. Where Munby saw theses images as erotic the *Report* shows a persistent rejection of women's working in terms of sexuality, and Arthur Munby opposed its provisions bitterly. He too saw female work in terms of sexuality, but wished to keep women working to fulfill his own desires. The Mines Act passed as a result of this report stated that no females at all were to be employed underground, and set the minimum age for boys at 10. The legislation thus protected women as a group and young male children but did not address the problems of mining as a dangerous and exploitative form of labor for men. Since men were supposed to work they were not in danger of being corrupted in the same way as women.

Women's bodies in both Redgrave and Hood are understood therefore as vehicles of sin when in contact with work (which is, as we shall see, the opposite of the effect of work on men). While both Redgrave and Hood may have wished to improve the working conditions of women, their representation of these women is short-circuited by an underlying assumption that for women to work is to enjoin them to sin. Only by dying and going to Heaven will these women be released, not by the intervention of government policies based on blue books. The appropriate emotional response in this case is to 'mourn' these and all working women. Men such as the anonymous letter writer can imagine women from their own families in this situation, think of them as dead, and mourn them. However, as Jeffrey points out, readers of Hood poems 'would be moved to feeling but not necessarily to efficacious action' (145) and the representation allows the male viewer to experience sympathy for the plight of the woman depicted, but not necessarily feel that anything more was required than this feeling.

In this context the promise of the anonymous letter writer to go shirtless to his grave takes on a rather more sinister gloss. His reaction is entirely couched in terms of what he will do in reaction to his feelings, and while the promise to go shirtless was a noble and dramatic gesture, it was impractical; it's extremely unlikely that a Victorian male could have boycotted wearing shirts. While the letter writer may have experienced a surge of emotion at the spectacle of a distressed needlewoman, his reaction is not likely to improve the women's working conditions. The male is also not the one who dies because of work in these or any other representation of labor in this period; it is women who die. Therefore the only ones going to their graves are women, either literally through starvation or imaginatively when their male relatives imagine them as dead. While Redgrave and Hood may have wished to provoke outrage and consequent government reform, their representations actually provoke thoughts of death and mourning, and lead to emotions that do not find outlet in any action. The images also place women firmly within the family, and represent any move to leave the family as fatal. Hood explicitly blames the lack of family for the prostitute's death:

> Sisterly, brotherly,
> Fatherly, Motherly,
> Feelings had changed:
> Love, by harsh evidence,
> Thrown from its eminence. (Hood 206)

The prostitute is thus isolated and estranged by being outside the family. In the 'The Song of the Shirt' and 'The Bridge of Sighs' the focus is on a single woman outside of any social context who should have been incorporated under the rubric 'sister' or 'child' but is not. Hood encourages readers to think of the woman as a potential member of the family, just as Redgrave does in his painting. It is for this reason that Redgrave has the woman in *The Poor Teacher* reading a letter from home, and a song on the piano entitled 'Home, Sweet Home' to locate the problem as the displacement of the woman from the domestic setting. For women therefore to work in the commercial sphere is seen as fatal; for men to work is implicitly the natural state of affairs.

The difference between the treatments of women's and men's work can be seen most dramatically in the contrast between 'The Song of the Shirt' and Hood's poem 'The Lay of the Labourer.' The poem was written after Hood read about a young worker who, in an anonymous letter that was traced back to him, threatened to burn down the Huntingdon Assizes and commit robbery and other violent acts if he wasn't given work. Rather than a passive victim, the male worker in Hood's poem is shown as strong and independent and rejecting any kind of charity:

> No parish money, or loaf,
> No pauper badges for me,
> A son of the soil, by right of toil
> Entitled to my fee.
> No alms I ask, give me my task:
> Here are the arm, the leg,
> The strength, the sinews of a Man,
> To work, and not to beg. (Hood 233–4)

Hood glosses over the threat of violence in the original letter and focuses on man's 'right of toil,' or his natural destiny as a worker. This is Hood's version of Carlyle's formulation that men were born to work, and that not to work is not to be man. Where his poems on women workers invoked sympathy and eulogy, his poem in defense of male laborers emphasizes muscles and strength. The poem focuses on the 'sinews' of the worker's arms and the muscles that are developed in manual labor. A visual analogy for this poem would be the paintings of Hubert von Herkomer later in the century, who emphasized upright masculine figures in his depictions of working-class men. In a painting like *On Strike* the emphasis is upon muscular working-class men on whom women and children are dependent (1891; reproduced in Treuherz 100). 'The Lay of the Labourer' failed to inspire the same range of representations as 'The Song of the Shirt' and was not canonized in the same way. Where 'work, work, work' is seen as an appropriate rallying cry for men, it is seen as deadly to women who must be rescued from work. However, the image of a muscular laborer crying 'work, work, work' did not have the same emotional impact as a seamstress lamenting 'stitch, stitch, stitch' and the poem was not canonized like the 'Song of the Shirt.'

Just as Hood's poem 'The Lay of the Labourer' was not canonized, the reception of Redgrave's painting can be contrasted with that accorded a painting of social protest by his good friend Charles West Cope. Cope's *The Board of Guardians* was based on his first-hand observation of a woman and child appealing for aid to a meeting of such a body. Cope says that his painting attracted crowds when exhibited at the Royal Academy and was also cited in several *Times* editorials because there was a political struggle over the Poor Law at the time (142). However, despite its popularity, Cope could not find a buyer for the painting, nor was it as widely reproduced as Redgrave's painting.

Cope's *The Board of Guardians* differs from Redgrave's 'The Sempstress' and Hood's 'Song of the Shirt' in important respects. Cope's painting does not focus on a single woman in a domestic setting but rather on a woman in a highly charged public space. Rather than evoke individual feelings of protectiveness from men for distressed women, the painting shows a politically charged process at work with men in positions of authority and power over the woman. Rather than allow men to imagine themselves in the abstract as saviors of distressed women, the painting brings forcefully to the fore questions of political power and the distribution of resources in society. The painting leant itself well to a political debate carried on in the newspapers during this period, as Cope notes, but this very political relevance may have doomed its chances for sale and popular success.

Hood himself had similar difficulty gaining acceptance for a social protest poem that addressed politics directly. Also appearing in the Christmas 1843 Punch issue with 'The Song of the Shirt' was 'The Pauper's Christmas Carol.' This poem was much more directly political in its commentary on the Poor Laws and workhouses, invoking 'warden, clerk and overseer' as instruments of oppression in the treatment of the pauper. Where 'The Song of the Shirt' was anthologized and turned into song, 'The Pauper's Christmas Carol' was ignored and is hardly even mentioned even in studies of Hood, although Jeffrey does assert that 'there are some good things in it' (135). The poem's problem is that, like Cope's painting, it combines an appeal for sympathy with a more direct acknowledgment of the political and social forces that gave rise to the pauper's problem in the first place.

Cope's painting is closer in spirit to G. F. (George Frederick) Watts' painting *The Song of the Shirt/The Seamstress* (1848) which does not emphasize the woman's features. Her face is partially obscured by her arm and she rests her head on it in a gesture of despair. The painting is very dark, emphasizing the woman's isolation and despair. Visually the painting is far less appealing than Redgrave's attractive seamstress. Watts is, however, closer to Redgrave in his emphasis upon a woman isolated in a domestic setting rather than in a public venue like Cope's *The Board of Guardians*.

I am not suggesting that either Redgrave or Hood were acting in bad faith. Rather, these cases shows how in Victorian culture in the 1840s the range of representation of labor was constrained by ideological forces that prevented Hood's 'Lay of the Labourer' or Cope's *The Board of Guradians* from becoming popular successes like 'The Song of the Shirt' or *The Sempstress*. While Hood and Redgrave wished to express sympathy for the oppressed of the working classes, they could only do so through the representation of single, dying women. Implicitly the debate on working conditions in the 1840s was framed as a question of the threat posed to women only by having to work. Public support could be rallied for the separation of the categories of 'women' and 'work' through the figure of the dying seamstress, but not for men and not in overtly political terms.

Both Redgrave and Hood were viewing women from the perspective of men who had a natural right to work who were concerned to protect women from labor. Their depictions of women at work corroborate Tosh's assertion that 'men...were the invisible subject directing attention to women as object' (45). I would add to this observation that representations of the unsuitability of women for work implicitly strengthened the claim that men were naturally suited for labor. Their representations thus helped reinforce the idea also being articulated by working-class men that they had the right to a wage as the heads of families and protectors of women. The message from both middle-class men and trades unionists cemented men's position as breadwinner and *pater familias*.

An ideological redefinition of work along gender lines was therefore carried out in artistic representations government reports and the demands of male working-class organizations which increasingly used the demand for a living wage to mean enough for a male head of household to support a wife and children. The images, texts and reports of the 1840s mark the beginning of the articulation of the ideology of 'separate spheres' that denoted a male space of work in opposition to a feminine domestic space. As I will show, this ideological redefinition of work had profound repercussions for both men and women. While the effect of defining the domestic as feminine space has been well documented, much less attention has been paid to the effect of making masculinity coincide with the term 'work.'

The ideological limits of Redgrave's and Hood's representations of work emerge most strongly in contrast to William Bell Scott's painting *Iron and Coal* (1861). This is one of a very few paintings that attempted to eulogize the kind of industrial manufacture of which Redgrave had first-hand experience. While Redgrave did in fact have knowledge of manufacturing, he did not produce a painting like Scott's 'Iron and Coal' that actually tries to depict industrial production. Scott's picture was part of a series commissioned and designed to highlight the industry of northern England, and Newcastle in particular. As such it depicts George and Robert Stephenson's workshop, and particularly a process that involved several workmen striking a metal plate in unison. The resulting image is a unique representation of industrial labor in aesthetic terms. It is also a strikingly masculine image of labor.

Paul Usherwood remarks that this is a Newcastle that 'seemingly only values men's work' because examples of women working are pushed to the margins and made almost invisible, such as the figures of the fishwives and milkmaid on the quayside (50). The emphasis in the picture is upon the muscular, coordinated labor of the men hammering out metal in the workshop. The only female presence is a little girl who has brought her father's lunch. Where Redgrave focused on labor in the domestic space, Scott focuses on work as a masculine endeavor and through the figure of the child suggests that the domestic has no place in this world. 'The little girl may be bodily present in the man's world, in Stephenson's workshop, but clearly this is not where she properly belongs' (Usherwood 50), since the female domestic presence is out of place in this industrial workshop. In Scott's painting 'industry' is masculine, and also linked to male muscles. The workers are shown as beefy individuals, and their size and strength is emphasized by the diminutive little girl sitting in the foreground.

The incongruity of the little girl's presence is further underscored by her proximity to artillery shells and the design for a new piece of artillery produced in Newcastle arms works. In a previous version of the painting Scott had actually had the little girl playing with the shell. The girl is dangerously close not only to a male world of industry, but also to weapons and military conflict which are emphatically the preserve of masculinity. She seems an extremely odd element in the picture, and is an anomaly rather than an integral part of the work going on around her.

Scott's painting, like Ford Madox Brown's *Work*, makes working-class labor into a heroic, muscular enterprise. In contrast to Hood and Redgrave, however, Scott focuses on male labor in a very public space. The workshop is represented as if it were open to the rest of Newcastle, not as a closed environment. Thanks to his emphasis on muscles and strength in industrial labor, Scott is able to represent work as a cooperative effort among men that sets it apart from the female and domestic. Women are marginalized and infantilized in this world of masculine work. Where women were implicitly situated as dependents in Redgrave and

Hood's images, in Scott's painting they are explicitly placed in the position of the child in relation to men's work.

Scott represents a space that Redgrave, for all his knowledge of industry and his sympathy for the working classes, could not enter. Creating *Iron and Coal* later in the century than Redgrave, Scott can assume that 'industry' is a purely masculine enterprise and take for granted the separation of the domestic sphere and work. The cultural work of the 1840s in separating women from work and industry enables the representation of the masculine space of Stephenson's workshop. Similarly, when Ford Madox Brown comes to represent work in the 1860s; he can assume that work is a heroic, masculine, working-class enterprise, best represented by muscular men with women as marginal presences.

The marginalization of women from the world of work was part of a broad cultural process in the 1840s. Women were associated with abandonment and exploitation, and men with heroic enterprise in this period generally; Casteras notes that in Redgrave's paintings male figures faced 'manly challenges' while women were shown as in need of sustenance and care (22). This separation of women from heroic, manly work presented problems, however, for later artists and writers. The problems are revealed most strongly in Ford Madox Brown's *Work*, which attempts to show a panorama of Victorian society, but has difficulty encompassing women and intellectual labor in its scope. Like Scott, Brown shows a group of working-class men engaged in a very public form of labor, but his idealization of his working-class subjects is contradictory, as we shall see in Chapter 3.

Work and sexuality were linked in the Victorian imagination. Women working brought forth images not only of prostitution but also of a threatening female independence that could be expressed both sexually and financially. Work and sex are not normally now thought of as coterminous and sex would most probably be viewed as a leisure pursuit, unless one is a 'sex worker' which is a less pejorative term for prostitute that has not gained wide currency. In the Victorian discourse on labor, work and sex were often implicated in each other, especially when representing women at work. The specter of unregulated sexuality informs male representations of women and work, especially in Charles Dickens' *Hard Times* and *Bleak House*, as I argue in the next chapter.

**Notes**

1. *The Poor Teacher* was first exhibited at the Academy in August 1843. The painting was shown in 1845 with the title *The Governess* and the caption 'She sees no kind domestic visage here.' In the 1843 version teacher has a single cup and plate showing a meal taken alone. *The Sempstress* was first shown at the Royal Academy in 1844 and was accompanied by lines from Hood's 'Song of the Shirt' which had appeared the year

before in *Punch*. See Casteras and Parkinson for a detailed history of the many different versions of these paintings that Redgrave produced in his lifetime.

2. This is of course, part of a larger narrative of sexual danger and working women that assumed that earning money in any form led to prostitution. This connection was underscored in the section of Henry Mayhew's *London Labour and the London Poor* in which he drew upon the statistical work of Bracebridge Hemyng. See the section 'Those Who Will not Work.'

3. Redgrave is also part of the general cultural association of women and death noted in Jan Marsh's chapter 'Pale Ladies of Death' in *Pre-Raphaelite Women*. Elisabeth Bronfen has explored the use of the female body to represent death in *Over Her Dead Body*.

4. This chapter was written before the publication of Alexander's book. Her analysis is an invaluable contribution to our understanding of the seamstress figure. Her book focuses on the proliferation of seamstress images in the nineteenth century rather than the relationship between the males who created the images and their subjects, which is the focus of my own analysis.

5. A painting like Eyre Crowe's *The Dinner Hour, Wigan* (1874) presents a good contrast with the solitary woman. While it focuses on a moment of leisure outside the factory, the painting shows a group of working-class women in a social situation as a group.

6. Gallagher gives a cogent analysis of how analyses of social relations in Victorian discourse were couched in metaphors of family in her *Industrial Reformation of English Fiction*.

7. See Elaine Hadley *Melodramatic Tactics: Theatricalized Dissent in the English Marketplace, 1800–1885*.

8. David Meakin in *Man and Work*, to contrast with Hood's sentiment, quotes Ure's utopian vision of a society devoid of human labor as a 'vast automaton' (22).

9. A visual analogue to the Hood poem is the George Frederick Watts painting *Found Drowned* (1848–50) which eroticizes the body of a dead woman after her suicide.

# Chapter 3

# Dickens, Work and Sexuality

## Fire and Sex in Coketown

Work is found as a theme in many of the Dickens novels that are populated by clerks, lawyers and the occasional police inspector.[1] I will focus on two of Dickens' novels in which work is a more than usually explicit subject. These novels do not, like *David Copperfield*, draw upon Dickens' own experiences of life and work but use a working-class man and a woman to explore the value of labor in Victorian society.[2] *Hard Times* address industrialization directly and is most obviously concerned with the fate of the English laborer, as Dickens' Introduction makes clear; however, it actually represents labor not in terms of the worker but in terms of the regulation of female sexuality. Like Redgrave and Hood in the previous chapter, Dickens uses the female body to represent the need to separate work and sexuality.

The other novel I consider in this chapter also uses female labor to represent its theme. While *Bleak House* is not so obviously interested in issues of labor I argue that, through the figure of Esther Summerson, Dickens examines the status of all kinds of work carried out in the home, including writing. Mary Poovey has analyzed *David Copperfield* in terms of male labor, but I would suggest that *Bleak House* is even more centrally concerned with the issue of the representation of male labor through the intermediary of a female character.[3]

In both *Hard Times* and *Bleak House*, Dickens' attempts to represent work are displaced into a debate on the regulation of female sexuality. In particular, the characters of Louisa Gradgrind and Esther Summerson take on symbolic weight as female representatives who must enact Dickens' difficulties with defining the status of his own work as problems of sexuality. Even the heroic working-class figure of Stephen Blackpool is implicated in unregulated sexuality through his ill-advised marriage to an alcoholic and adulterous wife that leads eventually his downfall, and his death in Hell pit. Blackpool is in Katherine Kearns' terms a man who 'yearns toward...productive action' but is reduced to 'impotence' (858); as her vocabulary implies, male work is viewed in terms of a failure of male sexuality in *Hard Times*. Dickens' problems with male sexuality and with work lead him to idealize women and to see them as separated from both work and sex. The same kind of anxiety, that women working would somehow become sexualized, as was betrayed in the 1842 Mines Act, informs Dickens' representation of women and work in these novels. This effort to separate women from work leads to the idealization of Sleary's Horse-riding in *Hard Times* and of Esther Summerson herself in *Bleak House*.[4]

My analysis has a similar starting point to Johnson's in *Hidden Hands*, where she raises the issue of an 'anomaly' in the industrial novels that 'none of the women whose lives those novels use as templates for industrial transformation works in – or even enters – a factory' (1). As she says, the designation 'working men' to refer to factory 'hands' 'repressed the actual gendered makeup of the factory workforce' (4). Where her analysis leads to a consideration of the status of the 'factory girl' in the industrial novel, my own approach is to analyze the relationship between the male writer and the subject of work. The 'anomaly' identified by Johnson in terms of the representation of work is intrinsic to and a feature of the Victorian industrial novel. In Dickens' case in particular, I am interested in why he would often represent labor issues through the figures of women rather than men working in a factory.

The key to this conundrum lies, I believe, in Victorian masculinity. Sussman has analyzed the importance of male self-regulation and John Kucich in *Repression in Victorian Fiction* has addressed the general drive toward repression as a tool of consciousness in the Victorian novel. I would add to their analyses of Victorian masculine subjectivity the mechanism of displacement through which the bodies of women and the working classes come to symbolize a divided and contradictory identity. I am concerned here with a method of displacement that operates in a way similar to the Irish widow in Carlyle's rhetoric as a figure of disorder. Dickens' position as a male is defined through the threat of unregulated female sexuality. Work is read as sexuality in both novels, and the proximity to work threatens to create 'fallen' women who are dangerously close to the anathematized figure of the prostitute, rather than the governess, to adapt Poovey's title.[5]

*Hard Times* and *Bleak House* were written in sequence, the former in 1852–53, the latter in 1854. Both tackle the issue of work but from very different perspectives. Issues of work in *Bleak House* are represented primarily through the character of Esther Summerson, and in *Hard Times* ostensibly through Stephen Blackpool, but also through the figure of Louisa Gradgrind. When Dickens wrote *Hard Times* he had hoped to take a holiday from writing after completing *Bleak House*, but was pressured by declining sales of *Household Words* to take up the pen again. He wrote to a friend that 'I did intend to be as lazy as I could through the summer, but here I am with my armour on again.'[6] The metaphor of armor recalls Carlylean images of men doing battle against the demons of chaos and idleness. Like Carlyle, Dickens compares work to male combat and alludes to laziness as an alternative and rejected form of behavior.[7] The specter of indolence that haunted Carlyle's prose also informs Dickens' approach to hard work. Writing *Hard Times* was work undertaken in the face of the threat of indolence.

*Hard Times* is the Dickens novel most directly inspired by Carlyle. The book is dedicated to Carlyle, and the title '*Hard Times*: For *These* Times' is a reference to 'Signs of the Times.' Overtly the book is part of the 'condition of England' debate that addressed the effect of the industrialization of the country on the working classes. However, the novel seems in many respects unsympathetic to the working classes *en masse*, as the characterization of Slackbridge (with the suggestion that he is just trying to avoid work by 'slacking') shows. The division that animates the book seems much more to be between work and sexuality; work is represented by the mills and factories of Coketown, and leisure and play by the sexually loose denizens of Sleary's Horse-riding. In a very Victorian dichotomy, the alternative to an appealing but dangerous sexuality is a self-denying and self-punitive emphasis on work and duty.

Sussman has termed *Hard Times* a novel 'that works out in scathing comedy the emotional logic of Carlylean industrial manliness' in its 'definition of bourgeois manhood as sublimated sexuality rather than heterosexual erotics' (66).[8] As Sussman's reference to comedy implies, he finds Mr. Bounderby to be the most 'Carlylean' figure in the plot and analyses the novel from this perspective. Sussman's astute comments, however, point to the way in which sublimated sexuality marks the novel's two central characters, Louisa Gradgrind and Stephen Blackpool, who both must repress their desires for other people. Furthermore, the novel defines a Carlylean 'Gospel of Work' not in terms of labor but in terms of regulated sexuality. The novel works out a libidinal dynamics in the contrast between 'work' as regulated sexuality and 'play' as a marginal but alluring zone of desire.

Dickens names the distinction between work and play specifically as part of his novel when he introduces the figure of Stephen Blackpool. He says, in ironic vein, that:

> I entertain a weak idea that the English people are as hard-worked as any people upon whom the sun shines. I acknowledge to this ridiculous idiosyncrasy, as a reason why I would give them a little more play. (*Hard Times* 99)

Dickens, hard-working himself, would like to valorize 'play' as the opposite. In the 'condition of England' debate he sees excessive work as a problem, and presumably regards it as particularly acute for the working classes. Dickens tries to construct an alternative to the English problem of overwork in *Hard Times*. However, as many commentators have noted, Sleary's Horse-Riding is a marginal alternative at best to the severely workful Coketown. The circus functions well as an escape from the daily grind, but does not represent a meaningful alternative to the factory discipline embodied in the buildings of Coketown. What Sleary's does effectively represent is a certain sexual license and ease with sexuality. Where the workers of Coketown are defined as 'hands,' the inhabitants of Sleary's world seem defined almost entirely by their legs. 'Legs' in this case represent sexuality, so that the circus is an alternative world of sexual freedom that focuses on a different part of the body from manual labor. Sissy Jupe

is struck by the company being 'so scant of dress, and so demonstrative of leg' and
their general lack of inhibition in displaying their bodies (*Hard Times* 300).[9] The
contrast then is not between 'work' and 'play' here but work and sex, and between
the workers of Coketown as 'hands' and the members of Sleary's as 'legs.' The
human body in Coketown is divided into 'hands' and 'legs' by the division of
labor, which is represented in terms of work and sexuality.

In this context it may be asked what Louisa Gradgrind has to do with
industrialization or mechanization. Partly of course the narrative works out the
consequences for Louisa of her father's mechanical approach to education, an
austere pedagogy that excludes all imagination. At another level, however, Louisa
is connected to industrialization by fire as a metaphor for sexuality. Louisa is
identified consistently by her habit of staring into fires. The fire represents
imagination, which her father's system of education and the rigid, mechanized
buildings of Coketown seem designed to abolish. However, there is also a
consistent association made between the fires of Coketown and sexuality; the ideas
of smoke, flame and serpents occur repeatedly in Dickens' description of
Coketown:

> It was a town of machinery and tall chimneys, out of which interminable serpents
> of smoke trailed themselves for ever and ever, and never got uncoiled. (*Hard
> Times* 60)

> The Fairy palaces burst into illumination, before pale morning showed the
> monstrous serpents of smoke trailing themselves over Coketown. (*Hard Times*
> 104)

> The lights were turned out, and the work went on. The rain fell, and the Smoke-
> serpents, submissive to the curse of all that tribe, trailed themselves upon the
> earth. (*Hard Times* 105)

> The bell was ringing, and the Serpent was a Serpent of many coils, and the
> Elephant was getting ready. (*Hard Times* 114)[10]

The smoke serpents of Coketown seem an odd feature of industrialization
initially; the smoke is a sign of industrial work, but this smoke is connected with
sexual transgression. References to the curse of Genesis 3.14 invoke sin and
transgression and seem to have little in common with Dickens' social criticism.
Why should industrial labor be associated with serpents and the Fall? Part of the
answer is, of course, the traditional association of work with the 'curse of Adam,'
and the idea that work was a direct result of the discovery of sexuality in the
Garden of Eden. However, the fires also invoke the plot of Louisa's temptation by
Harthouse, and her own almost literal 'fall' as she edges closer and closer to
infidelity. This subplot pits the repression of desire and a devotion to duty against
the twin temptations of sexuality and idleness. The story thus becomes about the

regulation of desire in general, but the presence of fire also marks a debate about masculinity and sexuality that Sussman also finds in Pater's uses of fire as 'sexualized male desire' (146).

Catherine Gallagher has noted in passing the importance of desire in general in *Hard Times*, calling Coketown 'a world driven by rapacious desires, especially the desires of an incestuous 'unnatural' family' (164). Gallagher sees the origins of sexuality in the patriarchal family and an Oedipal relationship between Louisa and her father, who delivers her to Bounderby. However, the origins of sexuality in the book lie not in the family but in work. Far from being 'sexually exploited' as Gallagher asserts, Louisa is in danger of becoming sexualized because of her proximity to the fires of Coketown, which are linked to sin and death. Dickens thus explores issues of masculinity, sex and work through Louisa, just as in *Bleak House* he explores issues of professional versus women's work through Esther Summerson.

The connection between Louisa and the Coketown is made directly by Tom when he asks her what she sees when she is looking at the fire. Louisa talks in terms of 'unmanageable thoughts' that occur to her when she stares at the flames (*Hard Times* 90). Louisa's management of her thoughts, initially concerned with the unsatisfied 'fire' of her imagination, becomes as the novel progresses a question of her management of her sexuality. This sexuality is linked to the fires of Coketown again by another question from Tom:

> Removing her eyes from him, she sat so long looking silently towards the town, that he said, at length: 'Are you consulting the chimneys of the Coketown works, Louisa?' (*Hard Times* 133)

Louisa has a special connection to the fire of Coketown, remarking to her father that 'there seems to be nothing there but languid and monotonous smoke. Yet when the night comes, Fire bursts out, father!' (*Hard Times* 133). Just as the narrator recognizes 'serpents' in the smoke of Coketown, Louisa recognizes the fire smoldering in the depths of the factories. The narrative makes insistent connections between her stifled imagination and sexuality, and the fires of industry in Coketown. This imaginative connection between Louisa, sexuality and fire finds its ominous culmination in the Hell pit as Stephen pays the ultimate price for his own sexuality; Louisa escapes punishment because she resists temptation, but Stephen suffers because of the wayward sexuality that is embodied in his wife. This is underscored by numerous reference to the fires of Coketown in terms of Revelation 2.18 and 'the kindling of red fire' which invokes fiery images of Hell. Like the serpents, the fire imagery refers to images of sin and damnation as central aspects of life in Coketown. While the narrative clearly does address issues of regimentation and the repression of imagination as central problems, the repeated references to fire, smoke and sin make a discussion of the place of workers in industrialized England more of a debate on the management of sexuality than the need for reform of workers' conditions of labor.

Within this Biblical framework, work becomes the consequence of sin, particularly the fall of Adam and Eve. This is an echo of the language used to represent work by Carlyle. Hearkening back to an older religious tradition that viewed work as a necessary evil visited on the world by God in reaction to human transgression, the linking of smoke and serpents makes industrial labor a part of a general human condition. While Dickens may make appeals for the plight of the worker, on a symbolic level the text suggests that work is an unavoidable consequence of a general human fall from grace. All the workers in Coketown are by implication paying for the sins of their forebears.

Louisa is not a worker; *Hard Times* cleaves to a Victorian gendered division of labor in that Harthouse represents the 'Idle Dilettantism' of the upper classes castigated by Carlyle. Louisa is tempted by this idleness because she is a woman, and thus separated from the sphere of work. Stephen Blackpool, by contrast, is the severe, self-disciplined male worker who must rein in his desires.

The worker in *Hard Times* is thus represented by a male, in what by the time Dickens was writing was an anachronism. If Dickens were to reflect the real composition of the workforce in the Coketown mills, he would have a young woman as the central character. Stephen Blackpool is described as a power loom weaver, but by the 1850s most power loom weavers were young women. Advances in technology meant that what was previously a male skill was now a task that could be carried out by relatively unskilled and lower paid young women. However, rather than make his central character a female power loom weaver, Dickens makes him instead a forty-year-old man, and one considerably older than most female power loom weavers at the time.

Dickens is, however, unable to represent Louisa as a female mill worker. The contradictions between her gender identity and the representation of labor in the novel as a masculine enterprise mean that she must be separated from the 'men at work.' Louisa is connected to the world of work via her sexuality, but the connection is oblique and symbolic instead of direct. Instead of the world of work, she inhabits the domestic sphere and the threat to her identity comes from sex and leisure, not sex and work. Stephen Blackpool thus pays the ultimate price for transgressive sexuality as a worker, not Louisa. It is simply impossible for Dickens to represent his heroine as a worker, in contrast to, for instance, Elizabeth Gaskell in *Ruth*, whose heroine redeems herself from the taint of transgressive sexuality through redemptive work. Ruth dies thanks to her labors at the end of the novel, but the self-sacrificing work that she carries out leads to her redemption from the taint of sexuality.[11] There is no such outcome for Louisa because the contradictions she represents cannot be reconciled within the representational schema of the novel. The same is true of Esther Summerson in *Bleak House*.

Esther Summerson in *Bleak House* does find a work role in the novel, though it is not overtly recognized as such, and she is also rescued from the taint of her mother's wayward sexuality by the disease that transfigures her face and separates her from her mother. Unlike Louisa who flees marriage with Bounderby, Esther is shown as benefiting from her socialization into female domestic labor by marrying Dr. Woodcourt. The common feature of the two characters is their indirect connection with labor, and the intermingling of work and sexuality in their roles.

Esther Summerson functions as a mirror image of the male writer working in the domestic sphere. Just as Ford Madox Brown had difficulty representing intellectual labor as work, so Dickens indirectly represents his own position through Esther, but cannot directly represent the labor of writing. The problem for male intellectuals who worked at home lies in the separation of the domestic and labor. Work cannot be carried out at home. Work and home are antithetical concepts because of the long process of separation of women from work that began in the 1840s. Just as 'work' and 'masculinity' were synonyms, so were the 'home' and the feminine. The separation of spheres was not just an economic organization, but also organized consciousness, as John Ruskin's famous formulation in 'Of Queen's Gardens' in *Sesame and Lilies* made clear:

> But the woman's power is for rule, not for battle,—and her intellect is not for invention or creation, but for sweet ordering, arrangement and decision. She sees the qualities of things, their claims, and their places. Her great function is Praise: she enters into no contest, but infallibly adjudges the crown of contest. By her office, and place, she is protected from all danger and temptation. The man, in his rough work in open world, must encounter all peril and trial:—to him, therefore, the failure, the offense, the inevitable error: often he must be wounded, or subdued, often misled, and always hardened. But he guards the woman from all this; within his house, as ruled by her, unless she herself has sought it, need enter no danger, no temptation, no cause of error or offense. (Ruskin *Sesame* XI: 99–100)

Such passage as these were frequently reprinted and 'cast a long shadow' over the period (Tosh 149). Feminine consciousness and 'rough work' are completely separate in Ruskin's formulation, so that it would be impossible to represent the categories of 'woman' and 'work' under the same rubric.

For men the opposite is true in that identity can only be won through constant work which for Ruskin is expressed in the metaphor of battle. The corollary of this battle metaphor is that work will quite often kill its subjects, but this is an inevitable result of any 'battle.' Men in Ruskin's formulation must always be ready for battle and to vacate the domestic sphere completely. Like Dickens donning his armor to work on *Hard Times*, they are engaged in an incessant struggle against idleness.

It is impossible for men to stop working, and also impossible for them to remain in the domestic sphere. As Isabella Beeton's *Book of Household Management* makes clear, the domestic space is an ordered hierarchy of female labor; no men are present. While the *Book of Household Management* represents plenty of female labor being carried out, it is not recognized as 'work' in the same sense as masculine labor. Dickens, as a man who did 'housework' represents the contradictions in the Victorian relationship between work and domesticity most directly in the figure of Esther Summerson in *Bleak House*. As Graver points out, however, Dickens' attempt to write Esther's narrative in 'a womanly way' opened up a field of questions that disturbed him deeply, and made *Bleak House* one of his most difficult novels to write (13). Dickens found himself faced with irreconcilable contradictions in attempting this, however, in that his work as a professional writer bears close similarities to Esther's work as a housekeeper. In her analysis of *David Copperfield*, Mary Poovey suggests that Dickens carries out similar strategies of representation in portraying the labor of a housekeeper and of a professional writer:

> In both his representation of David's writing and Agnes's housekeeping...Dickens displaces the material details and the emotional strain of labor onto other episodes thereby conveying the twin impressions that some kinds of work are less 'degrading' and less alienating than others, and that some laborers are so selfless and skilled that to them work is simultaneously an expression of self and a gift to others. (Poovey 101)

Like Morris, Dickens as writer and intellectual turns work into play, and chooses women to represent labor that is undertaken voluntarily and without pay. Dickens, however, comes dangerously close in his representation of Esther's work to naming the contradictions in his own position as a professional writer and the recognition of his own work as potentially alienated. Dickens carries out his labor in the home, labor that as 'brain work' itself has an uneasy relationship with the manual labor of the factory. Just as Dickens represented Esther's work as 'labor that is not labor' (Armstrong 75), so he views his own work as a writer as somehow more autonomous and less alienated than other forms of work, especially working in a blacking factory. Dickens' own position as a professional writer is marked by contradictory ideologies, just as is Esther's as a housekeeper. He finds his own subject position within the Victorian gendered hierarchy of labor to be as problematic as that of a woman performing domestic labor as a feminized form of work.

## Working at Home

The contradiction for literary men who worked at home contributed to their fear of 'effeminization' within a society that conflated 'public' with masculine for the middle class and differentiated the competitive marketplace from the private 'feminine' space of the home. As Tosh notes in *A Man's Place* Carlyle, in placing his study at the top of the house and having it soundproofed, reinforced his identity as a 'professional writer' in opposition to the domestic space (17); however, Carlyle's study, while it was 'over' the rest of the house, was not a separate structure.[12] Carlyle played out on a material level in his house the contradictions inherent in Dickens' narrative.

Dickens' investment in the ideology of domesticity involved him in the same set of contradictions around work and the home as the site of leisure as he inscribed in Esther Summerson. Although we apparently have in Dickens' portrayal of Esther what Julia Swindells has termed 'the professional writer in his professional art idealizing the unprofessional woman' (84) the case is actually more complex than this because Dickens identifies with Esther in interesting ways. Dickens himself is caught within the same disabling dichotomies as the character Esther Summerson. Swindells describes this dichotomy as inscribed by 'a particular kind of masculine professionalism' and represented in terms of 'work and home, felt and thought, women and men.' (59) In writing *Bleak House* however, Dickens represents such ideological distinctions as unstable. Even though for Dickens 'respectable' women didn't work, Esther does indeed carry out various forms of unacknowledged labor in the book. Her labor's ambiguous status reveals the contradictions in Dickens' own masculine professional ideology, contradictions that made him unable to recognize certain forms of work as work.

Dickens therefore represents the contradictions inherent in the Victorian division of labor along gender lines through his representation of women and their ambiguous relationship to wage labor. The contradictions in Esther's character bespeak the ruptures in Dickens' own masculine identity, which was not as secure as it might at first seem. This is an aspect of the relationship between the 'professional' male and the 'unprofessional' female that Swindells does not consider in her otherwise excellent analysis; a man's relationship to the ideal of professional work could be fraught with contradictions similar to those of women, especially women fiction writers. The gender distinctions Dickens espouses overtly in *Bleak House* are subverted by his own uneasy awareness of the contradictions inherent in his own position, and the fissures in the hegemonic definition of work along gender lines. Chris Vanden Bossche has described Dickens' position *vis à vis* his female characters particularly well. Characterizing Dickens' attempts to differentiate the domestic haven of the home from the competition of the marketplace as revealing his desire to represent his work as 'unalienated labor,' Vanden Bossche describes Dickens' relationship to his female characters in suggestive terms:

> The paradox of the work ethic, however, produces discontinuities within the role of the writer. Even as the writer himself enters the home, writers are represented in terms of the woman who crosses into the marketplace: the philanthropist and the prostitute. (Vanden Bossche 104)

Vanden Bossche's analysis helps account for Dickens' vitriolic treatment of Miss Wisk or Mrs. Jellyby; both women threaten the distinction between the unalienated labor performed at home and the alienated labor of the factory by transgressing the gendered boundaries of private/public and work/home. Although Vanden Bossche claims that we as readers 'ultimately find that the realms are interdependent and implicated within one another' (102), Dickens overtly denies this fact. He attempts to represent women in ideal terms as separate from work. His vicarious identification with streetwalkers and other 'wayward' women shows, however, how divided his loyalties on this score were. Dickens attempt to write 'in a womanly way' in *Bleak House* involved him directly in questions of the gendered division of labor. The book raised troubling questions that exceeded Dickens' ability to answer. Although *Bleak House* ostensibly ends with Esther's marriage, the novel cannot come to a conclusion. *Bleak House* represents a fascinating counterpoint to David Copperfield. Poovey asserts that in David Copperfield '(masculine) gender is the constitutive feature of the subject' (90). In *Bleak House* by contrast, Dickens attempted self-consciously to fashion a female subject, thereby initiating an implicit critique of the hegemonic definition of work along gender lines in the Victorian period. The novel enacts a dialectic between two voices, one the authorial, impersonal, public and masculine voice of the narrative the other the tentative, self-denying feminine voice.

We see in Esther Summerson the embodiment of the ideas of domestic labor and the socialization of children in the concept of the housewife. The two terms imply the same relationship between woman as mother and woman as domestic worker. Ann Oakley's definition of housewife reflects the conjunction of these aspects of the gender-specific role:

> A housewife is a woman: a housewife does housework...the synthesis of 'house' and 'wife' in a single term establishes the connections between womanhood, marriage, and the dwelling place of family groups. The role of housewife is a family role: it is a feminine role. Yet it is also a work role. (Oakley 1)

As Oakley emphasizes, the term housewife denotes a particular form of work which, however, has an ambiguous status because it does not fit within the conventions of industrialized labor. Housekeepers work in the home, not in the factory, and they do not receive a direct wage for their work. Their labor is therefore not recognized as 'work' in the same sense as male forms of industry. For instance, when in the census of 1851 the Registrar General acknowledged the existence of a large segment of the population of Britain who performed such labor but were not paid for it, a '5th class' or category had to be invented to accommodate the data. In the 1851 census women were both confined to a class of their own, and separated from other forms of paid labor. The description of this new '5th class' emphasizes the different roles that women were acknowledged to play, but which did not fit the conventional categories of waged labor:

The 5th class comprises large numbers of the population that have hitherto been held to have no occupation, but it requires no argument to prove that the wife, the mother, the mistress, of an English family fills offices and discharges duties of no ordinary importance. (quoted in Davidoff and Hall 272)

While the labor that women performed is acknowledged, it is not in the same category as other forms of labor, and must have a special, separate rubric created to accommodate within the census. These 'duties' are important but are not actually work. Unable to unite the categories of wife, mother, mistress and work, the census must create a new class to accommodate women as people who do not have 'occupations' but rather 'duties.' Unlike the occupation of lawyer or doctor, the duties of the housekeeper or housewife do not have status in and of themselves but only in so far as they help reproduce and maintain the Great British Family. Feminist histories of housework have demonstrated how in pre-industrial households woman's work as housekeeper had prestige, and was directly related to the means of production, which was based in the extended family.[13] As factories replaced families as the sites of production from the late eighteenth century on, women's work became increasingly severed from direct market relations and devalued in consequence. The site of women's labor became a family increasingly defined in terms of consumption rather than production. Thus the roles of mother, wife, and housekeeper in the 1851 census are all firmly circumscribed within the domestic sphere and are separated from 'productive' waged labor. While the author of the Census may feel that the social value of these occupations needs no defense, he does not think that such services require payment.

While women continued to labor in the home, just as they had before industrialization, the labor they performed became progressively privatized and isolated from public forms of work such as being an operative in a factory. The role of wife was increasingly linked to not working as 'a non-working wife...might be a more convincing demonstration of his class status than a man's business of profession' (Tosh 24). The class status of the household depended on the woman not working, in other words.

As the family became a center for the reproduction of labor rather than the production of material goods, women's work suffered a consequent loss in social prestige. A 'gender hierarchy' of labor was created whereby women's work was given a lower social and economic value than that of men. This 'hierarchy of labor' is reflected in Dickens' novel by the status of Esther Summerson *vis à vis* the male professionals such as Dr. Woodcourt, the lawyer Tulkinghorn and Inspector Bucket. Esther's position is shown as subordinate to the prestige of these men. Her labor is not explicitly recognized as work in the same sense as the tasks performed by the male professionals. This lack of acknowledgment of Esther's labor results directly from the growing ideological separation of women from work in the Victorian period. The ideology of 'separate spheres,' however, was not uniform or completely coherent. As Dickens' representation of Esther shows, there were conflicting and contradictory images circulating in the Victorian discourse on work.

One prevalent Victorian image of women was the 'leisured lady' who incarnated the leisure most men could not afford. Upper- and middle-class women were not expected to work, because to be leisured was a marker of the wealth and success of their husbands. They were therefore told to devote their energies to maintaining the household and organizing a few servants to carry out the physical labor in the home.

So great was the separation of the notion of the lady from work that 'working ladies' was a 'contradiction in terms' (Holcombe 4). The association of women with leisure rather than work presented difficulties when Dickens tried to represent Esther in the role of housekeeper rather than leisured lady. Dickens subscribes to a middle-class work ethic. The 'lady of leisure' in the novel, Lady Dedlock, is part of the corrupt and stagnant aristocracy of Chesney Wold and therefore represents 'idleness' in Carlyle's terms. It is vital to the novel that Esther work in order to distinguish her from the corrupt world of aristocratic leisure, even if her labor is not explicitly acknowledged as work in the same sense as the tasks carried out by men. Rather than face a direct threat from a male as Louisa does in Harthouse, Esther must separate herself from her mother's idleness and sexuality. To recognize what she does as work, however, would masculinize her.

Although Dickens represents Esther in terms of her work roles as housekeeper, he cannot portray her as a working woman in the sense of having a definite profession that would take her outside the home and into the public sphere. Women at work 'lose the grace of sex' and become 'loose' signifiers out of place (Swindells 82). Thus 'for Dickens respectable women...simply do not perform professional work' so that 'his representations of female professionals are always hostile.' For Dickens a professional woman was by definition not 'respectable.'

Dickens therefore has Esther Summerson carry out a form of labor restricted completely to the domestic sphere and represents it in a way that does not acknowledge its status as work. Esther's work is seen as a natural extension of her biology, a genetic aptitude for looking after children and organizing domestic affairs that does not have to be learned because it is instinctive. Dickens in inscribing a maternal instinct in the character of Esther Summerson betrays the domestic ideology that Davidoff and Hall describe as asserting that 'women, whether biological mothers or not, had a maternal instinct' (335); this ideal is expressed directly in Brown's *Work* as we shall see in the next chapter. Dickens presents motherhood as an instinct to differentiate it from a trade or profession, which requires skills acquired through training or apprenticeship. Esther herself is therefore shown as unaware of how and why she does these things. Her narrative is peppered with gaps and elisions that denote the space of unconsciousness Dickens had to create to enable Esther both to work and not be damagingly aware that she is a 'working woman.'

These spaces of unconsciousness are products of the Victorian gender hierarchy of labor. Dickens' difficulty in creating the character Esther Summerson points ultimately to his unconscious recognition of contradictions in his own subject position as a male professional author attempting to represent a paragon of female subjectivity who both worked and was unaware that she did so. The space of unconsciousness that Dickens had to create in Esther Summerson betrays the way in which he represses the alienating aspects of both her labor, and his own activity as a male professional writer. Complicating Dickens' attempt to represent Esther's vocation as housekeeper is the repression of the labor involved in the upkeep of the Victorian household. Servants were supposed to be as unobtrusive as possible, and much of the 'dirty work' of the household was supposed to take place either 'below stairs' or when the householders were not around. For instance, Isabella Beeton's *Book of Household Management* (1861) emphasizes that the ideal servant is not seen and not heard from unless spoken to:

> A servant is not to be seated or wear a hat in the house, in his master or mistress's presence; nor offer any opinion unless asked for it; nor even to say 'good night' or 'good morning,' except in reply to that situation. (Beeton 1474)

A servant in a household is supposed to efface his or her presence and act as if he or she were invisible unless addressed directly. Servants, like their work, were supposed to be invisible to the upper-class inhabitants of the house. Even if the servant were involved in work that involved dirt or sweat he or she was supposed to stay clean. This was obviously a difficult feat to achieve, and for this reason the 'general servant' or maid-of-all-work is at the bottom of the hierarchy of servants. A maid-of-all-work such as Hannah Cullwick according to Beeton was the most to be pitied for her situation because she had to perform the hardest and most onerous tasks in the household (1485). Beeton states that this category of servant was 'subject to rougher treatment' and 'contains some very rough specimens of the feminine gender' (1485). By association with their labors, maids-of-all-work were classified as 'unfeminine' and 'rough' because they performed the dirtiest of household chores. They were actually closer to the masculine world of manual labor, as was Hannah Cullwick who was a 'maid of all work' in the Victorian household.

Maids-of-all-work were an anomaly even in the female domestic world depicted in the *Book of Household Management*. Each section of the text begins with a line drawing of the typical occupations of each category of person. The labor depicted in these drawings is carried out exclusively by women (Figure 4). The household is represented as an exclusively feminine domain; the male members of the household are conspicuous by their absence. They are the absent center of the household, the rhythms of the household being arranged around their business schedules. The domestic servants themselves are almost exclusively female, a result of the growing number of jobs in industry and the imposition of a tax on male domestic servants imposed in 1777 and not repealed until 1937.[14] Even when the practice of hiring domestic servants diminished, 'nobody questioned the assumption that housework was women's work and responsibility' (Davidson 182).

To increase the status of housework Beeton's text begins with a military metaphor. The mistress of the house is likened to 'the commander of an army,' turning domestic labor into a kind of battle akin to the enjoined on men by Ruskin in 'Of Queen's Gardens.' Like Carlyle's 'Captains of Industry,' this passage represents work in terms of military self-discipline. However, in this context Beeton is trying to 'masculinize' domestic labor and give it value that would allow it to compete in status with 'men's work.'

However, where work for men in seen in terms of sacrifice and 'hardening' of the male psyche, in Beeton's text work is turned into play, as the implications of the role of governing the house as work must be tempered by an appeal to pleasure:

> We may add, that to be a good housewife does not necessarily imply an abandonment of proper pleasures or amusing recreation; and we think it the more necessary to express this, as the performance of the duties of a mistress may, to some minds, perhaps seem to be incompatible with the enjoyment of life. (Beeton 1–2)

Rather than link work, duty and self-sacrifice as would be the case in remarks aimed at men, Beeton's text shows great anxiety about the potential loss of 'amusing recreation' in the catalog of 'duties and pleasures' that make up the section on the mistress of the house. Just as Dickens had difficulty reconciling work and play in *Hard Times*, the *Book of Household Management* tries strenuously, and not very convincingly, to argue that working from dawn to dusk can actually be fun. This kind of redefinition of work carries over into the illustration in Figure 4, in which the mistress, while she is supervising the labor of the household, is seated and being served a beverage; she looks more at leisure than at work. This is exactly the kind of split consciousness that is embodied in Esther Summerson; work must be represented as a joyful undertaking and a pleasure, and cannot be recognized as labor in the same terms as masculine activity. Rather than be assigned to a special '5th category,' housework here is redefined as play, just as play is represented as an alluring but marginal alternative in *Hard Times*. In both novels 'play' represents feminine labor as inferior to masculine work. A man working at home would therefore be implicated in 'play' rather than work and demasculinized in the ways that Nightingale suggested in the quotation in Chapter 1.

The same censorship of the realities of labor is found in the advice to servants in the *Book of Household Management*. The servants depicted in the text are invariably are clean, neat and well-groomed. The primary virtue in Beeton's hierarchy of domestic virtues is cleanliness, followed closely by order; the text therefore reproduces the conventional bourgeois horror at any suggestion of dirt or disorder. Cullwick's personal relationship to dirt, her frequent references to herself as being 'in my dirt,' show a dramatic reversal of the usual hierarchy of values. Both Cullwick and Munby inverted the usual Victorian hierarchy of cleanliness, and put dirt and labor on view in extremely transgressive photographs.

Figure 4 shows a striking parallel between the mistress and the housekeeper in terms of their respective roles and the text also emphasizes the similarities between the roles of mistress and housekeeper. The housekeeper 'must consider herself as the immediate representative of her mistress' and act 'as if she were at the head of her own family' (Beeton 20). This description of the housekeeper's role actually encourages some confusion of the two roles; the housekeeper is expected to act as a surrogate mother and mistress to the family. Both the mistress and housekeeper are involved primarily in the 'management' of household labor rather than in manual labor, and Beeton emphasizes that both act as role models for the servants under them. Beeton catalogues the responsibilities of the housekeeper in the following terms:

> She should...rise early, and see that all the domestics are duly performing their work and that everything is progressing satisfactorily for the preparation of the breakfast for the household and family. After breakfast...she will on various days set apart for each purpose, carefully examine the household linen, with a view to its being repaired, or to a further quantity being put in hand to be made; she will also see that the furniture throughout the house is well rubbed and polished; and will, besides, attend to all the necessary details of marketing and ordering goods from tradesmen. (Beeton 21)

The housekeeper is occupied from early morning to late at night by supervisory duties; as we shall see, this description is strikingly close to Esther's catalogue of her own daily labors in running a household.
The same professional/manual division of labor underlies the tasks appropriate to each class. Beeton's emphasis on cleanliness means that the more dirty the occupation, the lower its position in the hierarchy of labor. While both the mistress and the housekeeper perform labor in the household, it is seen as qualitatively different from the labor of the servants lower in the hierarchy. Needless to say, Dickens does not represent Esther as either sweaty or dirty in the course of her work. Partly this is because Esther is a 'manager' and not one of the household manual laborers. It is also because Dickens does not represent her work directly at all, but rather through symbols. The basket of keys is the primary symbol for Esther's work in the novel. It is a peculiar aspect of Esther's role in the novel that wherever she goes she is given keys:

> A maid...brought a basket into my room, with two bunches of keys in it, all labelled. 'For you, miss, if you please,' said she.

'For me?,' said I?

'The housekeeping keys, miss.' (*Bleak House* 52)

Upon her arrival at *Bleak House* Esther is immediately cast in the role of housekeeper and given two bunches of keys. She is initially surprised, but this surprise gives way immediately, and without any attempt at explanation on Dickens' part, to wonder at 'the magnitude of my trust.' This sequence is repeated when Esther goes in search of Necket's children and she is given a key by the landlady. No directions are given with the gift. On each occasion the giver of the key assumes that Esther will know what to do with it.

> I glanced at the key, and glanced at her; but she took it for granted that I knew what to do with it. As it could only be intended for the children's door, I came out without asking any more questions, and led the way up the dark stairs. (*Bleak House* 158)

Esther herself is portrayed as unaware of why people give her keys, but she inevitably ends up doing the right thing with them anyway. Her 'maternal instinct' is shown in this case leading her to the correct door, and she takes the children into her protective custody. The key is obviously a very important symbol for women's work in Dickens' novels generally, not just in *Bleak House*. For instance, in *Oliver Twist* when Fagin wishes to disguise Nancy as a suitable guardian for Oliver, he gives her two things; a basket, symbolizing her role as the purchaser of food for her fictitious family, and a large door key symbolizing her role as protector of the home's security and integrity. This, in Fagin's words, makes her look 'more respectable' and ensures that her impersonation of Oliver's sister will be more credible. The symbol of the key identifies both Esther and Nancy immediately as housekeepers and protectors of children, entitled to make a citizen's arrest of any vagrant and unprotected minors.

The symbol of the key also links Esther to the other male professionals in the novel who are entrusted with the duty of protecting the family, particularly the lawyer Tulkinghorn and the detective Inspector Bucket. Both men guard the secret of Lady Dedlock's adultery. Their protection of this secret is symbolized by the key. Tulkinghorn even has keys that unlock drawers that contain other keys. He 'takes a small key from his pocket, unlocks a drawer in which there is another key, which unlocks a chest in which there is another, and so comes to the cellar-key' (*Bleak House* 445). Inspector Bucket owns a key to Tulkinghorn's office (*Bleak House*, 239). Like Esther, these two characters use keys as part of their role in the novel as a means of gaining access to the domestic sphere. The key symbolizes their ability to enter and survey the domestic space of the family, and their guardianship of its material goods and secrets. They are all involved in the 'management' of the household and have access to all its rooms.

Jacques Donzelot characterizes domestic labor as taking the place of the dowry in nineteenth-century marriages, and asks 'What might take the place of this starting capital that they (women) could no longer supply?...It would be their labor, their domestic labor, raised to the level of a trade' (35). 'Trade' is however the wrong word to describe this substitute dowry. Esther is an orphan, with no family to provide her with a dowry. Her labor compensates for this lack in that she brings her role as housekeeper to the domestic partnership of marriage, but this labor cannot be recognized under the rubric of work. Like Esther, Agnes in *David Copperfield* contributes what Mary Poovey has termed 'the dowry of her middle-class virtue and efficient house-keeping skills' to her marriage with Dr. Woodcourt (99).

Esther's duties within *Bleak House* are both managerial and social; she summarizes her three weeks in the Jellyby household by saying 'so, what with working and housekeeping, and lessons to Charley, and backgammon in the evening with my guardian, and duets with Ada, the three weeks slipped fast away' (*Bleak House* 318). Esther is a manager of households as well as companion to Mr. Jarndyce. In her managerial role, she organizes and teaches servants. In one of the novel's most disturbing moments, Esther is 'given' Charley Neckett as a maid. Charley announces that 'If you please, miss, I'm a present to you, with Mr. Jarndyce's love...And if you please miss, Mr. Jarndyce's love, and he thinks you'll like to teach me now and then' (*Bleak House*, 255). As part of Esther's gradual socialization into her role she is given a personal servant, a marker of her class position. She will learn to 'manage' servants by her supervision of Charley, although she is represented as the one giving the education.

Esther monitors the inventory of material goods in the household, and also presides over family meals, moving rapidly from one role to another. For instance, Dickens describes her first morning's work as housekeeper in a list of labors of Herculean proportions:

> Every part of the house was in such order, and everyone was so attentive to me, that I had no trouble with my two bunches of keys: though what with trying to remember the contents of each little store-room drawer, and cupboard; and what with making notes on a slate about jams, pickles and preserves, and bottles, and glass, and china and a great many other things; and what with generally being a methodical, old-maidish foolish little person; I was so busy that I could not believe it was breakfast-time when I heard the bell ring. Away I ran, however, and made tea, as I had already been installed into the responsibility of the teapot; and then, as they were all rather late, and nobody was down yet, I thought I would take a peep at the garden and get some knowledge of that too. (*Bleak House* 70)

This dizzying catalog of activities represents only Esther's early morning schedule. While the rest of the household sleeps, she is already hard at work surveying her new domain, which she views with a proprietary pleasure. However, her activities here are not described as labor, but rather as a hectic but enjoyable romp just as the mistress's role is represented as pleasure rather than work in Beeton's text. Work is redefined as pleasure, or in Nancy Armstrong's terminology as 'labor that is not labor,' and by this means avoids the implication in alienated labor.

It is also work that she must be represented as undertaking willingly even though it is an enforced domesticity in the lacunae of her narrative. At the opposite extreme from the impersonal, authoritative and masculine third-person narrative, her narrative can record events only hesitatingly in personal terms. She records the effects of hegemony in the form of personal neuroses, such as her habit of jingling her basket of keys and saying to herself 'Esther, duty my dear' as she reminds herself of her social role. Esther's profession is represented as 'duty' rather than 'occupation,' a duty that she apparently imposes upon herself. The modesty tropes that Dickens uses to create the character of Esther Summerson correspond to her ideological position as a woman working within masculine terms, as a brief comment of D. A. Miller's underscores when he comments that 'like women's work, which is the external means to Esther's social regulation, the labors of modesty, its inner correlative, are never done' (101–2).[15]

Given the ideological constraints in operation in his creation of Esther Summerson, Dickens has to end his novel with a statement of what Esther does not know, rather than what she has learned in the course of the narrative. She cannot look back over the novel and summarize its moral content because she is a space of willed unconsciousness rather than a character. She represents Dickens' repressed awareness of the deep contradictions in Victorian domestic ideology and its relationship to other forms of work in the Victorian period. By the end of the novel Esther has been differentiated from ideas of beauty and sexual attraction, from ideas of work, and from images of women who abandon their domestic duties for evangelical causes. There isn't much Esther can be represented as knowing when all these areas of experience have been excluded. Dickens does not address the reader as author of the novel in conclusion because this would entail his facing his own doubts and uncertainties about his own gender position and his insecure tenancy of his identity as a masculine professional author of novels who 'worked' at home. He speaks through Esther, and presents her as hesitant and uncertain; his knowledge cannot be addressed directly.

The contradictions in Dickens' position as a writer are therefore recorded obliquely through his female characters. Louisa is drawn to the sexuality and bodily freedom of Sleary's Horseriding. She also sees within Coketown the hidden fires of sexuality. Esther is separated from sexuality by her illness that erases her connection to Lady Dedlock. In both cases issues of work are translated into issues of feminine consciousness and sexuality. Rather than represent male labor directly, Dickens uses female figures as representatives of excluded or repressed desires that cannot find expression directly within the world of masculine work.

Figure 1    Isambard Kingdom Brunel and the 'Great Eastern' (1857)

Figure 2    Richard Redgrave *The Sempstress* (1844)

Figure 3    William Bell Scott *Iron and Coal* (1861)

Figure 4    Illustration from *The Book of Household Management* (1861)

Figure 5    Ford Madox Brown *Work* (1852-1865)

Figure 6    Hannah Cullwick in Men's Clothing (1861)

Figure 7    Wigan 'Pit Brow' Girls

Figure 8    Ruskin's Ferry Hincksey Road Project

Figure 9    London Road Repairs (c. 1860)

Dickens wrestles in these novels with the division of labor that after the 1840s was expressed in polarized and gendered terms. A similar set of issues informs Ford Madox Brown's *Work* which is a visual analogue of Dickens' novels. Like Dickens, Brown attempts to represent an ideal of Victorian work, but includes in his canvas many figures who do not work, especially women who were not expected to perform productive labor. Brown expresses visually the uneasy relationship between 'men at work' and women's labor that informs Dickens' novels. Like Bleak House, *Work* is an attempt by a male artist to grapple with the ideological contradictions in the gender and class codes of the Victorian division of labor. Like Dickens, Brown represents the contradictory status of the 'man at work' located in the domestic sphere through the navvies at the center of the canvas and the women on the periphery.

## Notes

1. I might also add that most menial work carried out by women such as Harriet Carker, Little Dorrit and Mrs. Clennam is transformed through love into a noble form of female self-sacrifice. I am, however, interested in this chapter not in female labor as such, but the male imaginative appropriation of women's work in the novel.
2. See for example Spengemann's discussion of *David Copperfield* (199–231).
3. See Poovey on *David Copperfield* in *Uneven Developments* (89–125).
4. Dickens represents work in other novels such as *David Copperfield* and *Great Expectations*, but does so through autobiographical characters who find salvation through what Ruth Danon has termed 'the myth of vocation.' David Copperfield 'confronted with the need to work finds spiritual regeneration' in a realization of the Carlylean doctrine (Danon 74). I am concerned here with novels in which Dickens represents work through female and working-class characters in his effort to represent conflicts in the ideology of work for a male writer that are not resolved through the 'myth of vocation.'
5. Johnson traces a similar fate in the representation of the 'factory girl' (5).
6. Dickens letter to Émile de la Rue, quoted in *Letters II* (545).
7. See Kestner on knights in armor (92–140).
8. Kucich has argued compellingly that Victorian consciousness generally depended upon technologies of repression.
9. When Robert Williams Buchanan attacked the 'fleshly school of poetry' in 1871 he saw it as part of a morbid interest in the body, especially legs. See my article 'Dante Gabriel's Virtual Bodies' for an analysis of Buchanan's pamphlet.
10. Dickens also likens the town to 'the painted face of a savage' and uses similar imagery in 'Fire and Snow' in *Household Words* 8.53.
11. As Jill L. Matus notes, Gaskell has difficulty representing working-class sexuality through middle-class ideology; the redemptive force of work is part of this ideology, I would argue.
12. See Trev Lynn Broughton on men in their studies in 'Studying the Study.'

13. See Leacock and Safa *Women's Work: Development and the Division of Labor by Gender* and Harriet Bradley *Men's Work, Women's Work.*
14. See Davidson's discussion of domestic servants (181).
15. This is, unfortunately, the only instance in *The Novel and the Police* where Miller acknowledges the role of gender in *Bleak House.*

# Chapter 4

# Ford Madox Brown and the Division of Labor

A loathing of my vocation has seized me. I must rest. Work, work, work for ever muddles a man's brains and mine at times is none the clearest. What have I done today—worked in the garden and weeded the back yard. Yesterday I turned a servant out of doors and we walked far enquiring for another. The day before I forget, I only know I did not work. (Brown *Diaries* 86)

While engaged in painting his panoramic canvas *Work* (1852–1865), Ford Madox Brown was facing in his personal life, and recording in his diary, the contradictions inherent in the Victorian division of labor between the 'head' and the 'hands,' or between intellectual and physical labor. Brown constantly berates himself in his diary for idleness and records religiously in parentheses every day at the end of his entry the number of hours he has worked. In his use of the category 'idleness' he follows the template created by Thomas Carlyle, and attempts to be an industrious and productive 'man at work.' Unlike Trollope, who recorded his hours worked as a mark of his masculinity, Brown's diaries raise troubling questions about his 'vocation' and his productivity.

The diary entry above shows that Brown's experience of work while painting his canvas differed markedly from the idealized image he was creating. He had difficulty working and would lament his failing productivity when he did not paint. I will argue in this chapter that Brown idealized working-class, muscular manual labor as compensation for the experience of working as an artist, which was fraught with tension, self-doubt and anxiety. However, raising working-class men to the apex of work, although it was a commendable enterprise at one level, also devalued artistic and intellectual labor as a consequence. Brown wished to commemorate the virtues of industry in the manner of Carlyle, but his representation of work is fissured by multiple contradictions in terms of the class status of his subjects and his attempts to elevate their labor through oil painting. His painting is a visual equivalent of Smiles' argument that 'gentleman' was synonymous with 'worker' and Carlyle's attempt to construct an 'Aristocracy of Labour.'

Colin Trodd makes some suggestive comments on the relationship between Brown's art and his diaries in his essay on *Work*. As he says, there are two main subjects of the diary, work and the body (67). He also notes how the painting compensates for Brown's experience of labor in that 'the endless designing and re-designing of *Work* becomes an escape from his sense of the failure of his work as a painter' (68). However, the frame of Trodd's analysis is 'the relationship between vision and authority' (61), which leads him to miss the significance of the *Diaries* as clues to the ideological contradictions in the Victorian division of labor that caused Brown such difficulty. Like Carlyle, Brown has a conflicted relationship to work and the body. At one point he complains that 'all the week I have been ill with a tired brain and relaxed bowels. I think anxiety as well as work affects my head' (*Diaries* 151). Like Carlyle, Brown while he is making work into an aesthetic ideal, experiences anxiety and bodily disruption because of the strain of his labor; he experience his own version of Carlyle's 'misfunctioning bowels.'

John Ruskin gives an astute analysis of why an artist like Brown would struggle with the concept of 'work.' He opens his essay on *Pre-Raphaelitism* with an attempt to broaden the 'Gospel of Work' to incorporate an idea of happiness, rather than just the suffering emphasized in the Carlyle version:

> It may be proved, with much certainty, that God intends no man to live on this world without working: but it seems to me no less evident that He intends every man to be happy in his work. It is written, 'in the sweat of thy brow,' but it was never written, 'in the breaking of thine heart,' thou shalt eat bread. (Ruskin *Pre-Raphaelitism* VIII: 7)

Ruskin takes the same Biblical injunction to labor that Brown inscribed on the frame of his painting 'in the sweat of thy brow thou shalt eat bread,' but tries to reinterpret it in the context of 'happy work' rather than labor as a punishment for sin. This is an attempt to rescue the 'Gospel of Work' from some of its more grim implications as suffering and renunciation in Carlyle's dismissal of 'happy work.' He accepts that men must work and that this is part of a Biblical injunction. He still, like Carlyle, sees idleness as a source of sin and misery, so that he is not advocating the rejection of the category of 'work' itself as an integral part of masculinity. He also particularly wishes in his writings to restore the nobility of manual labor, which places him close in spirit to Brown's *Work*. Ruskin and Brown had very similar aims in using digging to represent masculine work at its best, as we shall see in the next chapter, but Ruskin was also acutely aware of the uncertain status of intellectual labor.

Ruskin's preamble on 'work' in his essay on Pre-Raphaelitism is meant to address the status of a particular kind of labor, that of intellectual work. His thesis is that great intellectual work should be achieved without great effort (*Pre-Raphaelitism* VIII: 10). This definition is linked to his ideal, inherited from Romanticism, of the existence of a genius that should make itself manifest naturally and without striving too hard (*Pre-Raphaelitism* VIII: 18). The purpose of Ruskin's essay was to raise the Pre-Raphaelites to this pantheon of natural greatness, on a par with the paintings of J. M. W. Turner; he does warn the artists in this school (including Brown) that they are 'working too hard' (*Pre-Raphaelitism* VIII: 51) and should show more 'freedom' in their brush strokes, but feels they show the possibility of genius. His most interesting comments, however, address the vexed position of the intellectual, including the Pre-Raphaelite artist, in comparison to such professions as being a lawyer or minister.

Ruskin catalogs the prerequisites for being a good worker, but then says that the Arts are a very difficult case when it comes to defining good work because of the peculiar conditions under which artists must labor:

> In general, the men who are employed in the Arts have freely chosen their profession and suppose themselves to have a special faculty for it; yet, as a body, they are not happy men. For which this seems to me the reason, that they are expected, and themselves expect, to make their bread *by being clever* (Ruskin's italics) – not by steady or quiet work; and are therefore, for the most part, trying to be clever, and so living in an utterly false state of mind and action. (Ruskin *Pre-Raphaelitism* VIII 12–13)

For Ruskin an artist should work 'quietly and steadily' as he advocates, but this is difficult because, unlike other workers, the product of the artist's labor is judged by the amorphous criterion of 'cleverness.' Ruskin sketches an ideal of 'industry' as hard, methodical work, but suggests that it is antithetical to the labor of art. This is the difficulty faced by Brown; in an era that valued the material and the tangible, he was trying to produce 'cleverness' that had no intrinsic weight or substance and was not recognized as work. Unlike the working-class navvies he represents in his painting, he cannot point to a quantifiable amount of 'cleverness' arising from a day's work, and it is even difficult to distinguish what in his daily activities could be defined as work. He tries to compensate for this by tallying the number of hours he has worked. This is a compensation for the amorphousness of the 'cleverness' that he is trying to produce.

Hueffer notes that in his copy of *Past and Present* Brown had underlined in pencil those passages 'enunciating the gospel of WORK' (*Ford Madox Brown* 195). He also incorporated Carlyle into the painting itself as one of the 'brain workers.' The canvas is therefore an attempt to represent the Carlylean ideal of work visually just as Dickens used words for the same end in *Hard Times*. As Gerard Curtis notes, there are also parallels between the painting and *Bleak House*, especially in the area of sanitation reform; Curtis argues that the painting shows excavations to install a water main, and that it therefore echoes the theme of sanitation through water works in the Dickens novel (624). The painting also echoes sentiments about cleanliness and purity through work that are found in Carlyle, such as metaphors of the benefits of physical labor as 'a free-flowing channel' that drains off 'sour, festering water' (*Past* 191). This emphasis on cleanliness, however, shows a middle-class set of values operating in the painting even as Brown raises working-class men to the top of a hierarchy of values.

The excessive cleanliness of the workers in the painting was remarked on by contemporary critics. Stallybrass and White in the *The Politics and Poetics of Transgression* analyze the middle-class emphasis on the separation of dirt as a moral imperative that made dirty, sweaty labor like that found in Munby's photographs into a transgression of boundaries. Brown, who aestheticizes work in the same way that Carlyle idealizes it in *Past and Present*, cannot represent his workers as dirty or sweaty. They contrast markedly, for instance, with the photograph of the workers constructing the road to be found in Figure 9. Brown's painting shows an ideological contradiction immediately in his attempt to represent work as 'purifying' and the effects of labor in terms of work and dirt. His emphasis upon work as 'pure' also leads to ideological contradictions in his diaries. As we shall see in the next chapter, Munby would have taken exception to removing dirt from working-class labor.

Brown in his diary attempts to quantify his productivity for the day as he fought off the demon idleness. He attempts to quantify the amount of work he has done in terms of hours; in other words, even though he is not a factory worker, he tries to tally the number of hours he has toiled. Brown internalizes a work discipline that ironically places him closer to a factory worker than a professional in that it is dominated by the number of hours labored as if he were paid by the hour. But what does Brown mean by 'work' when he counts the number of hours he has worked? Brown offers a definition later in his diary:

> This week I have worked steadily on neither Sunday but 42 hours in the week which is 7 hours per diem *pure* (Brown's italics) 'work' for I only put down the time I actually work at art, not the time lost in preparations. I am in reality employed at *business* (Brown's italics) all my time from the moment I get up till I go to bed—but I am dreary and slow in my movements (1 hour). (Brown *Diaries* 94)

This entry was written on Sunday, September 24, 1854 and shows a conflict in Brown's mind over the religious injunction to refrain from labor on Sunday and his drive to produce art. Brown attended church on this day, but he also 'worked some 2 hours at dressing up the lay figure for the man in *The Last of England*,' wrote letters, balanced his domestic accounts, and worried obsessively about money. As he admits in the last sentence of this diary entry, this was in fact a very busy day, filled from morning until night with 'business.' However, this 'business' is not the kind of work that he documents in his daily tally of hours worked, which he records on this day as lasting only one hour, despite all his activity.

Part of the problem here is of course that the work he describes, that of budgeting, was defined as women's work, most notably by Ruskin in the essay after 'The Mystery of Life and its Arts,' in which he calls cooking, sewing and 'casting accounts' appropriate work for young ladies (*Sesame* 49). The deeper issue is, however, that this is not 'productive' work for Brown; 'pure' work is 'productive' work. 'Pure' work is like the labor represented and idealized in his painting *Work*, but is an ideal that he finds impossible to realize on a regular basis because, as Ruskin predicted, he cannot work steadily and conform to an ideal of manly industry.

Brown is in 'pure' work attempting to represent that productive 'man at work' that I argued was embodied in the photo of Isambard Kingdom Brunel (Figure 1). For Brown real work is productive, physical labor but not 'being clever' in Ruskin's terms, or 'brain work' in his terms. Like Ruskin, Brown idealized digging as a symbol of redemptive labor that transcended class. Brown invokes the same idea as Ruskin's Ferry Hincksey road project that I discuss in the next chapter, seeing men digging as the epitome of heroic manual labor. His representation of labor, which Curtis characterizes as a 'common form of street excavation in urban England' (623), turns the act of shoveling into an aesthetic object that contrasts markedly with Munby's photographs of Wigan pit brow girls (Figure 7) and the road-mending project shown (Figure 9).

Brown's painting *Work* lends itself to a cross-reading with his diary because, like all the canvases on which he was engaged at this period in his life, it is autobiographical. In their study of Brown's art, Teresa Newman and Ray Watkinson have argued that *Work, An English Autumn Afternoon, The Last of England*, and *Cromwell on his Farm* all have autobiographical elements (65); they maintain that *The Last of England* is 'the most nakedly autobiographical of his works' because Brown represented himself as the young male emigrant in the painting and the same is true in the case of *Work*. Brown originally represented himself off to the side of the painting in the same position as Maurice and Carlyle watching the navvies excavating the street. Brown's representation of himself in the canvas underlines his identification with the navvies' labors as an imaginative resolution of the many difficulties he himself faced as a struggling artist attempting to define his career in an uncertain and capricious art market. However, placing himself in a position off to the side makes him a marginal observer of their labor.

In the entry with which I opened, Brown declares himself as filled with 'loathing' at his chosen vocation. Brown at this moment admits alienation from painting as work and his profession as a self-imposed discipline that 'muddles a man's brain.' His repetition of 'work, work, work' shows a brief rebellion at the need to produce original paintings, potboilers and other less prestigious forms of art as a way making money, imposed on him by financial necessity. At one point Brown notes laconically that he 'gave my first lesson for a guinea & am no longer a gentleman' (Hueffer 136), indicating his sense of loss of status thanks to his financial position. 'Gentlemen' do not have to work for a living. While Brown subscribes to a middle-class veneration of the work ethic, he is also aware of the definition of a professional and a 'gentleman' who does not work directly for money. While Brown has chosen art as his vocation, he is conflicted about the definition of art as a commodity. Nevertheless, the definition of art as a commodity underlies his work, even though he does not acknowledge this directly.

In the catalogue of activities Brown records in the opening quotation he includes 'worked in the garden.' While being in the garden is 'work' it is not the kind of 'pure work' that Brown includes in his daily measure of accomplishments; neither are the domestic duties associated with running a household, such as balancing the accounts and hiring domestic help. While Brown does not acknowledge this directly, the difference between these activities and the 'pure work' of art is that they don't produce income. Painting is the only activity that Brown undertakes on that day that will make him any money; Brown laments one day 'what a miserable sad thing it is to be fit for painting *only* & nothing else' (Hueffer 152). This comes after a discussion of his anxiety at not producing more 'saleable' art and thus gaining a livelihood from the only profession to which he feels himself suited.

By calling his activities in the garden 'work' Brown indicates that the term could be applied to labors that are not 'saleable' in the way that paintings are. Gardening, like housework, occupies an ambiguous position in the Victorian hierarchy of labor. Although gardening produces plants, it is not 'work.' The term 'work' itself is fissured and ambiguous in Brown's diaries, just as it in his painting. Although Brown sets out in *Work* to celebrate labor, he includes in his canvas many figures who do not carry out the 'pure work' which Brown himself has in mind when he measures his own daily labors in terms of hours. In the canvas he includes women who do not work, members of the upper classes, and the intellectuals Carlyle and F. D. Maurice.

Brown's identification with the women in his canvas is particularly strong because his own work and home were intimately connected.[1] His studios were always located in or next to his residence; he therefore did not experience the separation of work and home that comes with labor in a factory or office. He identifies with women, who were themselves closely associated with domestic labor, but he is also aware that their labor is not counted as work. He thus includes them in the canvas, but indicates their subordination to the sweaty, muscled masculine labor that he places at the center of the canvas. The idealized status of this form of masculine labor is indicated in the sonnet that he composed to accompany his painting *Work* depicts labor as a masculine ideal.

> Work! which beads the brow, and tans the flesh
> Of lusty manhood, casting out its devils! (Hueffer 189)

These lines invoke the Victorian ideal of work as antidote to idleness and the 'sins of the flesh' and assume that labor promotes the regulation of male sexuality, where it led to unregulated sexuality in women. While sweat and darkening of the skin as a result of physical exertion are appropriate for men, it would have been highly inappropriate for a Victorian woman to have been described in these terms. The results of physical exertion in a woman might have suggested blushing, which could be read as sexual excitement.[2] While man can be 'lusty' and drive out the devil of sexuality through work, the fact that women worked was construed as a threat to the middle-class standard of morality and dangerously close to prostitution.[3] Work is thus a way for the male subject to regulate desire for Brown, as it was for Carlyle. The connection between work and sexuality is what makes it inappropriate for women to be represented as workers in the canvas.

One figure in particular in the canvas, that of a young girl who is trying to care for her younger siblings following the death of her mother, raises acute questions about the status of women's labor in the nineteenth century just as did Esther Summerson in *Bleak House*. Brown described the characters on his canvas, all of whom he claims are 'representative types' of Victorian society, in detail in the catalog for his one-man exhibition in 1865.[4] Brown in his catalog calls the viewer's attention to a 'group of small, exceedingly ragged children' in the foreground of the painting:

> That they are motherless, the baby's black ribbons and their extreme dilapidation indicate...a mother, however destitute, would scarcely leave the eldest in such a plight...The eldest girl, no more than ten, poor child! is very worn-looking and thin; her frock, evidently the compassionate gift of some grown-up person, she has neither the art nor the means to adapt to her own diminutive proportions—she is fearfully untidy, therefore, and her way of wrenching her brother's hair looks vixenish and against her. But then a germ or rudiment of good housewifery seems to pierce through her disordered envelope, for the younger ones are taken care of, and nestle to her as to a mother. (Hueffer 192)

In Brown's panoramic depiction of Victorian labor, the mother is conspicuous by her absence. Brown could have drawn upon stock Victorian images motherhood as the pillar upon which the edifice of the family rested, as in John Everett Millais' *The Order of Release* (1853) for instance.[5] Instead he chooses to excise the mother and replace her with a small girl. His description of this girl is interestingly ambivalent. She is obviously completely unsuited to her task, which Brown indicates by having her wear adult clothes that are too large for her small body, but she has 'maternal instincts.'

Brown represents the girl as having an innate capacity to nurture children despite her youth and inexperience. Brown introduces the term 'housewifery' into his description of her tasks, a word that connotes the whole range of domestic skills expected of the Victorian mother.[6] This 'germ' of housewifery forms part of the girl's genetic code, emerging naturally simply because she is female, causing the children instinctively to cling to her 'as a mother,' just as they do to Esther

Summerson in *Bleak House*. Just as Esther is entrusted with keys automatically in *Bleak House*, Brown represents this young girl as being an instinctive 'housewife.'

By the end of Brown's description the mother killed off at the beginning has re-emerged through the surrogate of her child. The troubling question remains, however, as to why Brown would depict this street urchin caring for the children rather than represent their natural mother? Lucy Rabin in her study of Brown's life and work provides one clue. She jestingly suggests that the girl is 'perhaps the first baby-sitter to appear in serious historical art' (223). This joke unwittingly captures a great deal of the motivation behind Brown's painting. Calling the girl a 'baby-sitter' demotes her labor in precisely the way Brown demotes the labor of child-rearing generally. In a painting that celebrates the redemptive power of labor, work performed by women is given second place. Brown includes 'housewifery' as an aspect of Victorian labor, but does so only marginally and in terms that relegate it to a low position in the hierarchy of represented in the painting. In this he carries out a procedure similar to Dickens separating Esther from Lady Dedlock in *Bleak House*.

Rather than depict a middle- or upper-class woman as mother, Brown chooses a diminutive lower-class street urchin. By having a girl take the mother's place he implicitly changes mothering into baby-sitting, and by having the girl be a street urchin casts the role as a lower-class occupation. This is an accurate representation of the status of such occupations in the Victorian period, since caring for children as an aspect of women's work was of lower status than the masculine professions. Governesses, for instance, were referred to as 'decayed gentlewomen,' a delightfully euphemistic term that ascribed their loss of class status to natural rather than social causes' (Holcombe 14). 'Women's work' is 'almost by definition in the nineteenth century work of low status' so that single women's autobiographies record a process of 'losing caste' as they leave the parental home for low-paying jobs (Swindells 127). In comparison to the masculine forms of labor depicted on his canvas, then, Brown represents women's work as secondary and of distinctly lower social standing than the physical labor of the navvies, or the intellectual 'brain work' of Carlyle and Maurice.

Brown wishes to follow his 'attachment to the theme of women in history' (Rabin 236), yet realizes that ladies do not work. The view that women 'were and should be dependents' had become axiomatic by the time of *Work* (Davidoff and Hall 279). Brown thus faces a very similar set of contradictions to Redgrave in his image of the seamstress, wishing to express solidarity with working-class women yet subscribing to the division of labor along gender lines. The problem was that 'respectable women...simply did not perform professional work' and the 'feminine ideal...is located outside professional work' (Swindells 82). When it comes to celebrating caring for children as a form of labor Brown cannot depict a 'lady' performing work, but must choose a lower-class girl instead. He also could not depict child care as a chosen 'profession,' but as a role decreed by fate.

The dichotomy between women and work emerges most clearly in Brown's description of an upper-class woman who is distinguished by the fact that she does *not* have to work at all. According to Brown her sole occupation is to make herself attractive to men:

> In front of her is a lady whose only business in life is to dress and look beautiful for our benefit. She probably possesses everything that can give enjoyment to life; how then can she but enjoy the passing moment, and, like a flower, feed on the light of the sun? Would anyone wish it otherwise? Certainly not I, dear lady. (Hueffer 191–2)

Brown adopts the narrative voice of a man among men here. The 'our' in the first line quoted above signals his assumption that the viewer of the canvas is male. Furthermore his description of the lady is interestingly ambivalent. She may have a 'business,' but it is not the type of 'business' that a man would undertake. She essentially provides an unpaid service.[7] On the one hand Brown appreciates her as a beautiful object displayed for 'our' consumption, but on the other his description makes her sound more like a parasitic weed than a flower. While she may expend a good deal of time and energy on her social duty to look attractive to men, this 'emotional labor' is not defined as work.[8] Part of the problem for Brown is that the upper-class lady, like the 'ragged wretch who has never been *taught* to work,' is not redeemed by association with labor (Hueffer 191). Upper-class women and beggars therefore have similarly parasitic and dependent roles.

Women and the aristocracy do not work and therefore do not fit in with the bourgeois ideology of the sanctity of labor, which Brown, like Carlyle, portrays as a spiritual and redemptive activity. Ignoring the class basis of his ideal, he tries to read the navvies in its terms. He is unaware of the class bias in his representation in terms of the working classes, although he does recognize its inapplicability to the upper classes. Brown is particularly critical of the upper classes in his reference to the 'pastrycook's tray,' a symbol in his painting of the waste and redundancy of the wealthy. The pastrycook's tray is 'the symbol of superfluity' denoting those 'who have no need to work' (Hueffer 191). Brown scorns those who have no profession by which to define themselves. His criticism is very much like Carlyle's critique of the upper classes and their idleness. Not to work is to lose moral status even if one has high social status.

Brown views work in masculine terms. Women and work do not coexist easily within a world view in which certain kinds of work are assumed to have characteristics that make them unsuitable for one gender or the other. This is nowhere more apparent than in Brown's description of the woman trying to do 'good work' in the painting; 'good work' or voluntary and unpaid service, is equated with the feminine (Swindells 70). The well-intentioned woman distributing evangelical tracts is treated by Brown with a great deal of heavy-handed irony, and is introduced in conjunction with the upper-class lady who has no need to work:

> The elder and more serious of the two devotes her energies to tract distributing, and has just flung one entitled 'The Hodman's Haven; or Drink for Thirsty Souls,' to the somewhat uncompromising specimen of navvy humanity descending the ladder; he scorns it, but with good-nature. This well-intentioned lady has, perhaps, never reflected that excavators may have notions to the effect that ladies might be benefitted by receiving tracts containing navvies' ideas! (Hueffer 191)

This do-gooder woman is criticized for being an interfering busybody like Mrs Pardiggle in *Bleak House*.[9] Brown turns the tables on the woman by portraying the navvy as good-natured rather than reacting with a surly retort, which is the response one might have expected to such an uninvited intrusion, and by suggesting that he has ideas of his own quite at odds with those of the 'well-intentioned lady.' Unlike the figure of Maurice, who is described as 'a gentleman without pride, much in communion with the working classes,' this woman's interventions in the lives of the working classes are shown as inept and inappropriate.

Brown's painting, in short, is informed by gender and class-based categories of the division of labor in its depiction of work. In the hierarchy of labor in the picture, women occupy an uneasy and ambiguous position. They are admitted onto the canvas, but are subordinated to heroic images of masculine labor. He cannot represent women and work in the same terms as 'man's work' in his canvas, and implicitly casts women as second-class citizens. Therefore the work of raising a child is depicted as a job for a lower-class child, not for a professional governess or a mother.

However, there are also several masculine characters in the canvas who do not work, and in their lack of apparent activity approach the status of the women in the painting. Particularly interesting in this context is Brown's equivocal description of the roles of Carlyle and Maurice in a painting that celebrates manual labor. Brown links as opposites the ambiguous figure of the flower seller, to whom I will return later, and the two intellectuals:

> In the very opposite scale from the man who can't work, at the further corner of the picture, are two men who appear as having nothing to do. These are the brain-workers, who seeming to be idle, work, and are the cause of well-ordained work and happiness in others. (Hueffer 190)

Carlyle and Maurice appear as if they have nothing to do; in other words they come dangerously close to the vice with which Brown often accused himself, idleness. Like Munby posing with Grounds and her shovel, they have no shovel or tool to show that they are workers. Brown finds it dangerous that the men should 'appear as having nothing to do' rather than being 'men at work' which is what the artist wishes to convey. They corroborate visually Deirdre David's point that intellectual labor was seen by Victorian as perilously close to leisure. Their proximity to this sinful category is further signaled by the contradictory syntax of Brown's description; these two men 'seeming to be idle, work.' The sentence both affirms that they are working and subverts that statement, because if they 'seem' to be idle there are no external signs that they are in fact working, which is part of the difficulty of intellectual labor. Intellectual labor is 'idle work' or a contradiction in terms in Victorian ideology. This proximity of their occupation to idleness is further underlined by the similarity of their pose to the man leaning against the tree and smoking a pipe who stands to the left of Carlyle.

     As Sussman notes, there is a contradiction here as there was in *Past and Present* between the 'brain workers' and the heroic physical activity in the painting (118). E. D. H. Johnson has claimed that 'the pipe-smoking idler under the tree counterbalances the portraits of Carlyle and Maurice' (149). While Brown's intention may have been to 'counterbalance' the figures in this way, his intent is subverted by the ambiguous status of 'brain work.' Rather than 'counterbalance' the two brain workers, the pipe-smoking idler highlights their proximity to leisure rather than labor. This suggests that they are *not* working, at least not in the same sense as the navvies excavating the street.

     It is at this point that I dissent most strongly from Trodd's reading of *Work*. Quoting the same lines about Carlyle and Maurice, Trodd glosses them as 'the intellectual, absorbed by the sight of the labour is, so Brown seems to believe, sufficiently detached from it to evaluate its worth' (65). While Brown does claim that Carlyle and Maurice are 'the cause of well-ordained work and happiness in others' this does not negate the fact that they look idle. The difficulty within the Protestant work ethic that it elevated physical labor and denigrated intellectual labor causes the contradictions in both Brown's prose and his painting. Furthermore, Trodd assumes too easy a transition from 'vision' to 'authority' in his analysis. The fact that Brown placed himself initially in the same position as Carlyle and Maurice in the painting shows that he views his own labor, that of looking at and painting such scenes, as potentially marginal like theirs. The intellectuals are not just 'detached,' they are peripheral to the labor being carried on in the central tableau. The painting has a classic pyramidal shape (of which any member of the Royal Academy would have approved) with the upper classes on their horses at the apex (albeit in shadow) broadening out to the flower seller on the left and the ragged child on the right. The workmen's tools, with the upright sieve on the left and the wheelbarrow on the right, also provide a pleasing symmetry to the central structure.

     The intellectuals, by contrast, are not included in this central pyramid of labor. Just as the proximity of the shovel in the photograph of Munby and Grounds raises implicit questions about the relationship of manual to intellectual labor, so too the proximity of the wheelbarrow and its trowel raises symbolic questions about the role of Maurice and Carlyle. They are leaning against a railing, which implies relaxation, and this implication is reinforced by the sleeping bodies just visible to the right of Carlyle's leg through the railing. Their stance and placing in the painting aligns them far more closely with the unemployed than with the pyramid of labor that constitutes the central focus of *Work*.

Brown in using the navvies as the symbolic center of his pyramid is privileging manual, working-class labor as 'the outward and visible type of Work' (Hueffer 189). The problem with 'brain work' is that is it is inward and invisible. Rather than working, Carlyle and Maurice look as if they are enjoying a moment of idleness. Brown replicates his own difficulty in sorting out 'idleness' from work when representing intellectual activity in paint. He cannot count the preparation time involved in thinking about a painting as part of his 'work' in his daily tally; only producing actual, physical paintings that are 'saleable' can be valued as work.

The difficulty facing Brown here is another facet of the problem that led him to both include women in the canvas and devalue their labor. These two intellectuals perform work that does not fit easily into an economy based on the production of commodities. The intellectual males are like the women in the canvas in that they do not appear to 'work,' although they are indirectly providing service that produces 'well-ordained work and happiness in others.' They are not obviously 'men at work' in the way that the navvies are, and therefore do not seem to be engaged in 'productive' labor. The congruence between women and male intellectuals is signaled by the presence of one of the most enigmatic figures on the canvas; the flower seller.

In his analysis of *Work* Johnson has underlined the structural importance of this character in the canvas:

> Designated by Brown as a 'ragged wretch who has never been *taught* to Work,' his upright figure bounds the composition on the left, as the portraits of Carlyle and Maurice do on the right. The gaze which he directs at the viewer through the broken brim of his hat imparts an accusatory and distinctly menacing atmosphere to the painting. (E. D. H. Johnson 146)

The flower seller provides a counterpoint to the male intellectuals, but he is also a crossover figure between the women behind him and the 'brain workers.' The flower seller symbolically links the women, who do not work, and the intellectuals who do not look like they are working. My students are often confused as to this figure's gender; they usually assume that it is a woman, primarily because of a continuing association of women and flowers that Brown himself exploits when he compares the genteel lady in his picture to a flower. My students simply assume that, because both women and flowers perform ornamental functions in the Victorian period, the flower seller must be a woman. The figure is in fact male, which some astute observers ascertain from looking at the subject's masculine bare feet, but his labor makes him marginal in terms of both class and gender. He is in fact closer to the women behind him than to the navvies on whom the painting focuses, both structurally in terms of the painting and socially in terms of labor.

This flower seller took the place of a dandy or fop who Brown had in his place in earlier versions of the canvas. The dandy is characterized by an excessive concentration on clothes that aligns him with vanity and femininity, as Adams has made clear in *Dandies and Desert Saints*. The dandy is also a figure of studied leisure who makes a point of avoiding work. Both the dandy and the flower seller introduce a feminized male subject who symbolically connects the intellectuals and the women in the canvas. Brown underlines the transvestite potential of this figure in his catalogue description when he says that 'but for a certain effeminate gentleness of disposition and a love of nature he might have been a burglar!' (Hueffer 190). Both his effeminacy and love of nature separate him from the masculine world of labor and violence.

The flower seller is a more ambiguous character than the dandy in that he does earn a living, but does so in commodities that have little value. Like the artist, the flower seller is not paid very well for his labors. Brown identifies the marginal position of his own work as an artist through the flower seller and the intellectuals. Carlyle and Maurice take his place on the canvas, and embody the uncertain status of intellectual labor; the flower seller represents Brown's own attitude to nature, and the way in which it aligns him with the feminine. Brown gardens and paints landscapes, but neither occupation is renumerative. Brown complains frequently that landscapes are not worth the amount of time they take when compared to their monetary reward. The flower seller, like the intellectuals, expresses Brown's consciousness of his marginal and precarious position in the hierarchy of Victorian masculine labor.

The 'language of flowers' introduces another point of intersection between Brown and the subjects of his canvas. Curtis has commented at length on the flower symbolism in *Work* but misses one crucial aspect of the flowers when he notes that one worker has a rose in his mouth and that this emphasizes 'the laborer's physical attributes and the beauty of his labors' (626). The use of 'beauty' here emphasizes the way in which Brown turns working-class labor into an aesthetic object, and makes his navvies physically attractive.[10] This emphasis on 'beauty' implicitly feminizes Brown's masculine subjects and makes them like the 'unproductive' woman whose only work is to look attractive. It seems unlikely that many working-class men would dig with a flower in their teeth; the presence of the rose betrays ideological contradictions in Brown's definition of work and undermines the separation between men and women and work and idleness. The navvies are implicitly feminized by their inclusion in his canvas.[11]

Brown's depiction of the shovel-wielding navvy also contrasts with other images of working-class men from the period. Although Edwards asserts that Herkomer's *Hard Times* (1885) has much in common with the navvies in *Work* (79) the images are in fact very different. Herkomer represents a single, heroic figure in a rural landscape where Brown emphasizes the place of the workers in a social hierarchy (reproduced in Treuherz 97). The worker's tools are on the ground in Herkomer's painting, and represent both his unemployment and his status as an agricultural laborer migrating in search of work. As Edwards notes, this solitary figure embodies 'the values of a pre-industrial past' while Brown seems to celebrate the creation of an urban environment through manual labor. Unlike Herkomer, Brown does not acknowledge the existence of unemployment and represents the Irish as an example of the 'unemployed' tacitly drawing upon stereotypes of 'those who will not work' as not from English stock. He may well be drawing upon stereotypes of the Irish as profligate and idle, as Carlyle did in his prose works.

However, idleness and industry are not such easily separated categories as Brown would like to believe in his celebration of the sanctity of labor, despite the pronouncements of Carlyle on the subject. While the painting sets up a paradigm of manual labor as the epitome of work, Brown himself is uncomfortably aware that there are forms of work that do not fit his empirical and masculine definition of what counts as 'pure work.' The dichotomies within the Victorian ideologies of work are particularly acute for him as he was a male intellectual who 'worked' at home. Like Victorian male writers such as Dickens, the male artist found the domestic and professional spheres were intertwined and could not be separated as neatly as the ideology of separate spheres would suggest. He is himself structurally closer to the women in his painting than he would like to admit.

*Work* has been termed 'a veritable novel in paint' (Newman and Watkinson 119). The similarities between *Work* and Victorian novels run deeper than similarities in choice of themes, however. There is a basic structural similarity between *Work* and *Bleak House* because of the subject positions of Victorian male intellectuals like Dickens and Brown. The difficulties faced by Dickens are paralleled by Brown's attempts to represent 'work that is not work.' Brown both identifies with feminized forms of labor, and devalues them at the same time. In doing so he also denigrates the position of his own profession, which itself has an ambiguous social status.

Brown idealizes the social group of navvies also in part in compensation for the solitariness of his own labors. As Newman and Watkinson say, it is 'as if the workers' colorful life had the power to break through his gloom and isolation; as if he envied their *comradeship*' (67). This is an astute comment on the function of Brown's representation of working-class labor; the working classes are represented in such a way as to symbolize the sense of community that he felt was lacking in his own life. A troubling romanticization of the position of the working classes has to take place for them to fulfill this role, however. There is no doubt that Brown did indeed feel a great deal of sympathy for his working-class subjects; he was Socialist in politics, was criticized by friends for being too open-handed with the homeless and destitute, and was involved directly in the Working Men's College movement. This sympathy is subverted by a passage in the catalogue description, however:

Many stories might be told of navvies' daring and endurance, were this the place for them. One incident peculiarly connected with this is the melancholy fact that one of the very men who sat for it lost his life by a scaffold accident before I had yet quite done with him. (Hueffer 195)

While Brown obviously is troubled by the fact that one of the real navvies who sat as a model for the painting is dead, this does not interfere with his idealization of their labor. The work that Brown celebrates in paint was potentially fatal for those undertaking it, and would probably is represented quite differently by the working classes themselves. Brown elides the alienation he himself experienced in his own work, and that the working classes themselves understandably experienced. This elision is understandable given the differences in class between Brown and his subjects. Despite his comparative lack of money at the time he was painting *Work*, Brown was still in a position to hire and fire domestics, as his opening journal entry makes clear. As Hueffer himself points out, Brown's friends 'remained chiefly members of the intellectual classes' (Hueffer 109); he did not move in 'society' or working-class circles. He was a middle-class intellectual with a relatively comfortable financial position that did not entitle him to be considered wealthy, but he was also able to support an active social life in his own circle of friends.

Both Carlyle and Brown are involved in a simultaneous project; to embody an ideology in which work is sanctified and turned into the apotheosis of human endeavor, and to raise their status as professionals. While both were sincere in their idealization of the working-classes, their representational strategy could also be read cynically as an attempt to use the middle-class, anti-aristocratic doctrine of the sanctity of labor as a way to boost the cultural capital of artists and intellectuals.

Also, when they think about work, Brown and Carlyle do not appear to have in mind working in a factory or a coal mine. Brown chooses as his subject men working outdoors in sunlight, not in a factory. Like Munby who picks rustic heroines for poems like *Dorothy: A Country Story*, Brown chooses outdoor, muscled labor rather than factory work as his subject. Unlike Ruskin, he does not situate work in the country but rather chooses an urban setting for working-class labor but he stills wielding a shovel as the epitome of masculine labor.

In the forefront of the painting two dogs, one a lower-class mongrel, the other a sleek, red-coated upper-class greyhound, enact the inter-class aggression echoed in the exchange between the woman giving out tracts and the navvy. The dogs introduce class conflict into the apparently harmonious panorama of the painting. Behind Maurice's shoulder a policeman upsets an orange seller's basket as he forces her to move on, an incident to which Brown draws attention in his catalogue description. Faithful to his realist agenda, Brown incorporates the class conflict he knows takes place in his painting, but relegates it to the margins of the picture. Like Carlyle, Brown is drawn to work as the vision of work as a transcendent, pseudo-religious category that could unite the middle and working-classes in opposition to the idle rich and those who would not work. It is only with hindsight and with the benefit of Brown's diaries that we can see how much is left out in this idealization of the Victorian division of labor.

However, as the diary entry with which I began indicates, Brown was not as far removed from the working-class figures he celebrated as we might at first think. Brown registers in his attempt to account for the number of hours he 'worked' each day an outlook similar to the labor discipline of the factory. Brown has no supervisor or foreman, and thus at first sight appears to control his own conditions of labor. Brown is in reality a 'piece worker;' his income is tied directly to the number of paintings he sells, as he himself is acutely aware. Just as the woman in Redgrave's painting had to produce shirts, Brown must produce paintings or he will not receive any income. When Brown can forget the conditions of his own labor, as in the ecstatic feelings he experiences when painting *Work* for instance, he can subscribe to the ideology of the sanctity of labor.

Although Brown is not in a sweated trade or factory, he has internalized the compulsion to work to the extent that he polices his own activities and tallies his own hours of work. He has thus internalized work as part of masculine identity as outlined in my Introduction. Eliot Friedson defines work as a professional in terms of the conditions of labor; 'a profession is distinct from other occupations in that it is given the right to control its own work' (Friedson 71). In the quotation with which I opened Brown calls painting his 'vocation,' suggesting definitions of his career in terms of older organizations such as religious orders or craftsmen's guilds. Magali Sarfati Larson in her analysis of the ideologies of professionalism links them to 'a work ethic derived from ideals of craftsmanship, which finds *intrinsic* value in work and is expressed in the notion of a vocation or *calling*'(220). Brown, as a professional, looks to his work as an end in itself, and as having an intrinsic reward.[12] Brown represses the status of painting as a money-making activity at times, and sees it as its own reward. He separates his work as an ideal from the pressures of the market place, but is also aware of the pressure to produce 'saleable' art.

Brown betrays what Larson terms 'professional ideology' in the way in which he internalizes an image of his work as an end in itself, and organizes and polices the terms of his own labor. He exhibits the masculine self-discipline that was encoded in terms such as 'duty' and the doctrine of the intrinsic healthiness of work for the male body. Brown's apparent autonomy as a professional is illusory because, like any pieceworker, he is at the mercy of market forces of supply and demand. Brown notes in his diary the fates of fellow artists who were forced to declare bankruptcy or emigrate when unable to sell their paintings. He and his fellow artists are as much at the mercy of market forces as any laborer selling his ability to work to prospective employers.

The professional internalizes work discipline and has no need of overt surveillance from an employer. While Brown, the middle-class professional, may appear to possess more autonomy than his working-class subjects because of this self-supervision, he limits his own activities according to a pattern that is akin to piecework and factory labor. In choosing navvies as the epitome of work, then, Brown is unintentionally underlining the irony of his own position as a middle-class intellectual. He indirectly represents his own working conditions through the navvies who, like him, must work to earn a living. Neither he nor they fit the classic definition of a 'gentleman.'

Brown was not the only middle-class intellectual to idealize the working classes. The ideological contradictions that Brown underscore in *Work* were made even more explicit by Arthur Munby. Munby idealized manual labor, but unlike Brown he chose working-class women as the object of contemplation. Also, unlike Brown, Munby relished dirt in his subjects. While he is clearly a transgressive subject in Victorian terms, Munby thanks to his marginal position, asks some of the most subversive questions of the Victorian division of labor to be found in this period, as we shall see in the next chapter.

## Notes

1. Dorothy Mermin has argued that 'for the Victorians writing poetry seemed like woman's work, even though only men were supposed to do it' (43). This comment about the conflicting gender identities in writing poetry could be extended to painting too.
2. See Margaret Homans 'Dinah's Blush, Maggie's Arm: Class, gender and Sexuality in George Eliot's Early Novels' in *Victorian Sexualities* edited by Andrew H. Miller and James Eli Adams (16–37).
3. The report embodies the Victorian assumption that 'economic independence will automatically lead to sexual independence' (Poovey 153).
4. This catalog is reproduced in its entirety in *Ford Madox Brown: A Record of his Life and Work* (Hueffer 189–95).
5. Rabin has pointed out that Brown drew upon 'a madonna-like group from Wright of Derby's *Iron Forge*' in creating the scene with the children, thus transforming the archetype of motherhood into a small girl (234).
6. Sarah Stickney Ellis catalogues these duties in *The Wives of England* (1843).
7. Mary Poovey has convincingly analyzed the paradoxical status of the Victorian 'leisured lady in *Uneven Developments*. The Victorian 'leisured lady' was both 'economically redundant' and an incarnation of 'the leisure most men could not afford to enjoy' (159).
8. 'Emotional labor' is a phrase I derive from Poovey. She argues that women's 'most important work was increasingly represented as the emotional labor motivated...by maternal instinct.' (Poovey 10).
9. See Johnson on this connection between *Work* and *Bleak House* (149).
10. Gerard Manley Hopkins was well aware of this aspect of the painting, and in his diaries records the physical attraction he felt to the navvies. Dowling, in a very brief reference to the painting, comments on the men as an 'object of beauty' linked to Carlyle (90).

11. There is also the problem of the irreconcilable class differences between oil painting as 'high' culture and the use of the working classes as a subject for representation. See my 'Sexuality and the Representation of the Working-class Child's Body in Music Hall' for more on this issue in the context of Walter Sickert's paintings.
12. This distinguishes the professional work ethic from the middle-class work ethic which is seen as a means of capital accumulation (Larson 220).

# Chapter 5

# Perversity at Work:
# Munby and Cullwick

## Arthur Munby and Work

Arthur Joseph Munby was not a figure who commanded much attention until relatively recently.[1] Since the publication of excerpts from his diaries by Derek Hudson there have been a number of excellent analyses of his sexuality and his attitude towards women. While they are fine studies of sexuality, these analyses have difficulty coming to terms with Arthur Munby's most perverse trait, his fetishizing of work.[2] The connection between sexuality and work, which was so axiomatic for the Victorians, is occluded for us since sexuality is seen now in terms of leisure. For Munby, however, work was an erotic category. It was not this eroticizing of work, which for us would still seem perverse, that made him distinctive but his questioning of the class basis of the division of labor. His resistance to the growing division of labor, shown by his impassioned rejection of the Mines Act (see Chapter 2), was prompted by his own idealization of working-class women as symbols of work. Munby, with his clandestine marriage to his working-class 'servant-wife' Hannah Cullwick and his collection of photographs of and interviews with working-class women, crossed class lines in his tastes. This is, perhaps, his most significant contribution to the analysis of Victorian culture.

While Rick Allen asserts that Munby 'hardly ever writes about his job' and that he focuses instead on the results of his walks around London and his observations of working-class women, this is not accurate (267). Munby is nearly always writing about his work, but displacing his discussion onto the bodies of the working-class women he observes. Munby's fetish of work can be seen most vividly in the contrast between the images that he collected and the paintings of his friend Dante Gabriel Rossetti. Rossetti's highly eroticized images of women show them in leisured settings, and often as languid and passive. Munby by contrast liked images such as that of Ellen Grounds who is active and energetic and clearly proud of her own accomplishments as a mine worker. Rossetti's models are all clean and unblemished, whereas Munby liked his models to be dirty. Munby inverted the usual aesthetics of Victorian masculine desire. Indeed he was highly amused when Rossetti admired a photograph of Cullwick that had been hand

painted to resemble a portrait. Rossetti called Cullwick a 'lady' and Munby was
delighted by the thought of Cullwick, who that morning had been doing domestic
labor, being elevated to such a high social status despite her real class position
(Munby 127). Munby was acutely aware of the physical class markers that set
Cullwick's body apart from those of a lady and had given up the attempt to pass
Cullwick off as of the same class as himself. Rossetti would have had no sympathy
with Munby's tastes, and most literary critics have had trouble coming to terms
with his tastes as well.

As somebody who worked with his mind, Munby idealized physical
labor, especially if it led to the development of muscles. He shows anxieties about
writing as 'productive' labor that made him romanticize working with one's hands
in compensation for the frustration and anxiety he experienced when working as an
intellectual, a trait he has in common with John Ruskin and Ford Madox Brown.
Munby subverts, or perhaps better, perverts the Carlylean doctrine of work as a
masculine vocation by making explicit the erotic basis of Carlyle's formulations.
Munby turned the signs of physical labor visible in the bodies of working-class
women whom he interviewed and photographed into objects of erotic desire. Anne
McClintock has termed Munby's interest in collecting photographs of working-
class women 'pornographic;' while this is an anachronistic term, it does capture the
erotic charge that such pursuits held for him (126–31). Munby transformed the
conditions of working-class labor, and their effects on the body, into a fetish for
collecting representations of working-class women that eased his own deep
anxieties about his class and gender status.

Munby in his diary shows a persistent and subversive sense of the way in
which class and gender differences were relational, not fixed and immutable
categories. In one diary entry he muses on the way in which the significance of
class and gender markers shifts with the changing context:

> Are the relations of the sexes really inverted when three men sit at a table, with
> hands delicate and jewelled, and a woman stands behind and waits, offering the
> dishes with so large coarse a hand that makes her master's look almost lady-like:
> And is it the proper thing, that the women should sit as at a ball supper, drawing
> the gloves from their dainty fingers, and waited on by men whose hands that
> seemed so ladylike by comparison with Molly's look sinewy and laborious by the
> side of Blanche's tender tips? If this is right for one class is that for the other?
> (Munby quoted in Davidoff 117)

Munby was acutely aware of the way in which work shaped the body,
especially the ways in which manual labor roughened and hardened the hands of
working-class men and women.[3] He indexed his own diaries and created a heading
for 'hands' and, of course had a photograph of a pair of hands in his collection.
Munby in his long narrative poem *Dorothy* refers to Dorothy's hands as 'signs,
instruments, symbols of work' (line 568).[4] This signals the symbolic function of

hands in Munby's fetishization of working-class women; they are the signs of work as an erotic locus for him, and he 'reads' these signs of labor in their hands as sexual signals. They represented for him the most important locus of the signs of the subject's class and gender status.

As his meditation on the oddity of a group of men with 'lady-like' hands being served by a woman with rough, calloused hands shows, he was aware of the shifting and provisional nature of the gendered and class identities symbolized by hands. In one context his hands could appear soft and ladylike when compared to those of a working-class woman, but in another context compared to an upper-class woman's hand they could seem 'sinewy and laborious.' In the upper-class context Munby's hands could actually look muscular and even 'working class' where before they had been closer to a lady's hands. The adjective 'laborious' links hands directly to manual labor in his description and follows the convention of defining the workng classes as 'hands.' Munby is well aware of the power of 'inversion,' in which class and gender status can be subverted by its mirror image.

Where Victorian ideology mandated innate, unalterable characteristics, Munby found unstable class and gender markers that shifted according to their context. For both female writers such as Sarah Stickney Ellis and male writers such as Carlyle, gender divisions were absolute and unconditional. Munby's diaries, on the other hand, show a persistent awareness of the way in which gender identity shifts and changes, as does his interest in cross-dressing. Underlying his questioning of the oddity of a situation of a group of men being served by a woman, or of men assisting a seated woman, is an awareness of the indeterminacy of and permeability of gender and class distinctions. Such distinctions are not absolute but relational, and Munby's own subject position could shift with the changing context.

Munby frequently compared his own white, soft hands with working-class women's rough and reddened hands, implicitly drawing attention to the conventionally 'feminine' aspects of his body. For instance, Munby notes how one working-class woman's 'right hand lay, a large red lump, upon her light-coloured frock; it was very broad and square & thick—as large and strong as a sixfoot bricklayer...there was nothing feminine about it' (Munby 71) while his hand appeared 'quite white and small by the side of hers' (Munby 71). Munby describes the way in which this woman 'looked enviously at my hand....I could not then understand her vehemence; but remembering the difference between my fist and those small taper ladyhands one sees in drawing rooms, it did seem pathetic that this poor wench should envy my hands, and fancy that if her own were like them, she would have reached a ladylike pitch of refinement' (Munby 71). In a rapid series of identifications, Munby places himself in the relationship of someone with 'ladyhands' to this working-class woman with her hand envy. His hands, Munby implies, are 'ladyhands' in contrast to this woman's 'masculine' hands. Munby inverts gender identities by emphasizing the potentially feminine aspects of his subject position at this point. He also inverts Victorian class hierarchies by preferring working-class women's rough, reddened hands to the supposedly small, delicate hands of women from his own social circle.

Munby in his preoccupation with hands represents symbolically the relationship between professionalization and the proletariat, and the ways in which the Victorian division of labor was contradictory and fissured with inconsistencies. Where Ford Madox Brown represented the contradictions in his relationship to work through the heroic figures of working-class navvies, Munby does so through the hands of working-class women. Munby dramatizes the insecurities that writers such as Carlyle tried to efface in their celebrations of masculine labor as a heroic, physical enterprise. Munby inverts Carlyle's 'Aristocracy of Work' by identifying with working-class female labor. He expressed his awareness of ideological contradictions in his positions as a white, upper-middle-class male through his comparisons of his hands to those of working-class men and women—his pale, uncalloused hands were a visible marker of the different effects on the body of manual and intellectual labor. While their hands betrayed the destructive effects of unrelenting manual labor, his were preserved in a soft, 'feminine' form by his work as a writer and bureaucrat. Munby's hands in their uncalloused state were closer to 'leisure' rather than 'work,' and underline the problematic status of intellectual labor as an undertaking that appeared closer to the feminine and leisured rather than the masculine and laboring. In compensation for the sense of guilt that this comparison between his hands and working-class hands engendered, Munby eroticized working-class hands as a sign of his own insufficiency. Munby ironically underscored the different class statuses of manual and intellectual labor while attempting to express his erotic identification with the working classes. In Victorian and contemporary terms Munby's desires are 'perverse' in that he desires what is usually effaced or repressed in conventional representation.

The term 'perversity' denotes in one of its meanings a figure or image in which the right and left directions of the original are reversed, such as an image seen in a mirror; this is an apt metaphor both for Munby's fetish and for his relationship to contemporary criticism. Jonathan Dollimore uses the term 'perversity' to construct a theory of 'sexual dissidence' (*Sexual Dissidence* 27); the 'perverse' is culturally marginal yet discursively central in Dollimore's reading of the term. The 'perverse' also discloses a split, a contradiction within or about (in proximity to) the normal' and thus reveals contradictions in the construction of the subject (Dollimore 'Perversion' 101).[5] This is the case with Arthur Munby; his 'perversity' while apparently relegating him to the secretive margins of Victorian culture actually comments on its central beliefs. Munby is 'perverse' in the sense of 'turned away from the right way or what is good' but in this apparent turning away he subverts Victorian certainties. He 'perverts' Victorian masculinity and the ideology of work by reversing their central elements and making the rejected or excluded desirable. Munby is, in Dollimore's terms, a 'sexual dissident' who, like Oscar Wilde, performs an identity that critical theory has only just started to

name.[6] Arthur Munby holds up the mirror to Victorian culture and t
inverts the aesthetic hierarchies in both centuries.

Munby in performing a perverse or deviant masculinity re
famous depiction of a divided or fractured Victorian masculine subjᴏᴄᴛ...y,
Louis Stevenson's *The Strange Case of Dr. Jekyll and Mr Hyde*. As Stevenson
makes clear in a passage in *Jekyll and Hyde*, the horror in the story resides
principally in the fear that inside every upper-middle-class male body was a
working-class man waiting to break out and usurp the professional doctor's class
consciousness. When Dr. Jekyll wakes up one morning, he discovers that his hand
has spontaneously become that of Edward Hyde even though he is back in the
comfortable surroundings of Dr. Jekyll's West End home. He realizes the awful
truth of his condition when he recognizes that his hand has changed:

> Now the hand of Henry Jekyll...was professional in shape and size: it was large,
> firm, white and comely. But the hand which I now saw, clearly enough in the
> yellow light of a mid-London morning, lying half-shut on the bedclothes, was lean
> corded, knuckly, of a dusky pallor and thickly shaded with a swart growth of hair.
> It was the hand of Edward Hyde. (Stevenson 88)

Mr Hyde's hand is regressive in many ways, but principally because it
betrays the effects of manual labor in being 'corded' and muscled, and is 'dusky'
from working outside rather than inside. The class differences in the story are
registered geographically in that Dr. Jekyll lives in the West End and Mr. Hyde in
the working-class and seedy East End. Dr. Jekyll's 'professional' hand (described
as if his occupation were coded at the genetic level and visible in his body's
architecture) recalls Arthur Munby's comparison of his own white, uncalloused
hand to the muscled, dirty hands of working-class women. Mr. Hyde's 'corded,
knuckly' hands are like the 'sinewy and laborious' remarked on by Munby above.
Munby's fascination with hands is replicated in Stevenson's fictional tale by this
transformation of an uncalloused, upper-middle class hand into a working-class
one.[7] The tale is a literal embodiment of the ideology that Adams characterizes as a
product of Political Economy and Evangelical attitudes that defined masculinity in
terms of deferred gratification. The definition quoted in Adams by Archibald
Alison of the professional man's existence as 'an incessant scene of toilsome
exertion and of virtuous self-denial' describes Dr. Jekyll exactly, as does it antitype
the working class 'insatiable thirst for immediate enjoyment of the senses' (111).

The hand is the locus of anxiety for many representations of a crisis of
identity in Stevenson's story and in much Victorian fiction, as Richard Dury
notes.[8] However, it has not been noted before how the hand in Stevenson's story
registers a particular crisis in upper-class male professional identity in terms of
work. The professional man is 'toilsome' where the appeal of Mr. Hyde is that he,
as an archetypal working-class figure, indulges his senses. Mr. Hyde's hand

therefore marks him both as a working-class man and a sensualist. The working-class laborer is not idealized in Stevenson's text but rather represents a locus of horror. The working-class identity is housed within the body of the professional male, and his hand transforms from 'white' and 'comely' (the term registering the hand's proximity to the feminine) to hairy and muscled.

The parallels between Dr. Jekyll and Arthur Munby run deeper than simply a fascination with the class and gender markers encoded in hands, however. Stevenson's tale records one of Munby's primary strategies for managing the contradictions in his own subject position: compartmentalization. Hudson perceptively entitled his selection from the diaries *Munby: Man of Two Worlds*, underscoring the way in which Munby divided his life between his respectable, public persona and his private, perverse interest in working-class women. His is another version of divided masculinity, caused by the division of labor, that Tosh documented in his quotation from *Mark Rutherford's Deliverance* (140; see Introduction). Munby split his persona in two in the way that Stevenson has Dr. Jekyll divide off the perverse, socially unacceptable side of his desires in Mr. Hyde. In both these 'strange' cases (which are in fact not 'strange' but mundane in that they exemplify an everyday trait of Victorian masculine consciousness), these desires transgress class boundaries and are thus deeply troubling and divisive for the subject.[9] The division of labor along class lines leads to a corresponding splitting of the subject into conflicting work identities, one an intellectual, white collar worker and upper class, the other a blue collar, working-class manual laborer. It is as if in Stevenson's story Dr. Jekyll were to be divided into two different workers. The horror here is based in class anxiety in that the 'Dr.' could overnight become a 'Mr.' and lose the class status derived from his profession. Stevenson's tale expresses through horror the relationship between 'professional' and working-class hands that Munby registers in his diaries and photographs.

Munby in his diaries and photographs therefore registers the same professional, masculine class anxieties that Stevenson represented in the case of Dr. Jekyll. Through his anxieties about work, Munby dramatizes his insecure position within the Victorian division of labor, which supposedly privileged the masculine. Where in the early days of feminism men were lumped together as oppressors and beneficiaries of patriarchy, it is now becoming increasingly evident that the subject position of men is and was as contradictory and unstable as that of women within the division of labor. Munby in his photographs and diaries registers the entire panoply of masculine anxieties in the areas of race, class and gender. In particular, Arthur Munby uses what I will term 'negative identification' to question the very basis of his gender and class identity. Munby's collection of photographs in this context becomes a gallery of antitypes that help him subvert his interpellation by Victorian class and gender ideologies, and to imaginatively compensate for the division of his own subject position by the division of labor in Victorian society.

## Munby and 'Negative Identification'

In calling Munby's fetishizing of working-class women 'negative identification' I am adapting a term from Michel Pecheux's tripartite scheme of 'identification,' 'counteridentification' and 'disidentification.' In Pecheux's schema 'identification' is the position of 'good subjects who identify with the discursive formations that dominate them, 'counteridentification' the position of 'bad subjects,' the 'trouble makers' who reject such determination by discursive formations, and 'disidentification' the position of subjects (presumably represented by Pecheux himself) who 'work on and against the prevailing practices of ideological identification' (156–9).[10] Pecheux's binary opposition of 'good' and 'bad' subjects is not particularly helpful, as he himself seems aware, but the term 'disidentification' suggests the ways in which the subject is positioned within multiple ideologies in conflict with one another. Pecheux's term can help us situate Arthur Munby within conflicting class and gender ideologies that he both accepts and rejects.

Within Pecheux's scheme Arthur Munby is a 'bad' subject in his fetishizing of working-class women. His desire to keep his relationship with Hannah Cullwick secret shows his awareness of the extent to which he had transgressed class boundaries. He knew that, should his marriage become public, he would be the subject of scandal like other upper-class men he knew and whose fate he recorded in his diary. Munby is thus an ambiguous mixture of a 'good' and 'bad' subject in that he identifies inappropriately with working-class women as objects of desire, yet presents a public persona of the respectable bachelor.

Neither the adjective 'good' or 'bad' does justice to Munby's position. Munby in fetishizing work, sweat and dirt as they appeared on working-class women's bodies was inverting the dominant ideal of the clean, white and ethereal middle-class woman. Munby's identification with these women is a form of 'disidentification' in that he turns the gender categories of male and female, work and leisure, and dirt and cleanliness on their heads. Adapting Pecheux's terminology, I would designate Munby's fetishizing of working-class women 'negative identification.' In the context of the Munby collection this term is especially resonant because Munby collected photographs as 'negatives' of his own position; he is white, male and middle class; they are blackened by their labor, female and working class. Connell has described how the 'creation and imposition hegemonic masculinity...demands the repression of other psycho-sexual tendencies in hypermasculine men' (*Which Way is Up?* 58); rather than become 'hypermasculine' Munby became a bad subject who eroticized that which he was supposed to find repellent.

To fully become a 'man' in Victorian society required marriage and children. 'To form a household, to exercise authority over dependants, and to shoulder the responsibility of maintaining and protecting them–these things set the seal on a man's gender identity' (Tosh 108). In this context, Munby can be seen to be 'refusing to be a man' as far as this was possible for the Victorian male. He did not marry a woman from his social class, he did not have children and he did not set up a conventional household. In Victorian terms he was a failure as a man. Instead he expressed his resistance to Victorian masculinity through 'negative identification.'

When discussing 'identification' between a subject and an image it is usually assumed that the process at work is positive, and that the subject constructs a coherent identity from a constellation of possible models. 'Negative identification' suggests that identification can be used negatively to shatter conventional definitions of one's gender and class position. By identifying with his 'photographic negative' Munby subverts his own class and gender status. Munby's use of 'negative identification' shows the way in which a male subject can subvert ideologies of class and gender. Munby fetishized working-class women as a way of rejecting the definition of himself as a 'full social adult' (Davidoff 59), and as a good masculine subject. Thanks to his relationship with Cullwick, Munby was able to create a zone in which he could perform his rejection of himself as a productive, autonomous male and act instead as a 'bad' subject. He rejects, in other words, the definition of himself as a man long before Peter Stearns 'refused to be a man.'

Munby particularly enjoyed the inversion of their respective gender roles when he compared his relative lack of strength to Cullwick's muscles and great physical power (Munby 71). In their relations with one another Munby and Cullwick staged variations on the theme of dominant and subordinate, enacting the contradictions not only within their relationship but those within the dominant ideology generally. While he acted out the role of white master in some of their private theatricals, Munby also used his relationship with Cullwick as a way of questioning his own class and gender identity. His clandestine relationship with Cullwick allowed Munby to imagine himself as outside the social order and no longer bound by its system.

Munby's masculine subject position supposedly gave him power over dependents and 'inferiors.' However, Munby consistently admires Cullwick's prowess and muscular power; the inverse of these statements is his awareness of his own relative lack of strength, and therefore of his own proximity to a feminine subject position in the Victorian gender system.[11] Seeing Cullwick and other women performing physical labor helped anesthetize the disturbing implications of their muscular physical power by confirming his mastery over them. Munby's need for domination and 'mastery' is a symptom of his anxieties concerning his own class and gender status.

Munby and Cullwick also performed their rejection of conventional gender roles in their scheme to dress Cullwick up as a man and have her pose as Munby's personal servant (Figure 6).[12] Although they eventually rejected this possible configuration of their relationship, Munby had Cullwick photographed in mens' clothing. While this cross-dressing is a sign of Munby's repressed homoerotic desire, I would argue that it is also an example of the way in which Munby and Cullwick would collaboratively transgress gender lines and adopt conventionally 'masculine' and 'feminine' roles; the photograph of Cullwick as a man is much like the photo of Munby posing with Ellen Grounds in this respect. It also shows how work, in this case the role of manservant, could be used by Munby and Cullwick to enact what would be considered perverse desires. Work becomes a locus of disidentification for both of them. Again, Munby uses work to stage a transgressive performance of his own desires; like the women in the Mines, Cullwick dresses in men's work clothes.

Cullwick was proud of her muscular strength, and the fact that she could pick grown men up; she derived power and a sense of autonomy from this conventionally 'masculine' aspect of her body. Munby enjoyed being picked up and 'petted' by Cullwick and assumed a relationship with her that both infantilized him and made his position to her one of passivity and dependence. However, Cullwick thought of herself as a woman and rejected the idea of dressing as a manservant after one experiment. Like Munby, she could not fully reject her gender identity no matter how much she might play the sexual dissident in their private theatricals.

It is in the realm of dirt and cleanliness that Munby shows the most dramatic inversion of the usual Victorian aesthetic. His fetishization of the dirt associated with physical labor, and his interest in seeing Cullwick 'in her dirt,' show his rejection of middle-class standards of cleanliness. Cullwick's own diaries make it clear that the households she worked for attempted to make dirt invisible; nobody would take notice of her when she was sweaty and dirty after performing the work necessary to keep the household clean. Cullwick was conscious of the way in which her association with dirt made her anathema to her employers and to society generally; in one despairing moment she complained to Munby 'Everybody hates me!....I'm so dirty and shabby!' (115) She was well aware of the way in which her work, some of the dirtiest and most onerous in the Victorian household, made her a pariah in the houses in which she lived.

Munby, on the other hand, makes the invisible visible in his photographs of female colliers (Figure 7) and of Cullwick performing domestic labor. This is what makes the photographs in the Munby collection so unusual, and Munby such an interesting case. As Heather Dawkins points out, the photographs in the Munby collection are unique because 'they represent what is conventionally effaced in representations of the bourgeois home and family ideal, yet which provide that ideal's material conditions' (167). Munby makes visible the 'dirty work' of the Victorian household and turns it into the object of erotic interest rather than a source of pollution. This work is usually rendered invisible, as Robbins has shown in *The Servant's Hand*.

Munby was trained as a lawyer, but found himself unable to enter the rough and tumble of the legal profession. Instead he secured a sinecure civil servant position that allowed him time to write his poetry on the side. Munby spent most of his time at work writing reports, letters and poetry, occupations which left his hands free from callouses. When he compared his hands to those of Cullwick or other working-class women he was comparing the gender implications of their respective kinds of work. Munby makes the conection between his fetish and work explicit in one striking diary entry in which he compared the sumptuous surroundings of a dinner being served to him, Dante Gabriel Rossetti, F. W. Burton and other members of Munby's literary and artistic circle:

> The glass, the china, are all antique: the dinner, elaborate and refined, is handed round by a single female servant; a robust, comely young matron, whose large strong hands, used to serving, contrast with the small hands of her master, used to pictures and poems. (Munby 297)

Munby's connection, and that of the other artists and writers around him, to a particular occupation implicitly feminizes them. The gender identifications and disidentifications in Munby's dairy entries relate directly to forms of labor and their effect on the body. Men who work on pictures or poems are feminized in comparison to the laborious bodies of working-class women.

Munby fetishizes the signs of physical labor in the working-class women he had photographed because of their connection to strenuous work and the way in which, particularly in the case of women mine workers, they transgressed gender lines by wearing men's clothing. The calloused hands and muscles that Munby admired in these women were marks of strenuous physical labor recorded at the level of the body that aligned them with men's work. He idealizes and aestheticizes them to compensate for his own insecurities about the manliness of his profession. Munby frequently complained about his lack of aptitude for the law, and his feelings of oppression at having to practice law:

> This is not a Diary of moods and 'experiences:' else I might say much of the wretchedness and selfdespair I have gone through this week—and all, or chiefly, because of some law business I had in hand! The practice, though not the grand and general principles, of Law is most hateful to me, from natural inaptness & from the miserable associations of home. Perplexed among its dry hideous subtleties, ever afraid to bring one's little knowledge to bear, for fear of some unsuspected trap which nothing can evade—one feels degraded by this, and by the hypocrisy one has to maintain. (Munby 54)

Legal work for Munby brought to the forefront deeply disturbing anxieties about his own autonomy and efficacy as a masculine subject. Law is for him associated with his home, and his damaging emotional and financial dependence on his father. Munby felt acutely his lack of income, and his consequent need for supplements from his father, who seems himself to have been preoccupied to an unusual extent with his finances. The law seems also for Munby to have brought to the surface his anxieties about his own intellect and competence that left him feeling 'degraded' and hypocritical. He clearly felt himself unsuited to the role of a masculine professional. These anxieties became less pronounced when he finally found an undemanding job with the Ecclesiastical Commission.

Munby's fetishizing of working-class women can therefore be seen as an imaginative compensation for his own feelings of inadequacy, and his attempt to square his own experiences with the middle-class ideology of the sanctity of labor, an ideology which he himself espoused fervently. Munby felt that work ought to be, and was for most people, a redeeming and ennobling enterprise. For instance he calls work carried out by Cullwick 'noble and sanctified' (Munby 329), echoing Carlyle's pronouncements about work as a divine calling. For him, however, work provided no satisfaction, and in fact made him feel insecure and unhappy. He therefore in compensation idealized the labor of the working classes as a sanctifying undertaking and tried to fashion Cullwick in his image of work as a redemptive activity.

Munby gave many lectures to the working class on the sanctity of their labor. There is an undeniable irony in this spectacle. Unable to find fulfillment in work himself, Munby spent his evenings trying to persuade working-class women that they should enjoy their menial labor and feel ennobled by their toil. Trying to convert his listeners to the Carlyle 'Gospel of Work,' he redefined work as a transcendent category. Munby records the results of one of his lectures, saying that 'I spoke plainly on the subject of servants' work and servants' hands; and several of the girls spoke, most of them agreeing that folk should not be ashamed of common work, but all in favour of soft white hands' (Munby 352). To Munby's chagrin his message was not well received by the women he was supposedly helping. The working-class women he lectured understood all too well the importance of such class markers as white, soft hands, and would not subscribe to his attempt to invert conventional Victorian class ideology. Unlike Cullwick, they were unwilling to refashion themselves in the image of Munby's program of inverting the class and gender hierarchy that placed clean, white hands at its apex. They wanted to be 'ladies' and to have 'soft, white hands.' While Munby was able to idealize working-class hands made dirty and calloused by labor, the women he addressed understood all too well the reality of such symbols and the way in which they marked them as working rather than leisured women.

Munby's 'negative identification' with working-class women did not stop with symbols of class, however. Munby's attitude to working-class women was also inflected by Victorian racial ideologies. Working-class women's labor for Munby made them closer to inhabitants of the colonies than to upper-class white males like himself. As McClintock has suggested Munby was engaged in a process of 'racializing class differences' (107) through his interest in the 'blacking' of the skin as the result of women working in mines or cleaning chimneys. While McClintock reproduces some of Munby's striking sketches of working-class women, I will focus on two photographs from the Munby collection that have so far received no attention from critics. They are, however, crucial in articulating the link between Munby and colonial uses of photography to reinforce the ascendancy of the white, masculine worker. Munby's photographs are a visual counterpart to Carlyle's imperial use of 'work' in 'Occasional Discourse on the Nigger Question.' (See Chapter 1).

### Munby, Work and 'Internal Colonization'

Munby and Cullwick enact what I term 'internal colonization.'[13] I am exploiting the ambiguity of the term 'internal' here to simultaneously refer to a geopolitical space of colonization and to consciousness, and wish to suggest that the ideologies necessary to maintain the Empire abroad were also mapped onto Britain's indigenous population, especially the working classes, and that working-class women such as Cullwick internalized a vocabulary of racial domination. In their relationship they play out the same process of power as are to be found in Carlyle's 'Occasional Discourse' essay, in which the category of work is used to justify the domination of the inhabitants of the West Indies. Carlyle decides that the people in the West Indies must be compelled to work for their own good. Work brings salvation from the demon of idleness; that this work also profits the plantation owners and the Empire is conveniently ignored.

Catherine Gallagher has analyzed the ways in which the working classes exploited the vocabulary of the anti-slavery movement to assert their own rights. The obverse of this process can be seen in the way in which slavery as a form of systematic domination of one group by another created a vocabulary that made absolute domination of a British servant by a 'master' acceptable and even natural. Arthur Munby and Hannah Cullwick drew upon just such vocabulary of domination and subordination in their intimate relationship. Cullwick reportedly said to Munby that 'Massa, I am your slave' to which Munby replied 'you are my wife you dirty darling!' (Munby 424)[14] In their relationship the domination of a slave by a master is superimposed upon that of a wife by a husband; Munby did not contradict Cullwick's naming of herself as a slave, and Cullwick used 'wife' as interchangeable with 'servant' and 'slave' (Munby 322, 427). Munby's domination of Cullwick is aided by the difference in their class backgrounds, he being a white, upper-middle-class, professional and urbane male and she a lower-class woman from a rural background. His power over her as her husband is reinforced by his class position and a racially inflected language. Calling her his 'dirty darling' indicates furthermore how dirt, blackening of the skin and eroticism were closely linked in Munby's libidinal economy.

This aspect of their relationship is represented in a photograph from the Munby collection that has caused particular controversy; the photograph shows Cullwick in blackface, acting out either the part of a chimney sweep or a slave.[15] This photograph resonates powerfully when laid alongside other photographs in the Munby collection. Included in the collection that Munby bequeathed to Trinity

College are two pictures of African men and women. These photographs have not as yet been addressed in any critical study of Munby or Cullwick, but they are crucial pieces of evidence in that they help situate Munby and Cullwick's relationship within the wider power relations of a colonial use of both anthropology and photography. Munby himself was interested in exhibitions by African explorers such as Paul Belloni De Chaillu (Munby 103). In one diary entry Munby even compared the hands of a specimen of a gorilla with those of working-class women he knew (Munby 105). Munby's dual interest in Africa and the British working classes is symptomatic of a wider cultural linkage of the two apparently separate geopolitical contexts. The photographs from Africa help situate Munby in the context of both Victorian photography and anthropological colonial encounters between Britain and Africa. They situate Munby's relationship within the growing use of photography to both document and control the indigenous populations of the British Empire;[16] where expeditionary photographers used photography on 'natives,' Munby used photography to document the working classes, especially working-class women, and his servant/wife Hannah Cullwick in particular.[17]

The extension of British power in the colonies and the increased interest in documenting the cultures of the African population were echoed in England in the increased attention paid to the working classes. George Stocking has noted the close correlation between descriptions of the working classes as 'savages' by such writers as Henry Mayhew, and anthropological descriptions of Africans. There was, Stocking says, 'a close articulation, both experiential and ideological, between the domestic and the colonial spheres of otherness...for Englishmen at home and abroad, domestic class and overseas colonial society were linked by the 'internal colonialism' of the Celtic fringe' (234). This connection between Africa and the working classes, mediated by England's long domination and colonization of the 'Celtic fringe' of Scotland, Wales and Ireland, is underscored by such texts as George Sims *How the Poor Live* (1883) which presents itself as a 'book of travel' into a 'dark continent that is within easy walking distance of the General Post Office' (Sims 12). Such identifications of London's working classes with the inhabitants of Africa suggest that Hannah Cullwick in blackface is being subsumed under a system of racial markers that implied the domination of the photographed by the invisible photographer just as the Africans in Munby's photographs were being appropriated as both 'native' and 'savage' and thus inferior to Western cultures.[18]

The critical discussion of whether the photograph of Cullwick represents her as a chimneysweep or slave is ultimately beside the point, because Cullwick is interpellated both as a chimneysweep, someone involved in a 'dirty' occupation that places the worker beyond the pale of polite society, and as a slave enmeshed in a colonial system of racism and oppression. Cullwick in this photograph is in 'blackface;' she is assuming a role in which she enacts her servitude to Munby by temporarily blackening her skin. Munby coming home one day reports that

Cullwick looked 'like a chimneysweep' and that she said to him 'I'm blacking myself, Massa...to do the stairs' (Munby 316). Their conversation indicates how closely the categories 'chimneysweep' and 'black' were interrelated for them. The blackening of the skin through soot was linked by the use of 'blackface' by street performers to the racial categories operative in the British Empire.

The photograph of Cullwick in 'blackface' underlines that she is performing an identity that aligns her both with a dirty, menial occupation and the pejorative connotations associated with dark skin color in a racist vocabulary. Munby refers to Cullwick in his diary as 'my sweet *blackfaced* Hannah' (Munby 346), and shows a persistent interest in blackfaced street performers (Munby 157). Munby's descriptions of Cullwick thus show the continuity between the street performers' use of blackface and their own private theatricals. Munby also describes Cullwick's 'absolute blackness' thanks to dust and dirt stirred up by her work and calls her 'the black woman' (Munby 361). Cullwick's position in the British class structure is thus defined by Munby through racial metaphors that place her, as a working-class white woman, in an analogous subject position to that of a slave in a plantation economy.

Munby and Cullwick in this photograph and in their relationship draw upon a racist vocabulary that equated dark skin with inferiority, dirt and pollution.[19] Cullwick assumed blackface as a metaphor for her absolute submission to Munby, in a disturbing equation of servitude and love.[20] Munby reports that she said to him that 'I love you, Master—and I will be your faithful drudge and slave!' (Munby 132). Love equals subordination in this statement in a deliberate self-debasement as Cullwick equates the labor of the maid-of-all-work with slavery. While the maid-of-all-work might be referred to as a 'drudge,' the epithet 'slave' was Cullwick's embellishment of the role. Munby and Cullwick on a microcosmic level reenact the domination of the colonies by the colonial government in the metropolis. This colonial vocabulary, based on race, shades imperceptibly into the 'internal colonization' of the British working classes within a class-based vocabulary. Cullwick aligns herself both with 'slaves' and 'chimneysweeps' in the photograph of her in blackface, both subject positions being interpellated by a vocabulary that equated whiteness, cleanliness and sanctity with the upper classes and dirt, pollution and sexuality with the lower classes.

Hannah Cullwick's voluntary assumption of the position of slave in her relationship with Munby must be understood as an attempt to achieve freedom through domination. While feminist analyses of Hannah Cullwick's position have emphasized the ways in which she resisted identification as a 'lady,'[21] her alignment of herself with chimneysweeps and slaves by assuming blackface dramatizes her simultaneous rejection of bourgeois standards of cleanliness and hygiene, and her voluntary subjugation to a racist order. Cullwick frequently used · the phrase 'in my dirt,' which expresses a personal and proprietary relationship with the grime produced by her work as a domestic servant.[22] Rather than reject dirt and define herself as a clean, proper middle-class lady, Cullwick makes dirt part of her identity as a worker and as a woman. Cullwick dramatizes her rejection of the conventional social order in deliberately undertaking the dirtiest and most onerous tasks in the household as a maid-of-all-work, even when she could have taken more prestigious and less demanding positions. However, this rejection of a conventional, middle-class order also lead her to equate love and complete servitude, and to fashion her own identity within the matrix of colonial power relations. She voluntarily participates in her own 'internal colonization' in calling Munby 'Massa' and herself a slave. She took pleasure in subjugating herself to Munby's program of servitude as a paradoxical way of asserting her own autonomy from conventional gender ideologies. For Cullwick, therefore, subjugating herself to this racial order held a seductive pleasure and proffered the ultimate reward of her emancipation from the conventional social category of 'lady.' It is possible to read her position as embodying domination and resistance simultaneously.

Munby himself also embodies in his erotic fascination with dirt a similarly unstable mixture of domination and resistance. For Munby identifying with dirty, lower-class women dramatized his rejection of his own white, clean upper-class body. For him sexuality was implicated in dirt and pollution and this made it natural for him to see Cullwick 'in her dirt' as erotic. Munby expresses discomfort with his own sexuality in eroticizing working-class women and their dirt.[23] He parallels Carlyle's rejection of the masculine body in his identification with women and dirt.

When Cullwick played the role of chimneysweep or slave she confirmed Munby as the white, powerful 'master' over his colonial/working-class subject. While this relationship is obviously repellent in its connotations, it provokes the question of why Munby needed this performance of mastery in the first place. It was necessary, I would suggest, because Munby himself was not secure in his position as a male, and needed this confirmation of his power and mastery as a way of denying his anxieties about his own masculinity. Catherine Hall has argued that Victorian masculine 'mastery' relied upon the subjugation of 'others:'

> Their (middle-class men's) search for a masculine independence, for a secure identity, was built on their assertion of their superiority over the decadent aristocracy, over dependent females, over children, servants and employees, over the peoples of the Empire, whether in Ireland, England or Jamaica, over all others who were not English, male and middle class. But this identity was rooted in an ever shifting and historically specific cultural and political world, where the search for certainty and stability...masked conflict, insecurity and resistance. (Hall 207)

As Hall emphasizes here, Victorian masculine identity was not fixed and secure but rather needed constant confirmation in the face of unsettling social changes. Munby registers this insecurity in his relationship with Cullwick. The question of domination and resistance in the relationship between Munby and Cullwick is not an either/or proposition. One can read obvious signs of his domination of Cullwick in their diaries, but Munby was not dominant in all areas of their relationship. Munby played the role of 'tyrant' in one series of photographs and in a dream he recounts in which he played the role of lord while Cullwick crawled to him and kissed his feet. Munby's attitude to this role-playing is ambivalent, however, as he says about this dream 'my lordliness is tyrannical and base' (Munby 182). Munby is still plagued with self-doubt even when playing the 'tyrant' in their relationship. McClintock notes that his relationship with Cullwick offered Munby 'the illusion of mastery over his contradictions' (145): what must be emphasized is the illusory nature of this 'mastery,' of which Munby himself was acutely aware, and his own contradictory position.[24] Even as he played the 'tyrant' he knew it was a theatrical device that did not resolve his anxieties.

Munby's anxieties here were common for Victorian men. Since his diaries were not intended for immediate publication, but bequeathed to posterity to be opened long after his death, Munby is more explicit about his anxieties than most published authors. Munby's case suggests how Carlyle's idealizations of work masked imaginative compensations for his own class and gender anxieties. This anxiety is particularly strong in such essays as 'Occasional Discourse on the Nigger Question' and 'Shooting Niagara: and After?' in which a racial and colonial other is invoked to confirm Carlyle's subject position as a white, male intellectual. As we have seen in Chapter 1, Carlyle in the 'Occasional Discourse' follows the logic of 'internal colonization' in that his discussion of the condition of the recently emancipated slaves in the West Indies leads to a consideration of Distressed Needlewomen in particular, and the British working classes in general.

Just as Munby and Cullwick move between racial and class vocabularies, so Carlyle links the West Indies and Britain's working class. Carlyle's attitude to Ireland, to the West Indies, and to the British working classes is similarly structured, and thus he can move easily from a discussion of freed slaves, to a reference to the starving peasantry in Ireland, and thence to domestic servants in England. Carlyle corroborates Catherine Hall's contention that Victorian masculinity was defined in opposition to both colonial and working-class 'others.' Carlyle also injects a gendered contrast into his discussion of slaves in that he feminizes the inhabitants of the West Indies. He refers to them as 'our beautiful Black darlings' ('Occasional Discourse' 295) and asserts that 'I decidedly like poor Quashee; and find him a pretty kind of a man' ('Occasional Discourse' 302). Both the terms 'beautiful' and 'pretty' align Africans with women, and implicitly eroticize Carlyle's racial attitudes. Just as Munby eroticized blackface in women so Carlyle projects his own sublimated desires onto a caricatured and eroticized portrait of his 'beautiful Black darlings' in the West Indies. Where Carlyle projected his anxieties about work onto colonial others, Munby used working-class women. Work for Carlyle, like work for Arthur Munby, therefore is not a source of satisfaction but the locus of anxiety about the status of masculine desire in the Victorian period and its relationship to racial and class categories.

The fear that haunts both Munby and Carlyle is that the dark, dirty 'other' may have its locus not in the far-flung colonies, but within their own psyches. Far from being a 'strange case' Arthur Munby, like Dr. Henry Jekyll, encodes in his desires the insecurities of Victorian masculine identity. Carlyle, Munby and Jekyll 'split off' unacceptable aspects of their desire for a class or racial other. At the root of this split is the Victorian division of labor. The division of the field of labor along class and gender lines was deeply contradictory in that the labor performed by working-class women could be conventionally 'masculine' while the labor performed by upper-class intellectual men placed them closer to ideals of the 'feminine.' The division of labor led Victorian males to split their own identities into masculine and feminine, and to repudiate the feminine. This imaginative disidentification led them to disavow some of their deepest desires, particularly sensuous desires, and to demonize them as symbols of a gendered or racial antitype. Arthur Munby's 'perverse' desire for working-class women holds the mirror up to Victorian class and gender ideologies and shows the deep fissures in its supposedly uniform surface.

Arthur Munby's is not merely a 'strange case' that haunts the fringes of Victorian culture. Like Stevenson's cautionary tale, his photographs and diaries record the costs of maintaining a male identity in a culture in which work is the central, defining activity for men. Munby's diaries provide an ironic commentary on texts like *Past and Present* and Ford Madox Brown's *Work*. Far from finding that work reinforced his sense of masculine identity, Munby found it to be the locus of anxieties about his masculinity. As a result he fetishized muscles and dirt in working-class women as compensation for his own anxieties. While he lectured working-class women on the 'Gospel of Work,' he and Culwick played out roles that relied upon class and racial domination. Munby and Cullwick in their private dramas enacted the way in which 'work' could be sued as a category to reaffirm the white, upper-class male's ascendancy over women and colonial subjects. Munby's diaries also record, however, the insecurities that lead to this need for domination in the first place.

Munby's cache of photographs also provide an ironic commentary on Victorian visual images of work. The Wigan 'pit brow girls' immortalized in his photographs contrast in their dirt as well as their gender with the working-class men in Brown's *Work*. They show that digging could be 'women's work' as much as the 'men's work' that Brown idealized. The masculine symbol of the shovel in these images is displayed in conjunction with feminine labor. These photographs are a visual mirror image of Ford Madox Brown's navvies in *Work*, but unlike the male laborers they were not idealized in paintings. Their existence disrupts the Victorian ideology of the 'man at work' by mixing the codes of femininity and masculine labor; not only in the way that they wield shovels but also in their wearing of trousers. Munby, thanks to his own transgressive desires, could see this mixture of gendered codes as erotic and as the negative image of the male professional who, while these women were 'masculinized' in Victorian terms, were 'demasculinized' by their white, uncalloused hands.

The 'pit brow girls' also provide an ironic commentary on John Ruskin's philosophies of work as much as they do on Carlyle's. As we shall see in the next chapter, Ruskin idealized digging as a form of manual labor that would transcend class distinctions and rescue work from industrialization and alienation. Ruskin wanted young Oxford undergraduates to undertake manual labor as part of their education. These undergraduates would be far more likely to be photographed with a cricket bat or an oar, symbols of their leisure and sporting prowess, as they would with a shovel. The photographs of these working-class women were, however, not the kind of image he had in mind because like the other males in this study he saw digging as 'men's work.' These women simply would not fit into Ruskin's division of labor, or his attempts to overcome class distinctions between working men and Oxford undergraduates. These 'pit brow girls,' like Ellen Grounds, provide a visual reminder that digging was not confined to the 'man at work' and that the shovel could represent femininity as well as masculinity. For Ruskin, however, as for many intellectuals, digging was the epitome of manly work, and could form the basis for a regeneration of Victorian society in the face of industrialization and urbanization.

## Notes

1. Arthur Joseph Munby (1828–1910) was the eldest son of a York solicitor. Munby took a degree at Cambridge and was called to the bar, but never practiced law, securing instead a sinecure position with the Ecclesiastical Commission, where he worked from 1858–1888. Munby met Hannah Cullwick (1833–1910), a working-class woman who had moved from Shropshire to London to work as a domestic servant, in 1854 and after a long, clandestine relationship married her in 1873. Munby kept a diary for most of his life, and collected photographs of working-class women. He also asked Cullwick to keep a diary. Munby bequeathed his diary, Cullwick's diary and his photographs to Trinity College, Cambridge library under the condition that they not be opened until 1950. Selections from Munby's diaries have been published by Derek Hudson in *Munby: Man of Two Worlds: The Life and Diaries of Arthur Munby* and Cullwick's diaries have been reprinted in their entirety in Liz Stanley's *The Diaries of Hannah Cullwick, Victorian Maidservant*.
2. See Carol Mavor *Pleasures Taken: Performances of Sexuality and Loss in Victorian Photographs* and Anne McClintock *Imperial Leather: Race, Gender and Sexuality in the Colonial Contest*. Francois Barret-Ducrocq terms Munby's diaries an 'autobiographie érotique' in cataloguing his obsession with working women (35). See also Davidoff's excellent analysis of Hannah Cullwick's subject position in an early analysis of the case 'Class and Gender in Victorian England: The Diaries of Arthur J. Munby and Hannah Cullwick.'

3. The erotic power of hands for Munby is embodied in the plot of his long narrative poem *Dorothy: A Country Story*. *Dorothy* is clearly a thinly disguised dramatization of Munby's own erotic feelings, and a fictionalized version of his relationship with Cullwick. Hudson notes with some understatement that hands may well be a 'fetish' for Munby (Munby 70). Hands are an overdetermined site of erotic, gender and class issues for Munby as well as most other Victorian males. See for example William A. Cohen 'Manual Conduct in *Great Expectations*' for a discussion of hands as sexual symbols in Dickens and their relations to anxieties about masturbation.
4. Cullwick in her diaries also compares her hands to one of her mistress's as a sign of their respective class positions (Dawkins 159).
5. See also Buchbinder for a discussion of perversion/inversion in the context of the Victorian definition of homosexuality (57).
6. Dollimore says of Wilde that 'Wilde's transgressive aesthetic suggests that certain aspects of what post/modern theory finds so very contemporary about itself...are not so new, having been developed as subversive and defensive strategies and subcultures before more recent manifestations in the intellectual main stream' (25). The same can be said of Munby.
7. Robbins has an innovative theoretical approach to the history of the representation of working-class hands in Victorian fiction in *The Servant's Hand*.
8. Richard Dury gives an excellent overview of the various ways in which hands have been represented both in film versions of Stevenson's story and in other contemporaneous texts. His notes also give an admirably thorough account of previous scholarship on the subject.
9. In an intriguing argument, Adams has suggested that transgression is best characterized as the 'banal' or everyday, not as the 'strange' or aberrant. See Adams' 'The Banality of Transgression?: Recent Works on Masculinity.'
10. I am indebted to Diane Macdonnell's lucid exposition of Pecheux's theories in my discussion of his texts; Patrick Brantlinger also refers to Pecheux and 'negative identification' in *Crusoe's Footprints*, and Raymond Williams uses the term, in a slightly different sense from and independent of Pecheux, in *The Country and the City*.
11. As Stallybrass and White point out, 'Munby worshipped Cullwick's physical strength and contrasted it to his own puniness and whiteness' (156).
12. For a contemporary discussion of the gender subversion implied in Munby and Cullwick's relationship see Judith Butler's *Gender Trouble* and Marjorie Garber's *Vested Interests: Cross Dressing and Cultural Anxiety*.
13. I adapt this term from Michael Hechter's *Internal Colonialism: The Celtic Fringe in British National Development 1536–1966*. Patrick Brantlinger in *Crusoe's Footprints* translates 'interior colonization' into 'internal colonization' and links it to internalized racism and imperialism (132). Like Brantlinger, I have translated the term into 'internal colonization.'
14. Ironically Cullwick could also be claiming a superiority for her relationship with Munby as outside the 'cash nexus' of economic relations (Dawkins, 166).
15. There has been some debate over whether this photograph depicts a chimneysweep or a slave. Stallybrass and White refer to Cullwick in this photograph as a 'slave' (Stallybrass and White 151), as does Davidoff (Davidoff 45), while Dawkins refers to her as a chimneysweep (Dawkins 175). Based on the evidence in Munby's diary, it seems clear to me that Cullwick was acting the role of a chimney sweep (Munby 133).

However, it is also a form of 'blackface' in which Cullwick implicitly aligns herself with subjugated colonial subjects.

16. Brian Street has argued that 'for the general public at the turn of the century, images of other societies with their underlying associations of race, hierarchy and evolution, were most vividly experienced through exhibitions, photographs and postcards' (122).

17. Nancy Armstrong has suggested that in the 1860s 'photographers...began to capture the faces of madwomen, whores, and aborigines in a manner resembling the modern mugshot' (9). An example of this are photographs of Africans and Australian aborigines by such explorer-photographers as Desiree Charnay. Figures such as Charnay combine the roles of anthropologist, explorer and photographer, documenting the peoples who were feeling the increasing surveillance of colonial European power (McClintock 123).

18. McClintock also notes the Victorian use of 'coolies' in reference to working-class men (108).

19. Phyllis Palmer has noted that the epithet 'dirty' has been 'regularly applied to women, working-class men and women, and to women and men seen as racially different from the dominant group since the eighteenth century' (140).

20. Jessica Benjamin has provided the most astute analysis so far of this strain of masochism, which is not unique to Cullwick; she argues in that masochism is a paradoxical strategy 'in which the individual tries to achieve freedom through slavery' (52). See also my essay 'Male Masochism' (forthcoming). McClintock romanticizes this process when she states that Cullwick 'celebrates the peculiar freedom of ambiguity' in her voluntary submission to Munby (175).

21. Cullwick herself said that 'I wouldna be a lady for a thousand pounds!' (Munby 430).

22. In my discussion of Munby and Cullwick's subject position I am indebted to Julia Kristeva's concept of 'abjection'. Kristeva emphasizes that participation in the Symbolic order of language entails the definition of a 'clean and proper' body through a rejection of the defiling, impure, uncontrollable materiality of the subject's existence. These aspects of the body later become the objects of erotic interest. Abjection is what the subject must reject, but which also attests to the impossibility of maintaining the boundaries of the 'clean and proper' body. Both Munby and Cullwick reject the 'clean and proper' body in favor of dirt and pollution. See Kristeva and Grosz for a complete discussion of 'abjection.'

23. It seems that Munby and Cullwick did not have a sexual relationship in the conventional sense. While Munby reportedly liked sitting on Cullwick's knee and being 'petted,' they do not seem to have ever had intercourse.

24. McClintock also notes the 'illusion of mastery' that Munby gained from his role playing with Cullwick (124).

# Chapter 6

# John Ruskin, Digging

> And nearly every problem of State policy and economy, as at present understood, and practised, consists in some device for persuading you labourers to go and dig up dinner for us reflective and aesthetical persons, who like to sit still, and think, or admire. So that when we get to the bottom of the matter, we find the inhabitants of this earth divided into two great masses; – the peasant paymasters – spade in hand, original and imperial producers of turnips; and, waiting on them all round, a crowd of polite persons modestly expectant of turnips, for some—too often theoretical—service. (Ruskin *Fors* I: 144)

John Ruskin shows the same anxieties and contradictions in his writings on work as Carlyle in his prose, Munby in his diaries, and Ford Madox Brown in his painting. For Ruskin as for Carlyle work was a moral imperative that could overcome the spiritual threat of Victorian materialism. As in Brown's painting, Ruskin's anxieties are represented in the context of an idealization of manual labor, especially digging. Ruskin had great faith in manual labor as an antidote to most of the ills that he saw afflicting Victorian society. In projects like the Ferry Hincksey road-building scheme or the utopian Guild of St. George, Ruskin hoped to bring about the spiritual regeneration of Victorian society through vigorous outdoor work. In his aims for the Guild, Ruskin equated digging as agricultural labor with education and advocated that children be schooled in 'bodily exercise' (*Fors* I: 133–5). Ruskin's aims in these projects, no matter how quixotic they may seem in hindsight, were sincere and well meaning. However, they foundered on the class division of Victorian society in which manual labor, no matter what its aims, was indelibly marked as a menial activity. Ruskin's difficulty in advocating the nobility of manual labor is most apparent in *Fors Clavigera*.

*Fors Clavigera* has been criticized for Ruskin's apparent confusion as to his audience, but also defended as a unique political document. E. P. Thompson and Raymond Williams have both criticized the text from a Marxist perspective for its failure to recognize the identity of the industrial proletariat to which it was ostensibly addressed. Most recently, Judith Stoddart has defended the text as not 'fitting into neat categories of class;' she cites approvingly Anthony's reading of Ruskin's work as a corrective to deficiencies in Marxist theory (14). None of these readings, whether for or against the political practicality of the text and its failure to reach working-class audiences, recognizes the root cause of *Fors Clavigera*'s problems in addressing its audience; this problem has its source in Ruskin's own difficulty in trying to address the 'working classes' while excluding himself from the category of 'worker.' Unable to recognize what he does as 'work,' Ruskin subverts his own political program systematically in the text. To counterbalance his subversion of writing as labor, he idealizes another form of work, that of digging, as the epitome of masculine industry. The contradictions in his own position therefore led him into the political impasse that many commentators have noted.

The contradictions that I explore in this chapter are also to be found in the writings of William Morris, even though Morris would superficially seem to be at the other extreme of political opinion from Ruskin's self-described 'radical Toryism.'[1] However, substitute art for digging as the epitome of 'useful work' as Morris does and the same set of contradictions emerge. Neither writer questioned the idealization of manual labor on which their social programs rested. Morris also used sleight of hand both in *News from Nowhere* and in lectures such as 'How we Live & How we Might Live' by turning labor into leisure by saying that in his vision of a restructured society 'a great deal of the best work would be done in the leisure time of men relieved from any anxiety as to their livelihood' ('How we Live' 19). While it is an appealing vision, it ignores the toll that any labor, no matter how voluntarily undertaken, would have on workers, even in a Utopian society.

Morris in redefining work as leisure tries to overcome the emphasis on pain, suffering and transcendence in Carlyle. Morris, while in some ways close to Carlyle who he admired (and as he noted, many of the working classes admired), is at an extreme remove from his definition of labor. He does not see work as transcendent category but rather tries to define it in terms of the 'useful' and the beautiful, substituting a pragmatic and utilitarian approach for Carlyle's theology of labor. However, he is still located within the Protestant work ethic, albeit with the overtly religious aspects abandoned, and sees the need to be a useful 'man at work' as paramount. His definition of masculinity is still intimately connected to work. This made apparent in his lecture on 'Art and Socialism' in which he lays down a basic claim for all men:

> It is right and necessary that all men should have work to do which shall be worth doing, and be of itself pleasant to do; and which should be done under such conditions as would make it neither over-wearisome nor over-anxious. ('Art and Socialism' 194)

Morris clearly wishes to redefine work as pleasurable, and in fact make it a kind of creative activity like writing or painting. However, he does not question the foundation of masculine identity in the compulsion to work. For him the terms masculinity and work are the bedrocks of a man's identity and must not be confused with idleness. In 'How We Live' he says that 'in order that my leisure might not degenerate into idleness and aimlessness, I must set up a claim for due work to do' ('How we Live' 20). While politically he is very different from

Carlyle, he is still a Victorian man who must combat the spectre of 'idleness' that would make him degenerate into a category perilously close to sin.

Morris goes on to say that in a Socialist community the workers would carry out such labor from a sense of 'duty;' thus the work ethic would be so well internalized that no external compulsion would be necessary to force people to carry out dangerous or onerous work. He also does not question the connection between work and masculinity saying that 'I should think very little of the manhood of a stout and healthy man who did not feel a pleasure in doing rough work' ('How we Live' 21). Morris' ideas are, then, simply an intensification of the kinds of ideals of work and manliness found in many other Victorian thinkers. His definition of 'man's work,' despite his apparent political differences with Carlyle, does not diverge from the standard division of labor.

The problem with Morris' approach is that he does not question the compulsion to produce encoded in the ideal of the 'man at work.' Denoting work 'useful' is does not change the terms of the debate that Marx framed as 'use value' versus 'exchange value.' Marx did not entirely escape from the trap of 'production' as we have seen, but did sever commodities from being defined entirely in terms of 'use value.' Morris still sees commodities entirely in terms of their 'use value,' and therefore ties them to the amount and quality of labor involved. He has an ideal of a worker producing goods that are priced according to the amount of labor needed to produce them and how useful they are to the person buying them. These issues are irrelevant under capitalism, where value resides in their place within a system of exchange that is separated from and, as Marx noted, often repressive of, the very people who produce the goods. Morris may wish to improve the lives of the working classes, but his vision of transformed work does not overturn the means of production that created the oppressive conditions to which he objected.

As we shall see, Ruskin is actually more radical in his approach to this issue in *Unto This Last* than Morris in such essays as 'How We Live.' Ruskin wanted to sever wages from questions of the amount and quality of labor involved rather than transform conditions under which labor took place. Like Morris, however, he idealized manual labor and the working classes, especially the image of the heroic 'man at work' wielding a shovel. The same set of contradictions ultimately can be found in *News from Nowhere* as in the utopian visions of *Fors Clavigera* or the Ferry Hincksey road project.

Throughout *Fors Clavigera*, Ruskin's series of 'letters' to the working classes of England, he refers to himself as a member of the idle classes. Like all the other male intellectuals in this study, Ruskin has difficulty in naming intellectual work as 'work' at all. In contrast to manual labor, Ruskin feels that thinking and writing should be seen as 'play' rather than work. Since he does not work but only plays, he cannot see his own writing as on an equal level with the labors of the working classes. Ruskin states this most explicitly in a long passage that compares all the kinds of work going on around him to his own situation in his study at Brantwood.

Consider, for instance, what I am doing at this very instant – half-past seven, morning, 25th February, 1873. It is a bitter black frost, the deep in snow, and more falling. I am writing comfortably in a perfectly warm room; some of my servants were up in the cold at half-past five to get it ready for me; others, a few days ago, were digging my coals near Durham, at the risk of their own lives; another old woman is going to-day to fetch me my letters at ten o'clock….and my cook will be soon making pancakes, for it is Shrove Tuesday. Having written this sentence, I go to the fire, warm my fingers, saunter about the room, and grumble because I can't see to the other side of the lake. (*Fors* I: 398)

Ruskin is uncomfortably aware of the way in which his relative comfort is dependent on the labor of others who do not share his warm, cozy room. The contrast is made more uncomfortable by the fact that some of these workers are older women who are carrying out tasks he as a man is not. I can think of no writer in the period who can compare to Ruskin's honesty here as he implicitly argues that he is in a dependent and in some ways parasitic relationship with working-class labor. In his comments on 'rough work' for example, Ruskin insisted that no matter how much talk there was of work being 'noble,' some forms of manual labor took a terrible toll on the body (*Crown* XI: 24).

The image of him 'sauntering' aimlessly across the room to look out of the window and grumbling because his view is spoiled by the weather is another example of Ruskin's delicate, self-deprecating humor as he turns his formidable powers of analysis back on his own situation, sitting in his study writing his books. To call what he does 'sauntering' is to place it on a level with rambles and tourism, just as his grumbling about the weather spoiling his view shows his detached status, unlike those who must make their way though frost and snow. Ruskin's awareness of the kinds of work going on around him while he is writing leads him to devalue his own writing as work.

Ruskin asks his hypothetical working-class readership 'speaking to you then, as workers, and of myself as an idler, tell me honestly whether you consider me as addressing my betters or my worses?' (*Fors,* I: 397). In conventional social terms Ruskin is clearly 'better' than his imagined audience, but in the scenario that he constructs Ruskin is lower in status than the working classes because he is not 'working.' Like Smiles he wishes to overturn conventional class distinctions, but where Smiles wanted to elevate all workers to the status of gentlemen, Ruskin denigrates the status of writers and intellectuals. Even though he wrote volumes of words, and was revered because of his writing, he cannot recognize what he is doing in his study as 'work.' Unlike the coal miners or boot-maker, or the fisherman that Ruskin names in his list of people who are working, Ruskin is not performing any manual labor. By idealizing manual labor, Ruskin subverts his own work by turning it into 'idleness.' He does not in this rhetorical question address the working class as a fellow worker, but as an idle man. In reality he was far from idle, but his definition of work turns writing into a form of leisure.

The problems with Ruskin's approach to work are made most apparent in the two projects that failed despite his high hopes for them; the Hincksey road-building project and the Guild of St. George. In both cases Ruskin tried to overcome the gulf between his own work and the lives of the working classes in terms of manual labor. Despite his high hopes for these projects, they did not live up to his idealistic aspirations for them.

Ruskin's road-building project was an attempt to make intellectual and manual labor equal in importance at Oxford. In keeping with his definition of education as 'wholesome and useful work' and involving the body he chose a project that combined working in the open air with an immediate practical benefit, writing to Acland on 28 March 1874 that his objective was 'to let my pupils feel the pleasure of *useful* muscular work' (quoted in Hewison 25). In 1874 he asked a local landowner for permission to repair the lane past Ferry Hincksey. He proposed the scheme to some Balliol men at breakfast on 24 March, and his eventual gang of road-diggers included Alfred (later Viscount) Milner, Arnold Toynbee, and Oscar Wilde. The work began under the supervision of Ruskin's elderly gardener, David Downs (Figure 8). In a typically playful move, Ruskin asked Downs to be Oxford Professor of Digging. Ruskin explained that 'even *digging*, rightly done, is at least as much an art as the more muscular art of rowing' (quoted in Anthony *John Ruskin's Labour* 144).

The Hincksey road project grew out of a set of ideals that were articulated by Ruskin as early as 'The Nature of the Gothic' in *The Stones of Venice*. In his definition of the Gothic Ruskin encouraged the reading of a building as if it were a text for signs of masculine labor. A great building 'looks as if it had been built by strong men' and would give a 'sign-manual' of 'the massy power of men' in its character (*Stones* VI: 229). Gothic buildings for Ruskin symbolized the virtues of male manual labor that would be expressed in the very structure of the building. The 'redundancy' and imperfection of Gothic architecture are for Ruskin signs that the labor that went into creating the buildings was not alienated as it was in industrial production. Industrial production entailed the 'the degradation of the operative into a machine' whereas Gothic architecture showed 'the sign of life in a mortal body' (*Stones* VI: 163, 171). Using the body in work was the crucial factor for Ruskin, which is why men using their muscles in creating art or roads was an ideal for Ruskin both in architecture and education.

Ruskin naming Downs 'Professor of Digging' and his comparison of manual labor and rowing show him through the Ferry Hincksey road-building project attempting to overcome many of the divisions in Victorian society between manual and intellectual labor and work and play. On an abstract, ideal level one can see Ruskin's aim in this project of making Oxford undergraduates experience manual labor and to make digging as much part of the curriculum at Oxford as the Classics or rowing. Elsewhere he suggested that the upper classes would benefit from engaging in manual labor (*Time and Tide* XII: 47) and that a clergyman should try brickmaking (*Fors* I: 83). It is an idealistic realization of his desire to make the upper classes in England understand the real nature of working-class labor and to close the gap between the 'two Nations.'

The connection of digging and rowing in Ruskin's comments on 'muscular activity' above is a telling one. Oxford undergraduates would have their pictures taken with their oars. They would not, as Ellen Grounds does in the frontispiece of this book, pose with a shovel. This was a symbol of prowess in competition, not a symbol of work as it would be for a fisherman or Thames lightman. Like Ellen Grounds in the picture with Arthur Munby, the oar is a marker of a leisured class pastime, while the shovel is a symbol of imposed labor. For Oxford undergraduates the 'muscular art of rowing' would have no connection with digging. Grounds may be posing with her shovel just as Oxford oarsmen posed with their oars, but the two images have markedly different connotations.

The Hincksey project was defended in a letter to the *Times* by Acland but parodied in bad but astute verse in *Punch*:

> Acland writes to defend John Ruskin
> Who an undergraduate team has made
> For once, from May-term, morn to dusk, in
> Hincksey soil to set working spade.
> So very Utopian! So Quixotic!
> Such is the euphemistic phrase.
> Equivalent to idiotic
> For Athletes guided to useful ways. (Quoted in Abse 267)

The verse recognizes the utopian intentions behind Ruskin's road-building scheme, but also labels it 'idiotic' for thinking that gentlemen athletes could be led to exchange oars for a 'working spade.'

Ruskin himself carries out some sleight of hand when he considers sports such as rowing or cricket in opposition to work. In *The Crown of Wild Olive* he initially posits a radical separation between 'those who work and those who play' (*Crown* XI: 7–8). This distinction erodes rapidly, however, as he accuses people of 'playing at literature and playing at art' instead of working (*Crown* XI: 12). Some forms of 'work' can be categorized as play, it appears, and some play can have deadly consequences, as in war. The difference between work and play comes down to a distinction between productivity and idleness, as it did in Carlyle:

> Men will be taught that an existence of play, sustained by the blood of other creatures, is a good existence for gnats and sucking fish; but not for men: that neither days, nor lives, can be made holy by doing nothing in them: that the best prayer at the beginning of a day is that we may not lose its moments; and the best grace before meat, the consciousness that we justly earned our dinner. (*Crown* XI: 13–14)

Ruskin believes that 'holy work' erased class differences, which is why he was a passionate advocate of such schemes as the Hincksey project. His 'holy work' is another version of the 'pure' work found in Carlyle and Brown. Like Smiles, Ruskin tried to create a brotherhood of work that transcends class distinctions in Victorian society by asserting a common bond between men through work and the rejection of idleness. However, he recognizes that work is not a uniform category and that professional work may well seem like 'play' to the working classes. Also, work can have deadly results for the 'jewel cutter, whose sight fails over diamonds; the weaver, whose arm fails over the web; the iron-forger, whose breath fails before the furnace' (*Crown* XI: 12–13) all of whom show the cost of work in using up the body of the laborer.

For the Oxford undergraduates the situation is entirely different. Building a road at Ferry Hincksey, while it may involve exertion, is not the same as, say, building a road in London. Photographs abound of men digging roads during the rapid growth of urban London and the Oxford undergraduates could not be in the same relationship to the activity of digging as these men. Ruskin was making laudable attempts to compensate for class differences in Victorian England, but simply putting shovels in the hands of Oxford undergraduates was not the solution to the ills he so presciently diagnosed. Simply digging a road in time taken away from other activities could not simulate the life of a working-class laborer.

A photograph of road building from this period shows the difference between digging at Ferry Hincksey and working as a laborer (Figure 9).[2] The men in this photograph are not individuals who can be identified, like Wilde and his companions. They are anonymous and are all identified by the tools of their trade, not by their names. Unlike the undergraduates in the photo in Figure 8 they are not wearing white (which makes the undergraduates look as if they are just about to play cricket) but wearing rough work clothes. Each one is standing behind a tool used to smash cobblestones into place to create a road. Like Ellen Grounds and her shovel, they are identified as working class by their anonymity and their representation in terms only of their work. Arrayed around them are gentlemen wearing hats and expensive clothing whose relationship to the work is not explained, but who presumably are supervising the operation. This photograph does not erase class differences simply because these men are working. The 'holy labor' of road building is still taking place in the context of Victorian class divisions, which could not be overcome as easily as Ruskin wished.[3]

Like the photograph of the Wigan 'pit brow girls' (Figure 7) in the previous chapter, this photograph presents a visual contrast with the image of heroic labor in Brown's painting. The men in this photo are not individuals but rather all made into identical subjects by posing with their tools in front of them. Implicitly they are identified by what they do rather than who they are. Unlike Ruskin's Ferry Hincksey project, this labor is undertaken in an urban setting with not a tree in sight, and so it would presumably not be redemptive labor in Ruskin's view. Also, other photographs of road building from the 1870s show increasing use of machinery on a scale that begins to dwarf the individual workers. Both Ruskin's and Brown's image of working-class navvies ignores the way in which labor was becoming mechanized in this period. This photograph from 1860 is itself a record of a kind of labor that was disappearing in that cobblestones were used less and less frequently to build roads, and machinery was beginning to supplant the force of male muscles.

Ruskin himself did briefly attempt to maintain a road in an urban setting, choosing a street in St. Giles', London as the site of his personal beautification project. This time instead of Downs he hired a 'staff of two men and a young rogue of a crossing-sweeper' to keep the street clear (*Fors* II: 305). Ruskin blamed the failure of this experiment on the traffic and the passivity of the inhabitants, which presumably was their way of expressing their indifference to Ruskin's scheme. As in the Hincksey project, but for different reasons, Ruskin's road-maintenance project foundered on class distinctions and the reality of manual labor recorded in such photographs as that of road menders in London.

The photograph underscores why the Ferry Hincksey project, while admirable in its aims, could never live up to the utopian vision of digging as a tool of social renovation in Victorian Britain. Ruskin chose digging a road in Ferry Hincksey for both personal and symbolic reasons. The road was in an agricultural and depressed area, and as he made clear in the Guild of St. George, he thought of manual labor in the country as a good end in itself. Putting Oxford undergraduates in the open air and having them dig was in itself a piece of social engineering for Ruskin. The attraction of digging had deep personal roots too, however, as his diaries from Brantwood make clear:

> April 22nd 1873
> Yesterday entirely radiant as days of old, all day long. I actually enjoyed myself, harbour-digging and planning garden terraces. Meadow all blue with violets. To-day misty, but lake calm. (*Brantwood* 744)

> April 25th 1873
> Yesterday an entirely good day. Made out wing, in second diagram. Worked with Burgess and Downes on harbour: found it much nicer in company than alone. Chopped path from gate of garden up to my own nest-garden with my own hand, in exquisite twilight. (*Brantwood* 745)

There are many despairing entries in the diaries from Brantwood; these are noteworthy because they recorded times of happiness. Working with Downs, the 'Oxford Professor of Digging,' the Professor of Art finds contentment. This is hardly surprising on one level. When Ruskin is digging his harbor he is working at changing a landscape he both loves and owns. Ruskin emphasizes 'using his own hand' in clearing a path 'to my own nest-garden.' The use of 'my own' in both these statements indicates the direct relationship between Ruskin's labor and his ownership of the landscape. Unlike the working-class men digging a road in the photograph, he has a personal, direct relationship with the land on which he is working. He achieves here something of the idealized relationship between the worker and artifact he described in the Gothic cathedral in which the presence of an animating human hand is visible. Building his harbor provides a marked contrast to Ruskin's intellectual labors as a writer. In building the harbor he is combining work and pleasure in that the harbor is for the boats he uses to cross Coniston and brings him into social contact with his domestic staff, as opposed to the solitude of writing. Ruskin's mood, as ever, is reflected in the descriptions of nature he includes—in both cases the weather is good, either because of signs of spring or because of the exquisite twilight, and these entries present a dramatic contrast to the black wind of the storm-cloud lectures.

Ruskin admitted in *Fors Clavigera* that activities like digging were his final bulwark against insanity. Responding to a letter writer who asked if it ever occurred to Ruskin that he were mad, he responded that he would become so 'if it were not for my *work* (Ruskin's italics)...but it must be manual work' (Ruskin *Fors* II: 306). 'Manual work' is associated by Ruskin with 'honest country people patient in their task of maintaining the rascals in the towns,' even if the task to which he referring is drawing (*Fors* II: 306). All good art for Ruskin is manual labor, and an activity like digging is the highest form of manly manual work.

Ruskin digging his harbor seems a mixture of work and play, and the scene recalls his own remarks on the relationship between physical activity in work and play. In *The Crown of Wild Olive* Ruskin defined play 'as an exertion of body or mind, made to please ourselves and with no determined end; and work a thing done because it ought to be done, and with a determined end' (*Crown* XI: 8). In this light it is difficult to decide whether digging the harbor is work or not, since it is the exertion of the body that pleases Ruskin, but it also has a determined end. In later remarks it seems that digging the harbor should be classified as a 'play' through its association with rowing which makes it an unserious exercise in comparison to work:

> In your own experience most of you will be able to recognize the wholesome effect, alike as body and mind, of striving within the proper limits of time, to become good batsmen or good oarsmen. But the bat and the rower's oars are childrens' toys. Resolve that you will become men in usefulness, as well as in strength, and you will find that then also, but not till then, you can become men in understanding. (*Aratra* IX: 83)[4]

In this formulation ideas of play and recreation are associated with children's toys, while manliness is equated by implication with adult seriousness. Ruskin also moves easily from 'strength' in body to a more metaphorical strength of understanding which he equates with a full-blooded masculinity. Ruskin is of course drawing upon a familiar set of Victorian assumptions about work, seriousness and masculinity. Real men put aside children's toys and get on with the serious business of life, and do not play. Therefore, Ruskin asks Oxford undergraduates to put aside their oars and bats and become diggers of roads, and thus become 'real' men. The act of digging is itself supposed to produce the change from 'boys' to 'men' in the Hincksey Road project.

This passage from *Aratra Pentilici* draws upon an overall argument in the lectures that society itself is emerging from a technic 'childhood' and becoming more 'manly' (*Aratra* IX: 28). The Hincksey project is therefore for Ruskin a microcosm of his overall plan for social reformation in which all men will abjure oars for shovels. He calls for his Oxford audience to shun all technology, even in the construction of buildings as 'degrading to the intellect' and 'vulgar exhibitions' (*Aratra* IX: 128). Machinery subverts the 'hands' that are crucial for Ruskin because in Victorian society 'our hands are dexterous with the vile and deadly dexterity of machines' (*Aratra* IX: 71). Ruskin therefore calls on his Oxford undergraduates to engage in manual work:

> And I would, in all sober and direct earnestness advise you, whatever may be the aim, predilection or necessity of your lives, to resolve upon this thing at least, that you will enable yourselves daily to do actually with your hands, something that is useful to mankind. (*Aratra* IX: 83)

When Ruskin says something 'useful' he actually has in mind something artistic because for him 'all fine art requires the whole strength and subtlety of the body' especially 'the action and the force of a strong man's arm' (*Aratra* IX: 127). For this reason Ruskin tried to raise activities like digging to the same status as art and architecture and saw manual labor as producing strong, healthy men as well as a healthy society. His artistic program is based upon the development of the male body rather than the rejection of the body as in Carlyle. His attempts to elevate digging to a higher artistic status parallel Brown commemorating the bodies of working-class men digging in *Work*.

Even though rowing also develops the body, Ruskin equated 'bats, balls and oars' with childhood, both in society and the individual and thus dismissed sport as an activity (*Aratra* IX: 51). Rowing, however, was an increasingly acceptable form of displaying masculinity, as were all such competitive sports in the English educational system. As J. A. Mangan and Callum McKenzie explain, there were two competing ways for young men to display their masculine prowess in school and college: through traditional aristocratic pastimes such as hunting and beagling (where the hunter ran on foot after a beagle) and the emerging 'sports' and athletic contests. In broad terms the new sports tended to reflect a middle-class image of success through merit rather than through inherited rank. The distinction should not be overstated because many newly-rich families enthusiastically entered their sons into hunting and beagling clubs as a way of elevating their social status. Nonetheless, from the 1850s on prowess with oar or bat was increasingly a way to exhibit one's masculinity and status for young men from the upper and middle classes. Thus Alton Locke, even though he is from a working-class background, is shown as becoming caught up in the excitement of rowing and could see 'that it was no child's play;' he identifies with the rowers 'for I, too, was a man' (Kingsley *Alton Locke* 132). While Ruskin dismissed rowing as child's play, Kingsley linked it to manliness and the battle of Waterloo and saw no contradiction between masculinity and sports.[5]

Ruskin's Hincksey project was an attempt to translate sport-playing masculine prowess into work. By substituting a shovel for the oar, Ruskin was endeavoring to get his undergraduates to redefine their social status; not only did he want an Oxford Professor of digging, but he also wanted to make digging into a sign of masculinity on a par with rowing. Unlike Brown, he did not try to turn navvies into aesthetic objects but rather tried to raise the social status of digging itself.

While it is obvious that Oxford undergraduates may have wanted to raise their social status by imitating the upper classes and by taking up hunting or beagling, there is no evidence of a fervent desire on the part of Ruskin's students to profess an allegiance with the working classes by taking up picks and shovels; in fact, Oscar Wilde was caustic in his remarks on the attempt to elevate manual labor in this way, as we have seen. The same difficulties with class identity that bedeviled Ruskin's attempts to address working men in *Fors Clavigera* also subverted his Hincksey project. While Ruskin idealized working class labor, the audience he was addressing in both cases did not. Ruskin's message was too cerebral for the working classes, and the middle and upper classes were extremely unlikely to identify with the working classes simply because Ruskin said they should.

The Hincksey road project shows in microcosm the problem with all of Ruskin's political program, but especially the Guild of St. George.[6] The Guild of St. George was in its aim the Hincksey road project turned into a national and nationalistic scheme. Ruskin's principle was that 'no great arts were practicable by any people unless they were living contented lives, in pure air, out of the way of unsightly objects, and emancipated from unnecessary mechanical occupation' (*Fors* I: 123). Partly Ruskin was continuing the Romantic rejection of industrialization that can be found so strongly in Wordsworth, and following a typical English idealization of the countryside. He showed in such texts as *The Stones of Venice*, especially in 'The Nature of the Gothic,' his rejection of 'machinery' and industrialization in favor of a direct relationship between the artisan and his product. Morris, like Ruskin in his studies of the Gothic, idealized the 'free workman' who was exempt from market relations; Ruskin sees the 'redundancy' of Gothic architecture as a sign that laborers who built were not 'slaves' who for Ruskin are linked to mechanical reproduction (*Stones* VI: 172). The Ruskinian twist in this ideal is that the inhabitants of areas purchased by the St. George's Guild were supposed to be following a particular occupation that was the antithesis of a 'mechanical occupation.' The opposite of a 'mechanical occupation' for Ruskin was digging, especially if it was digging meant to produce food. As he says in the quotation with which I opened this chapter, the entire well-being of the State relies upon digging up turnips.

This was made even more clear when Ruskin announced a sub-company within the Guild of St. George called 'Monte Rosa' that was to combine, like the Hincksey project, the work of digging and education:

> And they are to be entirely devoted, according to their power, first to the manual labour of cultivating pure land, and guiding of pure streams and rain to the places where they are needed; and secondly, together with this manual labour, and much by its means, they are to carry on the thoughtful labour of true education. (*Fors* I: 229)

The 'guiding of pure streams' is reminiscent of Ruskin at Brantwood digging his harbor (and his various other projects to cleanse rivers and streams), and of the use of water as 'purifying' in Carlyle's *Past and Present* and Brown's *Work*. While digging may have been redemptive for Ruskin, most people recognized that the 'Monte Rosa' was more of a vision than a practical program. Just as the Hincksey road project could not transcend the class implications of manual labor, so the Guild could not overcome the dichotomy between working the land as an ideal and the reality of an industrialized landscape and industrialized labor. Working on the land could be as 'mechanical' as working in a factory when all is said and done, but for Ruskin, because it is an outdoor activity and connected with growing food, it is innately superior.[7]

The men digging a road in London, or carrying out manual labor in Ford Madox Brown's *Work*, do not conform entirely to Ruskin's ideal, partly of course because they are not digging in the countryside and they are not producing food. However, they are representative of a country in which the majority of people after mid-century lived in urban areas and who were engaged in activities related to increased industrialization and urbanization. It is not clear that these people would have welcomed an effort to send them back to rural occupations since moving to London may well have meant an increase in their standard of living in comparison to working in the country.

Ruskin's whole approach to work was characterized, as was Carlyle's, by a rejection of the 'cash nexus' of payment for work. Especially in the realm of intellectual labor, Ruskin felt that 'none of best head work in art, literature, or science is ever paid for' (*Crown* XI: 31). Such a resistance led to further confusions between work and play, since the definition of leisure was increasingly that it was activity for which one was not paid. So extreme was Ruskin's resistance to defining work in terms of money that he made it a biological imperative for an educated man not to recognize the connection, saying that 'it is physically impossible for a well-educated, or brave man to make money the chief object of his thoughts' (*Crown* XI: 17).

Ruskin's idealization of the agricultural labor, like William Morris' in *News from Nowhere*, undercuts the political program he wishes to pursue through the St. George's Guild. What Ruskin was really objecting to was the increasing mechanization of labor, and the way in which, in the new industrial economics, the worker was becoming indistinguishable from a machine. Ruskin's true enemy was not industrialization per se but the kind of approach epitomized later in the century by Frederick Winslow Taylor and his approach to the labor of digging.[8]

Taylor pioneered an approach to manual labor in an industrial setting that came to be known as 'Taylorism.'[9] In 1878 Taylor went to work for the Midvale Steel Company in Pennsylvania. While there he used a stopwatch and direct observation to observe the actions of men digging pig iron at the plant. He concluded that the men were not digging in the most efficient manner possible and began to formulate both ways for them to increase their rate of work and better designed shovels with which to dig. Taylor described his method in the book for which he is best known, *Scientific Management*:

> Briefly to illustrate some of the other elements which go to make up the science of shoveling, thousands of stop-watch observations were made to study just how quickly a laborer, provided in each case with the proper type of shovel, can push his shovel into the pile of materials and then draw it out properly loaded. These observations were made first when pushing the shovel into the body of the pile. Next when shoveling on a dirt bottom, that is, at the outside edge of the pile, and next with a wooden bottom, and finally with an iron bottom. Again a similar accurate time study was made of the time required to swing the shovel backward and then throw the load for a given horizontal distance, accompanied by a given height. This time study was made for various combinations of distance and height. With data of this sort before him, coupled with the law of endurance described in the case of the pig-iron handlers, it is evident that the man who is directing shovelers can first teach them the exact methods which should be employed to use their strength to the very best advantage, and can then assign them daily tasks which are so just that the workman can each day be sure of earning the large bonus which is paid whenever he performs his task. (Taylor *Principles* 67–8)

Taylor's approach to 'the science of shoveling' is the opposite of Ruskin's idealized image of digging as redemptive work. Taylor himself was genuinely interested in both increasing productivity and in giving workers higher wages. As his last sentence shows, he wanted to reward the people who followed his directions with bonuses. However, this is exactly the kind of 'mechanization' of labor to which Ruskin was objecting. Taylor's vision of the 'science of shoveling,' however, is much closer to the realities of industrialized labor than the Hincksey road project. Taylor linked digging directly to money and pay, where Ruskin tried to sever the connection.

Taylor shared the antipathy of all Victorian writers to 'idleness,' but in his vocabulary this was glossed as 'underwork' (*Principles* 18). Taylor ascribed the existence of 'underwork' to a 'natural laziness' in workers rather than any resistance to discipline (*Principles* 20). For Taylor 'underworkers' were men who were not producing as much as they could under the piecework system but instead slowing down as soon as they had reached their targets. Taylor wanted to make these men more 'productive,' that is he wanted to make sure that they produced the maximum amount of work in the time available and so he set about creating a system that would prevent 'underwork.' Implicitly, like Ruskin, he wanted to promote the 'man at work' over idleness, but explicitly named the link between the worker and production.

Taylorism introduced time and motion studies into industry in which every movement of the worker was broken down into discrete steps and timed by stopwatch. An ideal of efficiency was then created in which the worker was supposed to follow the exact same steps at the exact same time to ensure optimum production. Taylor's ideas helped inaugurate the mechanization and deskilling of labor that also informed the creation of the Colt gun factory and the Ford production line.[10] In the Taylor approach the human body is treated as if it were itself a machine capable of performing the same task over and over without deviation. As Jacques Gleyse argues, 'man comes to be seen as a steam engine as a result of industrial discipline' and Taylorism is therefore a crucial stage in the industrialization of the masculine body (246).

Ruskin wished to combat forces like Taylorism by moving digging to the countryside. Digging as an activity, however, does not in itself carry any intrinsic potential for good or harm; the good or harm comes from the context in which the activity is carried out. Ruskin, because of his idealization of digging as an activity, could not recognize that what he was objecting to was turning workers into units of production and making them part of an exploitative system of labor. Taylor himself did not want to create this exploitative system, but 'Taylorism' became the vehicle for systems of piece work and repetitive labor that were dehumanizing in the extreme.

Ruskin's social program was thus subverted by his own idealization of activities like digging when placed in a rural setting. Because of his idealization of the countryside Ruskin felt that simply carrying out the activity in a different context would transform it from backbreaking work into an enjoyable activity. Ruskin in his writings reinforces a rural idyll that makes agricultural labor less alienated than work in the city. In this he is akin to William Morris in *News from Nowhere*. Morris inherited both Ruskin's social agenda and a damaging idealization of the capacity of the countryside to transform work into joyful activity. The Britain of Morris' future is agricultural and the major urban centers have been dismantled.

In essays such as *Unto This Last*, Ruskin took aim at Political Economy and protested against the exploitation of workers in industrialized Britain. Written 15 years before the Ferry Hincksey project, *Unto This Last* is in many ways a prescient analysis of the problems with 'production' that I outlined in the

Introduction. Ruskin assails Political Economy in the person of John Stuart Mill in terms of 'productive' versus 'unproductive' labor in his examples of a manufacturer of metal goods versus a silversmith. Ruskin questions very effectively Mill's use of 'productive,' and points out the moral and philosophical considerations that Political Economy wishes to exclude. It is this kind of cogent analysis of economics on humanitarian grounds that made Ruskin a hero for later readers such as William Morris.

However, Ruskin's objection to Mill is based on the premise of a silversmith, working with his hands, versus industrial manufacture. As in 'The Nature of the Gothic,' his response to industrialization is to valorize handicraft by skilled artisans. Indeed, as he says in a footnote his definition of 'skill' is 'united force of experience, intellect, and passion in their operation on manual labour' (*Stones* VI: 181). A silversmith would be an example of this kind of 'skill' in manual as opposed to mechanized labor. He does not question the ideal of the 'man at work' but instead promotes a certain form of work by hand, especially by male hands. He does not, for instance, think of women's labor under the rubric of 'productive' work. As he makes clear his definitions of 'production' and 'capital' are connected to agriculture and so the worker with a ploughshare is the basic unit of his system. His ideal society is agrarian, not industrial.

Ruskin compares Political Economy to a science of gymnastics that assumed that men had no skeletons and that 'it would be advantageous to roll the students up into pellets, flatten them into cakes, or stretch them into cables' (*Unto* XII: 19). While this is a joke, it does raise the concern in the essay over the effect of industrialization on the human body, especially the male body.[11] To his credit, Ruskin does not repress the male body in the way that Carlyle did in his writings on work, but rather promotes an ideal of the muscular male body at work. It is this working-class male body that is threatened by mechanization.

As far as Ruskin in concerned, both industrialization and Political Economy treat workers as machines. At another point in the essay he complains that Political Economy represents the worker as if he 'were an engine of which the motive power was steam, magnetism, gravitation, or any other agent of calculable force' (*Unto* XII: 23). This is of course precisely how Taylor approached the question of efficiency in digging; he treated the worker as if he were a machine. He also made the worker's wages dependent on a 'piece rate' of payment by results, which is the primary target of Ruskin's polemic against Political Economy. Ruskin uses the parable of the workers in the vineyard to argue that workers should be paid the same wage no matter how much they produce, and that their value lies not in their production, but in the fact that they work.

The healthy male body serves as a metaphor for the entire economy in Ruskin's *Unto This Last* in contrast to the use of the diseased body in Carlyle's prose that I analyzed in Chapter 1. A healthy Britain is compared to a human body after exertion:

> Thus the circulation of wealth in a nation resembles that of the blood in the natural
> body. There is one quickness of the current which comes of cheerful emotion or
> wholesome exercise; and another which comes of shame or of fever. There is a
> flush of the body which is full of warmth and life; and another which will pass
> into putrefaction. (*Unto* XII 50)

For Ruskin a healthy economy is like a body that has been exercised,
which helps explain his later support for projects such as Ferry Hincksey. They
were quite literally attempts to create a healthy 'social body' (to use the Poovey
phrase) and avoid 'putrefaction' which is a sign of both disease and idleness. As
with the artists and writers discussed previously, when Ruskin imagines the
healthy body at work he has in mind the male body. Political Science does not
address the problem of keeping the male body healthy, and so it does not address
'manliness.' His critique of 'value' is based on a definition of the 'valiant,' that is
those men who can use material with valor. Value is linked in his train of
association with masculinity and the problem that money threatens 'manliness:'

> This being so, the difficulty of the true science of Political Economy lies not
> merely in the need of developing manly character to deal with material value, but
> in the fact, that while the manly character and material value only form wealth by
> their conjunction, they have nevertheless a mutually destructive operation on each
> other. For the manly character is apt to ignore, or even cast away, the material
> value...And on the other hand, the material value is apt to undermine the manly
> character. (*Unto* XII 105–106)

Ruskin's discussion of what Marx termed 'use value' versus 'exchange
value' becomes fatally distracted at this point by the ideal of manliness as the
opposite of the 'cash nexus.' Rather than a critique of the 'commodity fetishism'
that was undermining the direct relationship between the worker and his product
that Ruskin valued, he sees the problem in terms of the male character not being
developed in Political Economy. He moves away from 'material value' into an
ideal of the healthy male body being developed in manual labor. While his
representation of the male body is radically different from Carlyle's, he shares
Carlyle's rejection of both Mammon and mechanization in terms that undermine
his critique of capitalism because it based on the body of the male worker.

Thus even in *Unto This Last*, written well before the Ferry Hincksey
project and arguably one of Ruskin's most incisive critiques of capitalism, his
political critique is subverted by the idea of the healthy working-class masculine
body as an antidote to the ills of Victorian society. While schemes such as Ferry
Hincksey and the Guild of St. George were designed to promote a healthy
masculinity through digging, the future of work was being charted by Taylor and
his stopwatch. The mechanization that Ruskin feared was proceeding apace, and
was accomplished ironically by observation of a man with a shovel. Far from

opposing the forces of capital, the man working with the shovel was enmeshed in the kind of definition of 'production' that Ruskin rejected.

Work was in the view of Ruskin, as it was for Engels, being 'demasculinized' by mechanization. This was certainly true if the muscular 'man at work' was your ideal of useful, practical labor, as it was for so many of those in this analysis. By the 1880s, the forces of mechanization and the development of a larger service and clerical industry were indeed 'demasculinizing' work as muscular power became irrelevant. As Engels noted, the introduction of machines into factories meant that women and children could carry out tasks that had earlier been confined to men. In the 1880s the mechanization that had transformed factory work began to transform clerical work.

New technologies led to the erosion of the 'separation of spheres' in the late Victorian period and the definition of work as a masculine prerogative. Women entered the middle-class work force in ever larger numbers thanks to the industrialization of writing through such inventions as the typewriter. The most obvious symbol of this change was the 'New Woman,' who was seen as a sexually liberated force. The rise of the 'New Woman' signaled a crisis in the definition of 'man's work,' a crisis that is registered most strongly in the novels of George Gissing. His novels record the end of the 'man at work' as an ideal in the face of the industrialization of labor throughout Victorian society.

## Notes

1. Morris himself named three authors as most influential on his thinking 'Sir Thomas Moore's *Utopia*, Ruskin's works (especially the ethical and politico-economic parts of them) and Thomas Carlyle's works.' (*Collected Works* XXII: xi). Morris locates himself within the same tradition as Carlyle and Ruskin, despite apparent political differences.
2. I am indebted to Stamp's *The Changing Metropolis* for this image (213).
3. This and other images of manual labor from Gavin Stamp's *The Changing Metropolis* emphasize the anonymity of working-class labor as the figures of the workers are dwarfed by the massive construction projects in which they are employed. This is especially striking in an 1866 photograph of the Paddington station construction (Stamp 218) in which the workers are dwarfed by machinery.
4. See Anthony *John Ruskin's Labour: A Study of Ruskin's Social Theory* for a further discussion of this passage (143–4).
5. Alton's cousin George self-consciously uses sports to raise his social status as well (Kingsley *Alton Locke* 68).
6. As Stoddart notes, Rosenberg and Speer dismiss the Guild as eccentrically nostalgic (75).
7. This is a small part of the overall Ruskin Edenic program, as Jeffrey L. Spear has noted (183).
8. Taylor is just as crucial an agent in the creation of industrial attitudes to the human body as the steam engine and factory (Gleyse 240).

9.  See Kanigel *The One Best Way* on the development of 'Taylorism.' Drucker ranks Taylor with Darwin, Marx, and Freud as one of the most influential nineteenth-century figures.
10. Kransberg notes that Taylor's rationalization of the use of the shovel is a paradigmatic moment in applying machine-like standards to the human body (156).
11. Ruskin's objection here parallels the critique of the mechanization of the 'social body' in Political Economy by Kay-Shuttleworth (quoted in Poovey, 85).

# Chapter 7

# Gissing and the Demise of the
# Man at Work

A man has no business to fail. (Gissing *Grub Street* 256)

Andrew Dowling in his study of *New Grub Street* correctly identifies failure as the central problem in Gissing's novel. As the quotation above indicates, masculinity and success are equated in Gissing's novel, so that the novelist is 'complicit with hegemonic masculinity' (Dowling 96). Dowling, like Sussman, would locate Reardon's failure in the novel as the result of a failure of 'manly discipline' or in Sussman's terms, masculine self-regulation.[1] I would, however, place the novel within the context of changes in the labor of male intellectuals in the 1880s as they faced challenges to writing as a craft thanks to the industrialization of writing. Gissing resists the redefinition of writing from art into a question of material production.[2] Where Ruskin in the previous chapter resisted mechanization with an appeal to masculine manual labor, Gissing registers the erosion of the Victorian ideal of the 'man at work.' The death of Reardon symbolizes the demise of work as an exclusively masculine enterprise, and registers Gissing's pessimism about the status of the male writer as more and more women entered the workforce.

Dowling claims that Gissing's novel is 'not really about literary production at all' (97) but this is in fact not the case; the novel is about male literary production and what happens when, in the new labor market of the 1880s, a man fails to be 'productive.' As Goode says of the book, Gissing 'portrays the relations of industrial production' (25) extremely well in his novels, and is centrally interested in the writer as a masculine producer of commodities. In this world, the writer is a pieceworker and struggles with the same contradictions that beset Ford Madox Brown as an artist. The new labor market created a direct threat to the ideal of the muscular 'man at work.' The change in the relations of industrial production and the redefinition of writing as a form of labor led directly to a crisis in the definition of masculinity. Gisssing records this crisis in the 'failure' of Reardon as a writer and as a man.

As Poole points out, Gissing registers the 'total industrialization of writing,' although I would add he also registers the domination of both masculinity and writing by the forces of production thanks to this industrialization (142). These forces, which Ruskin opposed earlier in the century in terms of mechanization, are seen by Gissing as the twin threats of the marketplace and of women's labor. Where Ruskin rejected the connection of manliness, valor and money, in the world of Gissing's novel masculinity is intimately connected with financial success. The novel is a commodity in Gissing's narrative, and although he would like to promote an ideal of art as autonomous from market forces, he traces a pessimistic trajectory for the writer when he does not become a productive worker. The success stories in the novel are men who adjust to the marketplace of literary production, or women who take advantage of new forms of labor that challenged the definition of work as a masculine prerogative.

Ruskin was resisting the industrialization of work through his idealization of digging. A similar mechanization is taking place in Gissing's novels, where the 'manual labor' of writing was turned into the mechanized production of typing and shorthand. This change in the production of writing was registered most dramatically in clerical work. As the governmental and private bureaucracies of the late nineteenth century expanded the number of clerical positions grew dramatically and these were increasingly staffed by women. Gregory Anderson documents the increase from 1851 when the census listed only 19 female clerks, to 1891 when the number was 17, 859 (56). These female clerks were in addition concentrated in London, the site of Gissing's novel, so that their presence and number would be more obvious than in other parts of the country. Anderson's book also contains cartoons in which women are pushing a male clerk out of the way to take over his position (entitled 'Elbowing Him out'), and the male clerk ends up staying at home looking after the children while his wife goes to work (entitled 'The Decay of Home Life' facing 57).

Late Victorian masculinity is under assault thanks to this redefinition of the terms of labor. The cartoons in Anderson's book on Victorian clerks represent graphically the fear that also informs Gissing's novels, that the entry of women into the marketplace, combined with the mechanization of writing, directly threatens the 'man at work.' Where the situation is portrayed as comedy in the cartoons, it is represented as tragedy in *New Grub Street*. Reardon's failure to become a productive 'man at work' leads to his death.

Gissing's portrayal of the downfall and death of Reardon presents a mirror image of the dying women in Redgrave and Hood. The incursion of market forces into femininity and the domestic sphere in Redgrave and Hood's images led to the death of 'distressed needlewomen.' In Gissing we have 'distressed male writers' whose livelihood is undermined by market forces, and who must compete with women who are entering the workplace thanks to the typewriter. The industrialization process 'demasculinized' intellectual labor and Reardon in the novel is steadily demasculinized as he succumbs to his loss of productivity and thus of income. His individual downward trajectory thereby represents the wholesale redefinition of writing as commodified labor in the period.

    The novel is especially concerned with the class status of the male writer. Reardon's 'failure' is marked by a rapid descent to the lower-middle-class rung on the Victorian social ladder. Reardon goes from being a self-employed writer thanks to his one successful publication to a clerk producing writing on demand for others. The novel represents this, which stands for a general devaluing of literary production, as his most egregious 'failure.' The conjunction of 'business' and 'failure' in the quotation above is therefore ironic, in that a man can only be a man by succeeding in business, which is seen as having less cultural capital but more real capital than being an artist or writer. There is an increasing clash in Gissing's world between the cultural status of the writer and his or her class status. The status of the writer as an autonomous professional is under assault by the pressures of commodification.[3]

    The history of professionalism in the nineteenth century is, as is widely recognized, the assertion of control by men over certain areas of labor. By means of accreditation and control of entry into the field, the 'professional' was made masculine, in the same way that the field of work was defined in gender terms earlier in the century. Perhaps the most obvious arena in which this took place was medicine, in which informal female practitioners were marginalized as the field became defined as a male domain. However, the 'professional' ideal was based not only on classification in terms of gender but also on an assertion of class status. The idea of the professional adds to the gendered division of labor the aspect of class differentiation. Professionalism denotes a certain class status, and bestows a prestige upon members of that profession. The professional tries to separate himself from the idea that services are based on money and to substitute an aura of prestige and skill instead; as Adams, quoting Perkins, says the professional tries to assert that his value 'cannot be measured by the market' (*Dandies and Desert Saints* 6). The professional is therefore not a pieceworker or waged clerk, supposedly, but somebody who operates independently based upon expertise that insulates his labor from market forces. 'Professional men as a class were characterized by their comparative aloofness from the struggle for income' so that to be identified too closely with 'money grubbing' would entail a loss of class position (Wiener 15).

    The male professional is distinguished above all from the working-class laborer. There is no particular reason that professionalism be defined in gendered terms, as became increasingly clear in the twentieth century, but class status is essential. Professional identity is above all class-based identity. A 'working-class professional' would be a contradiction in terms. The Victorian professional aspired to the status of gentleman, and even though he worked for a living would want to be viewed not as a wage earner but as someone with a skill who happened to be paid for his services. In Gissing's *New Grub Street*, as we shall see, to be a 'wage earner' in a clerkship is to become indistinguishable from the 'working man,' so that Reardon becoming a clerk is a fatal loss of class status.[4] The professional writer was not a laborer or a clerk because you could not be a 'working-class'

professional. As the novel progresses, Reardon loses professional status and
became more and more working class.

According to McIvor in his statistical analysis of the period from 1880,
the most striking feature was the growth of employment opportunities in the non-
manual sector of the economy (33). McIvor also characterizes the era as the
'deskilling' of work thanks to technological change (56). The effect of
technological change on writing is expressed in *New Grub Street* in Marian's odd
fantasy about a 'writing machine:'

> A few days ago her startled eye had caught an advertisement in the newspaper,
> headed 'Literary Machine'; had it then been invented at last, some automaton to
> supply the place of such poor creatures as herself to turn out books and articles?
> Alas! the machine was only one for holding volumes conveniently, that the work
> of literary manufacture might be physically lightened. But surely before long
> some Edison would make the true automaton; the problem must be comparatively
> such a simple one. Only to throw in a given number of old books, and have them
> reduced, blended, modernised into a single one for to-day's consumption. (Gissing
> *Grub Street* 107)

Marian had early been characterized as a mere machine because of her
labors for her father. Gissing's use of 'manufacture' and 'automaton' here betray
the spectral presence of technology turning the handicraft of writing into a type of
industrial production. Books are items to be 'consumed' and mass produced and
not individual works of art. Marian is herself an alienated laborer in the world of
literary production, so the idea of such a 'literary machine' is a labor-saving
device, not the source of horror that it would be for literary men like her father.[5] As
a woman, Marian actually stands to benefit from the introduction of 'literary
machines' like the typewriter into the workplace where for literary men it would be
threat to their status as producers of texts.[6] Marian is in the position of the
'urbanized worker' and her labors in the British Museum make her acutely aware
of commodification (Goode 120). She does not have a professional status to lose
and is aware of the industrialization of writing.

The industrialization of writing was a threat to male professional identity.
Gissing's text registers both the loss of class status suffered by the professional
writer, but also the commodification of labor and its impact on writing as work.
Professional working condition were increasingly becoming available to working
class men (Perkin 3), and this proximity placed pressure on the class basis of
professional work. Goode also notes that this was the period in which 'the
populace was beginning to erupt into the West End again and the armies of the
unskilled were beginning to organize' (13), so that in other words the pressure of
the working classes was being felt as a threat that had not been present with such
force since Chartism.

The locus for this anxiety was the figure of the clerk. George Grossmith's famous satire *The Diary of a Nobody* was a *Punch* series in 1888 that was published in 1892 as a book, and parodied the social pretensions of the lower-middle-class clerk. James Hammerton in 'Pooterism or Partnership?' has documented the many other fictional and autobiographical representations of the clerk, including George Gissing's own *The Town Traveler* of 1898. Hammerton focuses on the 'feminized masculinity' that marked both fictional and autobiographical representations of the clerk in this period (295). In the context of Gilbert and Sullivan's line from *Iolanthe* (1882) 'Bow, bow, ye lower middle classes' Hammerton introduces what he calls the 'paradoxical' convergence of different forces in creating this 'feminized masculinity:'

> Gilbert and Sullivan's immortal line...is most powerfully familiar in the feminization of the male white-collar worker, which developed, paradoxically, just at the time when clerical work was being defined in liberating ways for lower-middle-class women. (Hammerton 'Pooterism' 298)

As I will argue in conclusion, this 'feminization' of clerks was not necessarily new in the 1880s and 1890s; the work had already been 'feminized' in opposition to the ideal of muscular, sweaty labor carried out in the outdoors. Hammerton is right, however, to indicate the importance of the entrance of women into the clerical workforce. This led to crises on two interrelated fronts, firstly in terms of the threat to the domestic sphere and secondly the anxiety that English masculinity was increasingly becoming 'degraded' as 'an effeminate masculine identity built on servile employees and slaves to the domestic rule of women' (Hammerton 303). These anxieties have a fictional counterpart in Gissing's novels but rather than focus on the feminization of the domestic male, I will focus in this chapter on the loss of class status for the 'professional' writer in a marketplace dominated by women and men who define themselves in economic rather than artistic terms.

These class anxieties are registered also in Stevenson's *The Strange Case of Dr. Jekyll and Mr. Hyde*. *Jekyll and Hyde* is by its nature open to an extraordinarily wide range of interpretations because Mr. Hyde is figure of the return of the repressed. Exactly what Mr. Hyde does in order to act out the repressed desires of Dr. Jekyll is never made explicit, and so many possibilities, ranging from sex, homosexuality, masturbation, alcoholism and drug use have been proffered as possible secret vices. However, ignoring what Mr. Hyde does in secret, I will for the purposes of this analysis focus on his status as a 'Mr.' The transformation from Dr. Jekyll into Mr. Hyde therefore entails the loss of social status that attends Dr. Jekyll's profession. As I argued in Chapter 4, work-based divisions of the body are played out in the Jekyll/Hyde contrast, especially at the level of the hands, which were a central class marker. Stephen Arata has identified anxieties about his professional status as crucial for Stevenson when writing *Dr.*

*Jekyll and Mr. Hyde*, and this loss of social status is one of the most prevalent fears also in Gissing's novel. I have already analyzed the class conflict registered in Dr. Jekyll's hand in the context of Munby's fetish for dirty hands (See Chapter 5). The story also registers the loss of professional status entailed in the transformation from Jekyll into Hyde.

Dr. Jekyll is a divided man and a literal embodiment of Ruskin's claim in the *The Stones of Venice* that 'it is not, truly speaking, the labour that is divided but the men' (*Stones* VI: 16). The division of labor that informs Jekyll and Hyde is that between the professional and the working class, between the intellectual and the supposedly more primal manual laborer. Dr. Jekyll betrays the 'stigmata of degeneration' as Arata has argued (33–34), but these are signs of a descent down a class hierarchy rather than a Darwinian evolution in reverse.

The view of a threatening working-class masculinity is registered very strongly in Hubert von Herkomer's *On Strike* (1891; reproduced in Treuherz 100). The upright male figure has a threatening expression on his face and his body expresses pent up anger. It is not clear if the woman behind him is going to pull him back into the interior, and domestic space or whether he is about to leave behind home and family. He is poised ambiguously between these two courses of action as he stands in the doorway looking off into a landscape that we cannot see; it is also unclear whether he is an agricultural or industrial worker. He is a figure closer to the 'threat' of urban, lower-middle-class young men that Hammerton analyses in 'Men as well as Clerks' as the antitype to the domesticated and effeminate clerk. He represents the continuing fear of the violence of the working-class male.

The contradictory class codes in Dr. Jekyll's hand register the shift from a biologically based definition of class in which 'professional' status could be read from the shape of a hand, to one in which a working-class male could be latent inside the professional male. Dr. Jekyll's unstable identity is riven by a number of class-based fears, including the fear of the urban working class erupting into violence. However, the incident of the hand names the anxiety as specifically the relationship between the male professional hand and that of a manual laborer. Mr. Hyde is an interloper in the circle of male professionals in which Mr. Utterson and Dr. Jekyll move; as a result he must be brought out and destroyed.

Stevenson's text as a horror story registers many cultural anxieties, and I am certainly not claiming that this is the only contradiction encoded into the figure of Mr. Hyde. However, since the text does take place entirely in a world of male professionals, this aspect of the story is as important an element as that of repressed sexuality.[7] The men in the story seem to do a very good job of marginalizing women, with their access restricted to cameo roles as maids or landladies. The story is far more concerned with Dr. Jekyll's loss of status when he becomes a mere 'Mr.,' and is therefore primarily a horror story about the loss of class status.

The same loss of class status also haunts Gissing's story. Like *Jekyll and Hyde*, Gissing uses London to map class distinctions; where Soho and the West End provided a contrast in Stevenson's story, in Gissing's novel each of the different addresses used in the story maps the class status of both Reardon and friends like Biffen. It is the loss of class status that haunts the text and defines Reardon's 'failure.'

Where the specter of the proximity of the male professional writer to the domestic haunted earlier texts, in Gissing's story Reardon is haunted by the image of the writer as clerk, producing copy for money. Reardon works as a secretary when he finally gives up his dreams of being a writer, and is envious of the apparently anxiety-free life of the clerk:

> How I envy those clerks who go by to their offices in the morning! There's the day's work cut out for them; no question of mood and feeling; they have just to work at something, and when the evening comes, they have earned their wages, they are free to rest and enjoy themselves. What an insane thing it is to make literature one's only means of support! When the most trivial accident may at any time prove fatal to one's power of work for weeks or months. No, that is the unpardonable sin! To make a trade of an art! I am rightly served for attempting such a brutal folly. (Gissing *Grub Street* 50–51)

Reardon laments the difficulties of 'brain work' versus the supposedly much easier task of being a clerk. His comments here are reminiscent of Ruskin's remarks on the strain produced on artists by having to be 'clever' rather than being able to work steadily at a task. Just as manual labor was romanticized in earlier texts, Reardon romanticizes the ease, and ignores the stress and boredom, that accompany the waged work of the clerk, as compensation for his own anxieties. The key transition here is from writing as a vocation to a trade. If writing is a vocation then it is a lifelong pursuit similar to a profession. If it is just a 'trade' then to be a successful writer has more to do with the labor market than any innate genius.

Where genius was an inborn trait that you either had or did not, writing as a 'trade' is open to anybody from any social class who is willing to approach it in the right terms. Cross suggests George Augustus Sala as a 'case study' equivalent to Milvain, and quotes Sala as cheerfully admitting 'I knew perfectly well that I was altogether destitute of a particle of that genius without which I could never excel or become famous in pure letters; but, on the other hand, I was fully cognizant of the fact that I learned my trade as a journalist, and that I could earn a handsome income by it' (226); Sala sounds here like a mixture of Trollope in his *Autobiography* on writing as a trade, and Milvain on the income one could expect from journalism.

Reardon does of course undertake clerical work, both early in his career and when facing a financial crisis and a separation from his wife. However, this choice of occupation is seen by everyone, including Reardon himself, as a sign of his 'failure' and as an irremediable loss of caste. Even though Milvain early in the novel says that writing is 'just a trade' (*Grub Street* 8), he does not wish to lose social status by literally 'going into trade.' While Milvain quite cheerfully encourages his sisters to earn money by writing and seems to regard women as equally well suited to the 'trade' as men, he still views it as work with a higher social status than being a clerk.

Milvain is described early in the novel as having a face 'of bureaucratic type' (*Grub Street* 5). Like Dr. Jekyll's 'professional' hand, Milvain's face betrays his proximity to a kind of writing that Gissing associates with offices and journalism. He is marked from the outset as a member of a new world of commodified labor in which writing is tied directly to a salary. Reardon, although he is an artist, cannot find a place in this new world of commodified labor. Milvain marks himself as a member of the commodified world of writing when he remarks that Reardon 'isn't the kind of man to keep up literary production as a paying business,' whereas Milvain understands completely literary production as 'business' (*Grub Street* 6). His 'bureaucratic face' reinforces his connection with 'business' and a 'cash nexus' approach to the labor of writing.

Milvain's class status, as a new breed of professional, is ambiguous. Again, Gissing's initial description of him, like the 'bureaucratic' face, hints at the work-based features that he gives this character. Gissing writes that 'the clothes he wore were of expensive material, but had seen a good deal of service' (*Grub Street* 5), which indicates that Milvain has the initial capital to dress as a gentleman, but not the wherewithal to maintain his wardrobe; also when he is first introduced he seems to have the trappings of a gentleman and his sisters criticize his 'idleness.' He seems at one level to belong to the leisured classes so anathematized by Carlyle. However, Milvain is in search of work that will both give him an income and allow him to maintain the status of a gentleman. He is in search of a professional position that will allow him to maintain a household and work without losing class status. Another avenue open to him, as becomes clear, is to marry into money; either finding a professional position or marrying into money would secure his social status.

For both Milvain and Reardon their identities as men are defined by their work. In this logic, to 'fail' at work is to fail as a man, and conversations between Reardon and Amy move from a vocabulary of 'failure' to a vocabulary of masculinity, she calling his inability to write 'unmanly.' Failure to produce, rather than idleness, is the antithesis of masculine work in this text. Reardon laments his inability to produce anything, and as an unproductive writer is not a 'man' because he cannot get his brain to work. Milvain wonders if Reardon does not suffer from 'overwork' but rather than too much work is Reardon's problem is the inability to do any work at all. It is not his ambition to become a 'literary man,' with its suggestion that the 'literary' is a female term that is the problem here, but rather his definition of the 'literary' which is out of step with the new commodified definitions of literary production.

Reardon's failure in the story is therefore both as a producer of literary texts and as a man. He defines himself in the same way as the other figures in this study, in terms of a man whose identity is predicated solely on his work. Thanks to his identity crisis he begins to project his own anxieties onto Amy, expressing the definition of masculine identity in terms of work found throughout the nineteenth century:

> Do you only love the author in me? Don't you think of me apart from all that I may do or not do? If I had to earn my living as a clerk, would that make me a clerk in soul? (Gissing *Grub Street* 196)

While it would not presumably make Reardon's 'soul' any different to work as a clerk, the social construction of his identity would alter radically. The class status of a clerk is different from that of an intellectual or a writer, and there is no escaping the social construction of identity in Gissing's tale. If it were possible to distinguish 'soul' from social status then Reardon would be perfectly right, but Amy's response indicates that he would have become a 'downgoing man' if he were to undertake this occupation. Amy calls Reardon a 'working man' if he is a clerk, meaning that he would have joined the working classes, and be indistinguishable from a common man. While writing is work, its social status is very different from being a clerk.

When Reardon does in fact take the job as clerk Gissing's description is that his very behavior and posture, his *habitus* in Bourdieu's terms, changes also.[8] After Amy has left him Reardon looks for some food. Gissing describes the sequence in these terms:

> There was some food still in the cupboard, and he consumed it in the fashion of a tired labourer, with the plate on his lap, using his fingers and a knife. (Gissing *Grub Street* 256)

Almost immediately Reardon's behavior has begun to mark him physically as a member of a lower class. Just as fears of degeneration haunted Stevenson's text, with degeneration connoting a fall down the class scale as much as a return to a more primitive form of existence, so the fear expressed here is that a man may change in body as well as social status. Gissing makes this kind of fear explicit when he discusses the brains of the poor:

> A physiologist ought to be able to discover some curious distinction between the brain of a person who has never given a thought to the means of subsistence, and that of one who has never known a day free from such cares. There must be some special cerebral development representing the mental anguish kept up by poverty. (Gissing *Grub Street* 200)

Just as Lombroso reported to have discovered a difference in the brains of criminals,[9] Gissing speculates that Reardon's brain and those of people living in poverty are marked by the experience and thus differences in class become differences in physiognomy. The 'professional' is marked by a certain size hand, or presumably a larger brain, and so the lower classes can be distinguished at a physical level. Where Mr. Hyde carried the stigmata in his hand, Reardon evinces the effects of poverty at the level of the brain. This is particularly telling for him since he is a 'brain worker' whose very instrument is now fatally flawed. Reardon has ceased to be a 'brain worker' and become a working-class man.

Reardon and Biffen, thanks to their occupations as intellectuals, do not occupy an easily defined class position. Biffen says to Reardon that 'we are different types of intellectual workers' (*Grub Street* 375), making them neither upper nor lower class. Reardon's novels 'dealt with no particular class of society (unless one makes a distinct class of people who have brains)' and thus are not part of the conventional social hierarchy (*Grub Street* 62). Reardon's difficulties come from his being neither upper nor lower class, but part of a free-floating group of intellectuals who have cultural if not real capital. Biffen, even though he kills himself, is more successful than Reardon in that he has clear class aspirations to represent a certain lower-middle stratum of society.

Reardon's class status is defined by his love of the Classics. Knowledge of Classical literature had a long pedigree as the mark of education and being a gentleman.[10] Rather than mark Reardon as a gentleman, however, his love of ancient literature makes him an anachronism, as Selig suggests (Selig 191). More than this, however, his learning introduces a class incongruence between his financial status, his cultural capital and his downward trajectory as a failing artist.

Disturbingly the only way that Gissing can imagine as a way for Reardon to reclaim his masculinity, apart from being a successful novelist, is to become violent toward Amy. Gissing has Amy imagine that violence on Reardon's part would reestablish his masculine mastery over her:

> Blows and a curse would have overawed her, at all events for the moment; she would have felt: 'Yes, he is a man, and I have put my destiny into his hands.' (Gissing *Grub Street* 229)

Reardon is persistently described, even by Gissing, as 'weak' and by implication less than a man. However, if he were to erupt in anger and violence this would presumably rescue him from the effeminate category of 'weak' and put him back into the category of a 'man.' Unfortunately, Dowling quotes this same passage and merely comments that 'Reardon's sensitivity emphasizes his inadequacy in the struggle for life' (107). A normally astute reader, Dowling does not recognize here the equation of masculinity with violence, and Reardon's failure to use violence as a marker of his effeminacy in conventional Victorian gender ideology.

Reardon does not, however, erupt into violence; instead, he cries. Reardon becomes the conventionally 'effeminate' one in their relationship, showing 'weakness' and emotion that places him in the category of the feminine. Reardon thus compounds his 'failure' in class terms with a failure to be a strong, unemotional man at this point. The result is an imbalance in gender terms as Amy is the one who should conventionally have wept but 'never in her life had she been further from such display of weakness' (*Grub Street* 229). Amy does not follow the conventional narrative of female 'weakness' in the face of male strength, and their gender roles are reversed. Amy feels her 'superiority' over Reardon because he cries instead of cursing or hitting her.

It is at this point that the novel intersects with the theme of the feminization of the male clerk that Hammerton documents in his essay 'Men as well as Clerks'. As Reardon's failure becomes more and more obvious he is described in consistently less masculine terms. Reardon's situation comes to resemble the domestic scene satirized in *The Diary of a Nobody* in which the lower-middle-class man is dominated by a stronger wife in a reversal of the conventional gender hierarchy, or the cartoons reproduced in Anderson's book. Hammerton reproduces a quotation from a 'perplexed South Croydon housewife' who complained that her husband was 'altogether more like a woman than a man' which led to troubled sexual relations ('Pooterism' 312).[11] In contrast to the fictional representation of marriage in Gissing, this woman went on to say that she was able to help her husband overcome the fear that she saw as the basis of his 'feminine' behavior. Gissing presents a far less supportive domestic union in the relationship between Amy and Reardon.

Gissing, who is astute in questioning the changing gender roles in work in *The Odd Women*, reinforces conventional gender stereotypes in his portrayal of the relationship between Reardon and Amy in *New Grub Street*. Because Reardon fails as a man in both class and gender terms, Amy becomes the 'masculine' half of the couple. It is not until Reardon's death that the gender imbalance is rectified. Milvain notes that she had lost 'that suspicion of masculinity observable in her when she became Reardon's wife' after his death and appeared simply an attractive woman (*Grub Street* 511). With the death of the demasculinized Reardon, Amy can once again be a woman.

Reardon's 'effeminacy' does not only come from his failure as a writer, however, but also from his relationship to the domestic sphere. Like the clerks whose ranks he joins, he is criticized for his 'close to relationship to domesticity' where working-class men would be criticized for abandoning the domestic sphere (Hammerton 'Pootersim' 312). As a writer working at home Reardon is, like the other writers and artists studied here, located in the domestic sphere. Working as a clerk takes him out of the domestic sphere and realigns him with the world of masculine work; unfortunately his move also aligns him with the lower-middle-class, while Gissing portrays Amy as having aspirations to higher social status.

Amy is a harbinger of a new kind of woman made possible in Gissing's view both by the spread of literacy and new technologies. While Reardon's interest in the Classics and scholarship mark him as looking backward to an older ideal of the educated gentleman, Amy looks forward to a new mass readership and popular forms of writing. Milvain is her natural ally as a representative of the commodified labor of writing. Gissing says of Amy that 'she was becoming a typical woman of the new time, the woman who has developed concurrently with journalistic enterprise,' reading the kind of writing that Milvain and his ilk produced (*Grub Street* 361). Reardon's classical scholarship marks him as the 'old' kind of man just as Amy's reading marks her as a 'new' woman. The key transformation here is the intervention of technology in the writing process, especially the typewriter.

Gissing's eulogy for the 'old' kind of man is completed in *The Odd Women*, where new forms of labor are explicitly addressed. The issue becomes not men but women at work. Reardon registers this transformation as a loss of male power and social status. *New Grub Street* is informed by the romanticization of manual labor that has characterized so many of the male writers and artists of the nineteenth century:

> Oh, to go forth and labour with one's hands, to do any poorest, commonest work of which the world had truly need! It was ignoble to sit here and support the paltry pretence of intellectual dignity. (Gissing *Grub Street* 107)

Like Ruskin, Gissing represents manual labor as noble and writing as an ignoble enterprise. To work outside and labor with one's hands would give bodily and spiritual health. Biffen characterizes himself and Reardon as 'intellectual workers,' but such work has no status in *New Grub Street* where the choices are to be either a working-class man or a new professional writer like Milvain. Neither Reardon nor Biffen can find a place in this new social order. Gissing at one point tries to appeal to the reader's sympathy for these unhoused intellectual workers. He conjectures that the reader probably wonders why they do not, like Jasper Milvain 'bestir themselves, push and bustle, welcome kicks so long as halfpence follow:' He then appeals:

> But try to imagine a personality wholly unfitted for the rough and tumble of the world's labour-market. (Gissing *Grub Street* 425)

Gissing makes explicit the idea that 'artists' and 'intellectual workers' like Biffen and Reardon have no place in the social organization of work in late Victorian Britain. They are, in short, unable to find places as 'workers,' and by definition as men. Reardon fails in the new world of writing as business, and since 'a man has no business to fail,' he loses his masculinity.

Only one character in the novel seems to recognize what Reardon does as worthwhile work. The nurse's comment on Reardon is an obituary for the intellectual worker in *New Grub Street* whose labor turns out to be fatal:

> 'I always thought it must be hard work writing books,' said the nurse with a shake of her head. (Gissing *Grub Street* 451)

Unfortunately for Reardon, only the nurse recognizes that writing books is hard work that can take a deadly toll. The unrewarded, alienating work of writing claims Reardon as a victim shortly thereafter. He does not work, and so is not a man and death is the only release for which he can hope. Biffen has already committed suicide and Reardon joins him in death at the end of the novel.

At the beginning of this analysis of the 'man at work' I argued that it was women who were killed by work; by the end of the century it is men who are killed through work. Writers such as Reardon are worn down thanks to a nature supposedly unfitted for the world of market relations. Reardon is not really a man by the end of *New Grub Street* because he has failed and is by definition no longer masculine. The feminization of Reardon leads him to the same fate as the women killed by work in the first chapter. However, in a promising development for women, Amy and Milvain's sisters are not killed by work but can find a niche for themselves in the new journalistic writing and office jobs opened up by new technologies. The new woman was a working woman who left the 'old' literary man behind. With the demise of the muscular 'man at work' in the late Victorian period, new opportunities were being opened up for representation of 'the woman at work.' The 'Writing Machine' that Marian imagines in *New Grub Street* is on the horizon.

## Notes

1. It is undoubtedly true that a Carlylean ideal of 'the gospel of work' informs Gissing's novels, so that masculinity is seen in terms of discipline and industry; Goode analyzes the relationship between Gissing and Caryle extensively (121–5) as does Poole (106–8).
2. Nigel Cross characterizes the debate over the relationship between art and 'the market-place' (the Victorian term for commodification) extremely well in *The Common Writer*, especially in his comments on publishing practices in the 1880s and 1890s; as he notes, there was a dramatic increase in the production of cheap, single-volume novels (204–7). The importance of commodification for Gissing's novel is shown by the relentless focus on money; Selig in 'The Valley of the Shadow of Books' claims that money is mentioned in over half the pages of the novel (196); Dowling notes this assertion and lists a number of the pages on which money occurs (115). See also Thomas on Victorian 'commodity culture.'

3. William Trevor in calling 'literary men' 'middlemen' underlines their ambiguous class status and says that Gissing's writers 'are mercilessly out of place' (Trevor in Michaux 129–30).

4. As Selig says, the book is a 'vivid account of the profession of letters at a given time,' especially I would add of the status of the writer as a professional in the context of commodification (188).

5. Goode quotes Gissing from *Henry Ryecroft* on Trollope's *Autobiography* and the growth of the 'literary marketplace;' Trollope could 'manufacture' texts and so is the epitome of the productive man demanded by the commodification of literature (17). See Dowling's analysis of masculinity and work in Trollope, especially on Trollope comparing writing to the trade of a shoe or candle maker which makes him a 'manufacturer' of material goods for the marketplace (88). Selig in his Twayne *George Gissing* remarks that writers in *New Grub Street* are 'like humble nineteenth-century craftsmen such as carpenters, shoemakers or tailors' echoing Trollope's statement (51).

6. Her position is like that of Jasper Milvain who, as Dowling points out, produces writing with the regularity of a machine himself (103).

7. The classic analysis of the story in the context of male homoeroticism is of course Sedgwick's *Between Men*.

8. For Bourdieu *habitus* was a matter of 'taste' as it was in *Distinction* but also a matter of bodily carriage.

9. See Lombroso-Ferrara and the 'science' of criminal anthropology.

10. Reardon here approaches George Orwell's sketch of Gissing as 'a bookish, perhaps over-civilized man, in love with classical antiquity' trapped in a country 'where it was impossible to be comfortable without a thick padding of money between yourself and the outer world.' (Orwell in Michaux 196).

11. Orwell links Reardon's inability to write with sexual impotence in his remarks on *New Grub Street* (Orwell in Michaux 198).

# Conclusion

# New Women, New Technologies and New Work

Clerical work, which marks Reardon's loss of masculinity and class position in *New Grub Street*, is represented as a liberating possibility for women in *The Odd Women*. Miss Barfoot's school teaches the basics of office work as well as conducting discussions about the 'New Woman.' The list of skills needed for the office are linked with intelligence and social mobility, and as providing work for women in occupations that did not 'demand great physical strength.' (*Odd Women* 79). In other words, this is 'brain work' that does not require muscles, and is in fact directly contrasted to physical labor. The 'New Woman' enters the workforce thanks to technologies that are making masculine force irrelevant. New technologies undermined the gendered division of labor that had been in place since the 1840s, in a process that Connell has traced into the twentieth century. Connell links the growth of sport as a locus of masculine identity directly to the decline of 'pure labour' by 'masses of men with spades' being replaced by office work which does not 'test or signify masculinity' (*Which Way is Up?* 23).[1] The representation of the 'man at work' was redefined by new technologies.

The idea of 'working ladies' (an apparent contradiction in terms by mid-Victorian standards) promoted by Miss Barfoot would seem to contravene the separation of women from work enforced so strongly in previous decades. However, as we shall see, clerical work was already 'feminized' even before the 1880s, and so women were moving into an area that would seem suitable in terms of gender preconceptions. This is not to say that there was no resistance to the idea of women working. Indeed, Gissing records the conventional resistance to women undertaking paid labor in a letter written to Miss Barfoot that she reads aloud to her weekly meeting of young ladies in training:

> Not long since she had received an anonymous letter, written by some clerk out of employment, abusing her roundly for her encouragement of female competition in the clerkly world. The taste of this epistle was as bad as its grammar, but they should hear it; she read it all through. Now, whoever the writer might be, it seemed pretty clear that he was not the kind of person with whom one could profitably argue; no use in replying to him, even had he given the opportunity. For all that, his uncivil attack had a meaning, and there were plenty of people ready to urge his argument in more respectable terms. 'They will tell you that, in entering

the commercial world, you not only unsex yourselves, but do a grievous wrong to the numberless men struggling hard for bare sustenance. You reduce salaries, you press into an already overcrowded field, you injure even your own sex by making it impossible for men to marry, who, if they earned enough, would be supporting a wife.' (Gissing *Odd Women* 151)

The anonymous letter writer is shown as putting the forth the standard argument that women entering into clerical jobs are 'unsexing' themselves and leaving the category of 'woman' by working. Miss Barfoot makes explicit the basis of the letter in Victorian gender polarization in her acerbic comments on the 'view of us set forth in such charming language by Mr. Ruskin,' with the clear implication that its definition of 'woman' was outmoded (*Odd Women* 151). The letter also articulates the fear of competition for jobs raised when women enter the workplace, and the implicit threat to men as the 'breadwinner' of the family that was behind much labor agitation in the 1840s and beyond. The implication seems to be that a man undertaking such tasks is not 'unmanned' by office work, but the example of Reardon and others shows this not to be the case. Rather, Reardon abandons any hope of being a 'gentleman' or professional when he becomes a clerk. Reardon is not a real man when he works as a clerk, and his position in this is not unusual. James Fitzjames Stephen in 1862 specifically excluded clerks from the category 'gentleman,' and expelled them from the category of the masculine at the same time:

> It may appear paradoxical, but it is strictly true, that the manners of the English gentleman have much more in common with the manners of a labourer than with the manners of a mercantile clerk or a small shop-keeper....The language of the commercial clerk, and the manner in which he brings it out, are both framed on a quite different model. He thinks about himself, and constantly tries to talk fine. He calls a school an academy, speaks of proceeding when he means going, and talks in short, much in the style in which members of his own class write police reports and accounts of appalling catastrophes for the newspapers. (Gissing *Odd Women*, 401)

This formulation is indeed 'paradoxical' in that it creates an alliance between the upper and working classes that would seem to contravene the Victorian social hierarchy. However, Stephen in this argument is asserting a 'nobility of masculinity' that transcends social class and unites gentlemen and laborers because they are men. Just as Smiles tried to create an ideal that transcended class, 'gentleman' here is a term that unites men across class boundaries. Gentlemen and laborers exhibit 'truth and courage' where clerks show only an insecure social reaching. Of course, part of the virtue exhibited here for Stephen is that gentlemen and laborers know their social stations, and would not dream of trying to move up or down the social scale. The repellent aspect of clerks and shopkeepers for Stephen is their obvious social ambition, exhibited in a language that tries to move up the social hierarchy without the benefit of the capital or education of a gentleman.

This extract shows that governesses were not the only 'anathematized race' in the Victorian period; like governesses, clerks inhabited a diffuse and contradictory space in the hierarchies of social class and gender. Just as the governess was a troubling figure because she transgressed boundaries between the domestic and the world work and thus threatened the kind of female consciousness praised in 'Of Queen's Gardens,' so the clerk is a troubling figure. His work would seem to have high social status because it does not involve sweat and muscles, and requires education or at least some training. However, the work does not command enough pay to be 'professional,' and places the worker in the very ambiguous of the ranks of the lower middle classes; clerks were too educated to be working class but too poor to aspire to the status of gentleman.

This is the indeterminate work into which Miss Barfoot's young ladies are moving, or in the terms of the anonymous letter writer are 'invading.' It would therefore not be accurate to say that there was a distinct separation of genders in office work before the advent of schools like Miss Barfoot's, but rather that women were being allowed into an occupation that was not seen to be 'manly' in the first place.[2] Also, while women who moved into these occupations might be earning money, they would not be able to raise their social status beyond the ranks of the lower middle classes. While working in an office is an alternative to being a governess, it does not carry with it any more secure social position than the one available to the 'anathematized race.' As Charles Edward Parsons makes brutally clear, clerks have no hope of escaping from the lower end of the social hierarchy:

> He commences life as an ill-paid clerk, his ambitions are never encouraged, all the hopes of his manhood are thwarted, his employer can get numberless others to replace him at even less than he earns; and so he continues at the only calling he is capable of following and with nearly every feeling soured by adversity – he dies: a hard-worked, ill-paid clerk from beginning to end. (Gissing *Odd Women* 403)

This bleak summary of a clerk's life is remarkable for its depressing depiction of the clerk's fate. It also encapsulates the loss of 'manhood' or gender identity and 'prospects' or class mobility that are subverted by becoming a clerk. Whereas the social dilemma of the governess provoked measures to at least provide for them, Parsons seems to take a positive relish in portraying the most abysmal situation possible, with no remedy in sight. Just as there were widespread fears in the Victorian period that intellectual work would 'unsex' women, Parsons articulates a fear that being a clerk robs the worker of his 'manhood.'

Clerks are related to the intellectuals analyzed in this book, and suffer from the same idealization of manual labor as 'work' in opposition to 'brain work.' Thomas Suthert writes a desperate plea for parents not to let their sons or daughters grow up to be clerks. While it is encouraging that he views both sons and daughters as able to work, he argues that to allow them to become clerks is sentencing them to death:

> I beseech everyone having the custody of children to see that the education they possess is directed to the manipulating and fashioning of the products of the earth for the use and enjoyment of man, and not counter and quill driving. Of course there must always be clerks and assistants, and I have no fear of the supply being ever being inadequate to the demand. There are, however, grave reasons why the energies of young persons should be directed into healthier and more profitable channels. (Gissing *Odd Women* 404)

This expresses succinctly the kind of bias found in Ruskin toward outdoor manual labor over sitting at a desk or standing behind a counter. 'Quill driving' turns writing into an archaic and esoteric pursuit; however, even typewriting would not be allowed by Suthert because this too would lead to unhealthiness and disease in his opinion. The healthy male body is threatened by such sedentary and intellectual pursuits. Like Ruskin he would prefer men to labor outside in the country.

With the growth of bureaucracy, both in the State and private realms, the demand for office workers increased and sentiments like this became increasingly untenable. This was not, however, completely good news for 'brain workers.' It has taken a long time to recognize 'quill driving' as a valid form of work, and Gissing himself is caught in the Victorian valuation of some kinds of labor over others. Reardon's move into a clerk position is represented as an unmanly and demeaning role. Gissing himself sees clerical work as of lower status and less manly than manual labor. He subscribes, like Ruskin, to an ideal of the healthy male body and manual labor.

While Gissing is sympathetic to the demands of 'New Women' like Rhoda Nunn for new forms of employment, he is still caught himself in an older definition of 'man's work' that make his characters 'unmanly' in the conventions of Victorian labor.[3] It could be argued that these divisions of labor into 'manly' and 'unmanly' occupations are still with us. Terms like 'nurse' and 'secretary' since the Victorian era had become so completely defined as women's work that they had to be modified by having 'male' placed before them. As the example of the 'Caution: Men at Work' sign with which I began shows, the gendered division of labor continued well beyond the Victorian period. The primary difference between the Victorian period and later eras was the impact of the industrialization of many forms of labor, especially in the office, which continued the 'demasculinization' of work that Engels lamented in the nineteenth-century factory.

New technologies broke down older forms of the division of labor. The typewriter is clearly an agent of social change in Gissing, helping women enter the office on the strength of their ability to use the new machinery. As muscles became increasingly irrelevant to labor in all areas the older divisions between male and female work were overcome. This kind of change can have detrimental effects; as the anonymous letter writer in *The Odd Women* complained, women were introducing more laborers into the field. Opening up work to both men and women can initially be used as an excuse for lowering wages, since women have been and still are discriminated against in salary levels. However, the division of labor along gender lines cannot be maintained in the face of the industrialization of all forms of labor, including office work.

While Gissing entitles his book *The Odd Women*, the real oddity in the narrative is the social position of writing. In the context of the growing bureaucracy writing was becoming industrialized and commodified. The 'odd' women in his narrative were in fact the vanguard of new forms of labor, and Reardon an example of the older set of values that were rapidly becoming obsolete. While Gissing could recognize that Widdowson's attitudes to marriage were based on outmoded and ultimately disastrous assumptions about the gendered division of household labor, he could not recognize that a writer like Reardon's values might also be linked to a gendered division of labor that was increasingly being undermined by new technologies.

Where the typewriter helped break down the division of labor in terms of gender and 'demasculinized' clerical work, the computer may well have the same effect in terms of class. If 'literary production' becomes quite literally a mechanized process, then it will lose whatever cultural capital it may bring with it, as well as an erosion of professional status. Where the industrialization of labor in the nineteenth century created a new form of work for women, the increasing use of computer technology is mechanizing intellectual processes. As computers become more and more sophisticated the deskilling of manual labor will be extended to intellectual labor too. The aporias of Victorian intellectuals trying to come to terms with the demise of manual labor and the 'man at work' holds important lessons for 'brain workers' today.

It is for this reason that we urgently need a critique of the ideas of 'production' and 'work' as we have inherited them from the Victorian period. If the terms continue to be defined in material terms as quantity, and with connotations of the amount of effort expended, then the debate will remain in the Victorian realm of 'useful work' with its attendant ideological contradictions. Of all the commentators that I have analyzed, John Ruskin came closest to mounting a critique of work and production that avoided the contradictions inherent in defining it in muscular (and implicitly male) terms. His call in *Unto This Last* to decouple wages from effort severed the connection between 'production' and compensation and suggests a way in which we can avoid the aporias of the Victorian division of labor. From this perspective the question becomes not how much has somebody produced, but what they need to lead a decent life. This is a very different question, entailing a very different form of social organization, than asking how much a man or woman has 'produced.' While I have been critical of the limitations of writers such as Ruskin and Morris when they were not able to move beyond the gendered contradictions of the Victorian division of labor, their critiques of the definition of work in an industrialized society raise questions that remain germane to this day. Their effort to define work, whatever its limitations, has important lessons for those of us working in the 'information age.' We would do well to mount a sustained critique of the model of 'production' before all intellectual labor is mechanized in the same way as factory and office work in the Victorian period.

## Notes

1.  Roper and Tosh have expressed this in terms of a change from production to consumption, asserting that 'while the artisan of the 1880s gained manly pride from his breadwinning wage, the post-war manager...expressed masculinity directly in product fetishism' (12).
2.  Hammerton's otherwise excellent analysis needs to be tempered, therefore, by an acknowledgment that the subject position of the clerk was already ambiguous in terms of class and gender before 1880.
3.  Young has asserted that 'Rhoda Nunn is arguably the ideal new Woman' who is an 'odd hybrid of feminine and lower-middle-class conventions that cancel out each other's disabilities' (153). She has a social mobility that the male characters lack.

# Works Cited

Abse, Joan. *John Ruskin: The Passionate Moralist*. New York: Knopf, 1981

Adams, James Eli. *Dandies and Desert Saints: Styles of Victorian Masculinity*. Ithaca: Cornell UP, 1995.

——. 'The Banality of Transgression?: Recent Works on Masculinity.' Forum on Masculinity. *Victorian Studies*. 36:2 (1993): 207–13.

Alderson, David. *Mansex Fine: Religion, Manliness and imperialism in Nineteenth Century British Culture*. Manchester UP, 1998.

Alexander, Lynn M. *Women, Work and Representation: Needlewomen in Victorian Art and Literature*. Athens, OH: Ohio UP, 2003.

Allen, Rick. 'Munby Reappraised: The Diary of an English Flaneur' *Journal of Victorian Culture*. 5.2 Autumn 2000: 260–286.

Amigoni, David. *Victorian Biography: Intellectuals and the Ordering of Discourse*. New York: St. Martin's Press, 1993.

Anderson, Amanda. *Tainted Souls and Painted Faces: The Rhetoric of Fallenness in Victorian Culture*. Ithaca: Cornell UP, 1993.

Anderson, Gregory. *Victorian Clerks*. Manchester: Manchester UP, 1976.

Anthony, Peter. D. *The Ideology of Work*. London: Tavistock, 1977.

——. *John Ruskin's Labour: A Study of Ruskin's Social Theory*. Cambridge: Cambridge UP, 1983.

Applebaum, Herbert A. *The Concept of Work: Ancient, Medieval and Modern*. Albany: SUNY P, 1992.

Arata, Stephen. *Fictions of Loss in the Victorian Fin de Siecle*. Cambridge: Cambridge UP, 1996.

Armstrong, Nancy. *Desire and Domestic Fiction: A Political History of the Novel*. Oxford UP, 1987.

Arnold, Matthew. 'Culture and Anarchy.' *The Complete Works of Matthew Arnold Vol. V* Ann Arbor: U of Michigan P, 1973: 85–229.

——. 'Wordsworth' *The Complete Works of Matthew Arnold Vol. IX* Ann Arbor: U of Michigan P, 1973: 36–55.

Austin, Linda M. 'James Thomson and the Continuum of Labor' in *Victorian Literature and Culture* 20. John Maynard and Adrienne Auslander Munich, eds. New York: AMS P, 1993: 69–98.

Barret-Ducrocq, Francoise. 'Arthur Munby Mémorialiste: De L'Autobiographie Savante a la Pulsion D'Écriture' *Cahiers Victoriens & Édouardiens* 39 (April, 1994): 2–36.

Barringer, Tim. *Men at Work: Art and Labour in Victorian Britain*. New Haven: Yale UP, 2005.

Baudrillard, Jean. *The Mirror of Production*. St. Louis: Telos P, 1975.

Beeton, Isabella. *The Book of Household Management*. London: S. O. Beeton, 1861.

Bendix, Reinhard. *Work and Authority in Industry; Ideologies of Management in the Course of Industrialization*. New York: Wiley, 1956.

Benjamin, Jessica. *The Bonds of Love: Psychoanalysis, Feminism and the Problem of Domination*. New York: Pantheon Books, 1988.

Benyon, John. *Masculinities and Culture* Buckingham, Philadelphia: Open UP, 2002.

Berger, John. 'The Suit and the Photograph' in *About Looking*. New York: Pantheon Books, 1980: 27–36.

Bourdieu, Pierre. *Distinction: A Social Critique of the Judgment of Taste*. Trans. Richard Nice. Cambridge: Harvard UP, 1984.

——. *Masculine Domination*. Translated by Richard Nice. Stanford: Stanford UP, 2001.

Bowlby, Rachel. *Just Looking: Consumer Culture in Dreiser, Gissing and Zola*. New York: Methuen, 1985.

Bradley, Harriet. *Men's Work, Women's Work: A Sociological History of the Sexual Division of Labor*. Cambridge: Polity Press, 1989.

Brantlinger, Patrick. *Crusoe's Footprints: Cultural Studies in Britain and America*. New York: Routledge, 1990.

Breitenberg, Mark. *Anxious Masculinity in Early Modern Europe*. Cambridge: Cambridge UP, 1996.

Briggs, Asa. *Victorian People: A Reassessment of Persons and Themes 18–51867*. (Revised Edition). Chicago: U of Chicago P, 1970.

Bristow, Joseph. Review of Herbert Sussman's *Victorian Masculinities: Manhood and Masculine Poetics in Early Victorian Literature and Art*. In *Victorian Studies*. 39.3 (1996): 471–73.

Bronfen, Elisabeth. *Over Her Dead Body*. Manchester: Manchester UP, 1992.

Broughton, Trev Lynn. *Men of Letters, Writing Lives: Masculinity and Literary Auto/Biography in the Late Victorian Period*. London: Routledge, 1999.

——. 'Studying the Study: Gender and the Scene of Authorship in the Writings of Leslie Stephen, Margaret Oliphant and Anne Thackeray Ritchie.' *Mapping the Self: Space, Identity, Discourse in British Autobiography*. Frederic Régard, ed. Saint-Étienne: Publications de l'Université de Saint-Étienne, 2003: 247–67.

Brown, Mrs. A. 'The Proper Sphere of Men.' *Putnam's Monthly Magazine*. 4 (1854): 305–10.

Buchbinder, David. *Masculinities and Identities*. Melbourne UP, 1994.

Burke, Peter. 'The Invention of Leisure in Early Modern Europe.' *Past and Present* 146 (1995): 136–150.

Burnett, John. *Useful Toil: Autobiographies of Working People from 1820s to the 1920s*. Harmondsworth: Penguin, 1977.

Butler, Judith. *Gender Trouble: Feminism and the Subversion of Identity*. New York: Routledge, 1990.

Carlyle, Thomas. *Past and Present*. London: Chapman and Hall, 1872 [1843].

——. 'Occasional Discourse on the Nigger Question.' in *Critical and Miscellaneous Essays* Boston: Dana Esters & Co, 1869.

Casteras, Susan P. and Ronald Parkinson. Eds. *Richard Redgrave, 1804–1888*. New Haven: Published in association with the Victoria and Albert Museum and the Yale Center for British Art by Yale UP, 1988.

Castronovo, David. *The English Gentleman: Images and Ideals in Literature and Society*. New York: Ungaer, 1987.

Children's Employment Commission. *First Report of the Commissioners*. Mines. London: Clowes and Sons, 1842.

Christ, Carol T. 'The Hero as Man of Letters: Masculinity and Victorian Nonfiction Prose.' Thais E. Morgan. ed. *Victorian Sages and Cultural Discourse: Renegotiating Gender and Power*. New Brunswick: Rutgers UP, 1990: 19–31.

——. 'Victorian Masculinity and the Angel in the House.' *A Widening Sphere: Changing Roles of Victorian Women*. Martha Vicinus ed. Bloomington: Indiana UP, 1977: 146–62.

Clarke, Norma. 'Strenuous Idleness: Thomas Carlyle and the Man of Letters as Hero.' In Michael Roper and John Tosh, eds. *Manful Assertions: Masculinities in Britain since 1800*. London: Routledge, 1991: 2–543.

Clayre, Alasdair. *Work and Play: Ideas and Experience of Work and Leisure*. London: Weidenfeld & Nicholson, 1974.

Clubbe, John. *Victorian Forerunner: The Later Career of Thomas Hood*. Duke UP: Durham, 1968.

Coetzee, J. M. 'Idleness in South Africa.' In *The Violence of Representation: Literature and the History of Violence*. Nancy Armstrong and Leonard Tennenhouse, eds. London: Routledge, 1989. 119-139.

Cohen, Michele. *Fashioning Masculinity: National Identity and Language in the Eighteenth Century*. London: Routledge, 1996.

Cohen, William A. 'Manual Conduct in Great Expectations' *ELH*. 60.1(1993): 217–59.

Collins, Philip. ed. *Dickens: The Critical Heritage*. London: Routledge and Kegan Paul, 1971.

——. 'Dickens and Industrialism.' *Studies in English Literature, 1500–1900*. 4 (Autumn 1980): 651 – 673.

Connell, R. W. *Which Way is Up? Essays on Sex, Class and Culture*. Sydney, Australia: Allen & Unwin, 1983.

——. *Masculinities*. Berkeley: U of California P, 1995.

Cope, Charles West. *Reminiscences of Charles West Cope, R. A.* Charles Henry Cope, ed. London: Bentley, 1891.

Coustillas, Pierre and Colin Partridge eds. *Gissing: The Critical Heritage*. London: Routledge and Kegan Paul, 1972.

Cross, Nigel. *The Common Writer: Life in Nineteenth-Century Grub Street*. Cambridge: Cambridge UP, 1985.

Curtis, Gerard. 'Ford Madox Brown's *Work*: An Iconographic Analysis.' *Art Bulletin* 74.4 (December, 1992): 623–636.

Curtis, Liz. 'Echoes of the Past: The Victorian Press and Ireland.' *Studying Culture: An Introductory Reader*. Edited by Ann Gray and Jim McGuigan. London: Edward Arnold,

1993: 179–187.

Danahay, Martin A. *A Community of One: Masculine Autobiography and Autonomy in Nineteenth-Century Britain* Albany, NY: SUNY P, 1993.

——. 'Sexuality and the Representation of the Working-class Child's Body in Music Hall' *Victorians Institute Journal* 29 (2001): 103–132.

——. 'Dante Gabriel Rossetti's Virtual Bodies.' *Victorian Poetry* 36.4 (Winter 1998): 379–398.

Danon, Ruth. *Work in the English Novel: The Myth of Vocation.* Totowa, NJ: Barnes & Noble Books, 1986.

Davidoff, Leonore. 'Class and Gender in Victorian England: The Diaries of Arthur J. Munby and Hannah Cullwick.' *Feminist Studies* 5 (Spring 1979): 87–141.

Davidoff, Leonore and Catherine Hall. *Family Fortunes: Men and Women of the English Middle-Class, 1780–1850.* London: Hutchinson, 1987.

Davidson, Caroline. *A Woman's Work is Never Done: A History of Housework in the British Isles 1650–1950.* London: Chatto & Windus, 1982.

Dawkins, Heather. 'The Diaries and Photographs of Hannah Cullwick' *Art History* 10:2 (June 19987) 154–187.

Dickens, Charles. *Hard Times.* Edited by Graham Law. Peterborough: Broadview Press, 1996

——. *Letters.* Graham Storey ed. Oxford: Clarendon P, 1965.

Dollimore, Jonathan. *Sexual Dissidence: Augustine to Wilde, Freud to Foucault.* Oxford: Clarendon Press, 1991.

——. 'Perversion, Degeneration and the Death Drive.' In *Sexualities in Victorian Britain.* Bloomington: Indiana UP, 1996: 9–117.

Donkin, Richard. *Blood, Sweat and Tears: The Evolution of Work.* New York: Texere, 2001.

Donzelot, Jacques. *The Policing of Families.* Robert Hurley, trans. New York: Random House, 1979.

Dowling, Andrew. *Manliness and the Male Novelist in Victorian Literature.* Aldershot: Ashgate, 2001.

Drucker, Peter F. *Post-Capitalist Society.* New York: Harper Business, 1993.

Dupré, John and Regenia Gagnier. 'A Brief History of Work.' *Journal of Economic Issues* XXX, 2 (June, 1996): 55–559.

Dury, Richard. 'The Hand of Hyde' in William B. Jones, Jr. ed. *Robert Louis Stevenson Reconsidered.* Jefferson, NC: McFarland, 2003, 10–1116.

Easton, Malaina. *Victorian Philosophies of Useless Work for the Mind: Carlyle, Ruskin, Morris and Marx.* MA Thesis, Eastern Illinois University, 2000.

Edelstein, T. J. '"They Sang The Song of the Shirt:"' The Visual Iconology of the Seamstress.' *Victorian Studies* 23 (Winter 1980): 183–210.

Edwards, Lee M. *Herkomer: A Victorian Artist.* Aldershot: Ashgate Publishing, 1999.

Elias, Norbert. *The Civilizing Process.* Edmund Jephcott, trans. New York: Pantheon Books, 1982.

Ellis, Sarah Stickney. *The Wives of England, Their Relative Duties, Domestic Influence and Social Obligations.* London: Fisher, Son & Co., 1843.

Engels, Friedrich. *The Condition of the Working Class in England*. Oxford: Oxford UP, 1993.

Engels, Friedrich. *The Origin of the Family, Private Property, and the State, in the Light of the Researches of Lewis H. Morgan*. Introduction and notes by Eleanor Burke Leacock. New York: International Publishers, 1972.

Foucault, Michel. 'What is an Author?' in Josue V. Harari. Ed. *Textual Strategies: Perspectives in Post-Structuralist Criticism*. Ithaca: Cornell UP, 1979: 141–60.

——. *The Foucault Effect: Studies in Governmentality*. Edited by Graham Burchell, Colin Gordon and Peter Miller. Chicago: U of Chicago P, 1991.

Friedson, Eliot. *Profession of Medicine*. New York: Dodd and Mead, 1970.

Gagnier, Regenia. *Subjectivities: A History of Self-Representation in Britain, 1832–1920*. New York: Oxford UP, 1991.

Gallagher, Catherine. *The Industrial Reformation of English Fiction: Social Discourse and Narrative Form, 1832–1867*. Chicago: U of Chicago P, 1985.

Garber, Marjorie. *Vested Interests: Cross Dressing and Cultural Anxiety*. New York: Harper, 1992.

Gardiner, Judith Kegan ed. *Masculinity Studies and Feminist Theory: New Directions*. New York: Columbia UP, 2002.

Gaskell, Elizabeth Cleghorn. *Mary Barton*. Edited by Jennifer Foster. Peterborough: Broadview P, 2000.

——. *Ruth*. Angus Easson, ed. New York: Penguin USA, 1998.

Genna E. *Irresponsible Philanthropy, Being Some Chapters on the Employment of Gentlewomen*. London: Kegan Paul, 1881.

Gikandi, Simon. *Maps of Englishness: Writing Identity in the Culture of Colonialism*. New York: Columbia UP, 1996.

Gilbert, Sandra M. and Susan Gubar. *The Madwoman in the Attic: The Woman Writer and the Nineteenth-Century Literary Imagination*. New Haven: Yale UP, 1979.

Gill, Stephen. *Wordsworth and the Victorians*. Oxford: Clarendon P, 1998.

Girouard, Mark *The Return to Camelot: Chivalry and the English Gentleman*. New Haven: Yale UP, 1981.

Gissing, George. *New Grub Street*. Ed. John Goode. Oxford: Oxford UP, 1993.

——. *The Odd Women*. Edited by Arlene Young. Peterborough: Broadview Press, 1998.

Gleyse, Jacques. 'Instrumental Rationalization of Human Movement: An Archeological Approach' in *Sport and Postmodern Times*. Genevieve Rail, ed. Albany NY: SUNY P 1998. 239–260.

Goode, John. *George Gissing: Ideology and Fiction*. London: Vision P, 1978.

Graver, Suzanne. 'Writing in a 'Womanly Way' and the Double Vision of *Bleak House*' *Dickens Quarterly* 4:4 (1987): 3–15.

Grosz, Elizabeth. *Sexual Subversions: Three French Feminists* Boston: Allen & Unwin, 1989.

——. *Volatile Bodies: Toward a Corporeal Feminism*. New York: Allen & Unwin, 1994.

Hadley, Elaine. *Melodramatic Tactics: Theatricalized Dissent in the English Marketplace, 1800–1855*. Stanford: Stanford UP, 1995.

Halberstam, Judith. *Female Masculinity*. Durham: Duke UP, 1998.

Haley, Bruce. *The Healthy Body and Victorian Culture*. Cambridge: Harvard UP, 1978.

Hall, Catherine. *White, Male, and Middle-Class: Explorations in Feminism and History*. New York: Routledge, 1992.

Hall, Donald E. ed. *Muscular Christianity: Embodying the Victorian Age*. Cambridge: Cambridge UP, 1994.

Hammerton, A. James. 'Pooterism or Partnership?: Marriage and Masculine Identity in the Lower Middle-Class, 1870–1920.' *Journal of British Studies* 38.3 (July 1999): 291–321.

——. ''Men as well as Clerks': Normative Masculinity and the English Lower Middle-Class,1870-1920.' *Meridian* 15.2 (November 1996): 187-205.

Hamson, Austin. 'George Gissing.' Jean-Paul Michaux, ed. *George Gissing: Critical Essays*. London: Vision & Barnes and Noble, 1981: 22–36.

Harvey, John. *Men in Black*. Chicago: U of Chicago P, 1995.

Hechter, Michael. *Internal Colonialism: The Celtic Fringe in British National Development*. Berkeley: U of California P, 1975.

Heath, Stephen. 'Psychopathia Sexualis: Stevenson's Strange Case.' Colin MacCabe. ed. *Futures for English*. Manchester: Manchester UP, 1988.

Herreshoff, David Sprague. *Labor into Art: The Theme of Work in Nineteenth-Century American Literature*. Detroit, MI: Wayne State UP, 1991.

Hewison, Robert. *Ruskin and Oxford: The Art of Education*. Oxford: Clarendon Press, 1996.

Hobsbawm, Eric. *The Age of Capital*. New York: Pantheon, 1975.

Holcombe, Lee. *Victorian Ladies at Work: Middle-Class Working Women in England and Wales 1850 – 1973*. Hamden CT: Archon Books, 1973.

Homans, Margaret 'Dinah's Blush, Maggie's Arm: Class, gender and Sexuality in George Eliot's Early Novels.' *Victorian Sexualities* Andrew H. Miller and James Eli Adams eds. Bloomington, IN: Indiana UP, 1996:16–37.

Hood, Thomas. *The Works: Edited with Notes by his Son, Thomas Hood, jun., and Daughter, Frances Freeling Broderip. Vol. IX*. New York: Georg Olms Verlag, 1970.

Horrocks, Roger. *Male Myths and Icons: Masculinity in Popular Culture*. London: Macmillan, 1995.

Houghton, Walter E. *The Victorian Frame of Mind, 1830–1870*. New Haven: Yale UP, 1975 [1957].

Hudson, Derek. *Munby: Man of Two Worlds: The Life and Diaries of Arthur Munby*. Boston: Gambit, 1972.

Hueffer, Ford M. *Ford Madox Brown: A Record of his Life and Work*. London: Longman, 1896.

Jeffrey, Lloyd N. *Thomas Hood*. Twayne Publishers: New York, 1972.

Johnson, E. D. H. 'The Making of Ford Madox Brown's *Work*.' *Victorian Artists and the City*. Ira Bruce Nadel and F. S. Schwarzenbach, eds. New York: Pergamon Press, 1980:142–151.

Johnson, Patricia E. *Hidden Hands: Working-Class Women and Victorian Social-Problem Fiction*. Athens, OH: Ohio UP, 2001.

Joyce, Patrick. ed. *The Historical Meaning of Work*. Cambridge: Cambridge UP, 1987.

*Spectacle, 1851–1914*. Stanford: Stanford UP, 1990.

Robbins, Bruce. *The Servant's Hand: English Fiction from Below*. Durham: Duke UP, 1993.

Robson, Catherine. *Men in Wonderland: The Lost Girlhood of the Victorian Gentleman*. Princeton: Princeton UP, 2001.

Roper, Michael and John Tosh. eds. *Manful Assertions: Masculinities in Britain since 1800*. London: Routledge, 1991.

Rose, Sonya. *Limited Livelihoods: Gender and Class in Nineteenth-century England*. Berkeley: U of California P, 1992.

Rosen, David. *The Changing Fictions of Masculinity*. Urbana: U of Illinois P, 1993.

——. 'The Volcano and the Cathedral: Muscular Christianity and the Origins of Primal Manliness.' *Muscular Christianity: Embodying the Victorian Age*. Cambridge: Donald E. Hall, ed. Cambridge UP, 1994: 17–44.

Ruskin, John. *Sesame and Lilies*. *The Works of John Ruskin Volume XI*. New York: John Wiley & Sons, 1886: 1–186.

——. *The Crown of Wild Olive*. *The Works of John Ruskin Volume XI*. New York: John Wiley & Sons, 1886: 1–127.

——. *Aratra Pentilici*. *The Works of John Ruskin Volume IX*. New York: John Wiley & Sons, 1886: 1–181.

——. *The Stones of Venice*. *The Works of John Ruskin Volume VI*. New York: John Wiley & Sons, 1886.

——. *Pre-Raphaelitism*. *The Works of John Ruskin Volume 8*. New York: John Wiley & Sons, 1886: 149–156.

——. *Unto This Last*. *The Works of John Ruskin Volume XII*. New York: John Wiley & Sons, 1886. 17–138.

——. *Time and Tide by Weare and Tyne*. *The Works of John Ruskin Volume XII*. New York: John Wiley & Sons, 1886. 1–210.

——. *Fors Clavigera: Letters to the Workmen and Labourers of Great Britain*. (3 vols). New York: Greenwood Press, 1968.

——. *The Brantwood Diary of John Ruskin*. New Haven: Yale UP, 1971.

Scarry, Elaine. *Resisting Representation*. New York: Oxford UP, 1994.

Sedgwick, Eve Kosofsky. *Between Men: English Literature and Male Homosocial Desire*. New York: Columbia U P, 1992.

Segal, Lynne. 'Changing Men: Masculinities in Context.' *Theory and Society*. 22.5 (1993): 625–41.

Selig, Robert L. "The Valley of the Shadow of Books:" Alienation in Gissing's *New Grub Street*.' *Nineteenth-Century Fiction*. 25 (1970): 188–198.

——. *George Gissing* (Twayne's English Authors Series, #346, Revised Edition). New York: Twayne Publishers, 1995.

Shattock, Joanne. 'Work for Women: Margaret Oliphant's Journalism.' *Nineteenth-Century Media and the Construction of Identities*. Basingstoke: Palgrave, 2000, 16 –177.

Shaw, Christopher. 'William Morris and the Division of Labour: The Idea of Work in *News from Nowhere*.' *The Journal of the William Morris Society* 9, 3 (Autumn, 1991): 19–30.

Kanigel, Robert. *The One Best Way: Frederick Winslow Taylor and the Enigma of Efficiency*. New York: Penguin, 1999.

Kaplan, Fred. *Thomas Carlyle: A Biography*. Ithaca: Cornell UP, 1983.

Kearns, Katherine. 'A Tropology of Realism in *Hard Times*' *ELH* 59.4 (Winter 1992): 857–881.

Kestner, Joseph A. *Masculinities in Victorian Painting*. Aldershot, Hants: Scolar Press, 1995.

Kimmel, M. S. *Changing Men: New Directions in Research on Men and Masculinity*. Newbury Park: Sage, 1987.

Kingsley, Charles. *Alton Locke, Tailor and Poet: An Autobiography*. Elizabeth A. Cripps, ed. Oxford: Oxford UP, 1985.

Koestenbaum, Wayne. 'The Shadow on the Bed: Dr. Jekyll, Mr Hyde, and the Labouchère Amendment.' *Critical Matrix: Princeton Working Papers in Women's Studies*. Special Issue 1 (Spring 1988): 31–55.

Kransberg, Melvin. *By the Sweat of thy Brow: Work in the Western World*. New York: Putnam, 1975.

Kristeva, Julia. *Powers of Horror: An Essay on Abjection*. Trans. Leon S. Roudiez. New York: Columbia UP, 1982.

Kuchta, David. *The Three-Piece Suit and Modern Masculinity: England 1550–1850*. U of California P, 2002.

Kucich, John. *Repression in Victorian Fiction: Charlotte Bronte, George Eliot, and Charles Dickens*. Berkeley: U of California P, 1987.

Lane, Christopher. *The Burdens of Intimacy: Psychoanalysis and Victorian Masculinity*. Chicago: U of Chicago P, 1999.

Langland, Elizabeth. *Nobody's Angels: Middle-Class Women and Domestic Ideology in Victorian Culture*. Ithaca: Cornell UP, 1995.

Larson, Magali Sarfati. *The Rise of Professionalism: A Sociological Analysis*. Berkeley: U of California P, 1977.

Leacock, Eleanor and Helen I. Safa eds. *Women's Work: Development and the Division of Labor by Gender*. South Hadley, MA: Bergin and Harvey, 1986.

Lombroso-Ferrera, Gina. *Criminal Man, According to the Classification of Cesare Lombroso*. New York: Patterson Smith, 1972.

MacInnes, John. *The End of Masculinity*. Buckingham, Philadelphia: Open UP, 1998.

McClelland, Keith. 'Time to Work, Time to Live: Some Aspects of Work and the Re-formation of Class in Britain, 1850–1880, in Patrick Joyce, ed. *The Historical Meaning of Work*. Cambridge: Cambridge UP, 1987.

McClintock, Anne. *Imperial Leather: Race, Gender and Sexuality in the Colonial Contest*. New York: Routledge, 1995.

Macdonnell, Diane. *Theories of Discourse: An Introduction*. London: Blackwell, 1986.

McIvor, Arthur J. *A History of Work in Britain, 1880–1950*. New York: Palgrave, 2001.

McKibbin, Ross. *Ideologies of Class: Social Relations in Britain 1880–1950*. New York: Oxford UP, 1990.

McLaurin, Allen. 'Reworking "Work" in some Victorian Writing and Visual Art.' *In Search of Victorian Values: Aspects of Nineteenth-century Thought and Society.* Manchester: Manchester UP, 1988.

Mangan, J. A. and James Walvin. *Manliness and Morality: Middle-Class Masculinity in Britain and America, 1800–1940.* New York: St. Martin's P, 1987.

Mangan, J. A. and Callum McKenzie. 'The Other Side of the Coin: Victorian Masculinity, Field Sports and English Education.' *Making European Masculinities: Sport, Europe, Gender.* London: Frank Cass, 2000: 62–85.

Marsh, Jan. *Pre-Raphaelite Women: Images of Femininity.* New York: Harmony Books, 1988.

Marx, Karl. *Selected Writings in Sociology and Social Philosophy.* T. B. Bottomore, trans. London, McGraw-Hill, 1964.

Marx, Karl and Friedrich Engels. *The Manifesto of the Communist Party.* Edited by Frederic L. Bender. New York: Norton, 1988.

Masters, Joellen. *Bound by Duty: Women and Work in the Victorian Novel.* PhD: Boston University, 1996.

Matus, Jill L. *Unstable Bodies: Victorian Representations of Sexuality and Maternity.* Manchester: Manchester UP, 1995.

Mavor, Carol. *Pleasure Taken: Performances of Sexuality and Loss in Victorian Photographs.* Durham: Duke UP, 1995.

Mayhew, Henry. *London Labour and the London Poor.* Dover Publications, 1983.

Meakin, David. *Man and Work: Literature and Culture in Industrial Society.* New York: Holmes & Meier, 1976.

Mermin, Dorothy. 'The Damsel, the Knight, and the Victorian Woman Poet.' *Critical Inquiry.* 13 (1986–87): 64–80.

Michaux, Jean-Paul ed. *George Gissing: Critical Essays.* London: Vision and Barnes and Noble, 1981.

Michie, Helena. *The Flesh Made Word: Female Figures and Women's Bodies.* Oxford: Oxford UP, 1987.

Mill, John Stuart. 'The Negro Question' in *Collected Works of John Stuart Mill XXI.* John M. Robson, ed. Toronto: U of Toronto P, 1984: 8–96.

Miller, D. A. *The Novel and the Police.* Berkeley: U of California P, 1988.

Moers, Ellen. *The Dandy: Brummell To Beerbohm.* New York: Viking P, 1960.

Moi, Toril. *Sexual/Textual Politics: Feminist Literary Theory.* London: Routledge, 1985.

Morris, William. *News from Nowhere. The Collected Works of William Morris Volume XVI* New York: Russell & Russell, 1966. 3–211.

——. 'How We Live & How We Might Live.' *The Collected Works of William Morris XXVI* New York: Russell & Russell, 1966. 3–26.

——. 'Useful Work Versus Useful Toil.' In *The Collected Works of William Morris XXVI.* New York: Russell & Russell, 1966. 98–120.

Munby, Arthur. *Munby: A Man of Two Worlds.* Derek Hudson, ed. New York: Gamnit, 1972.

Nead, Lynda. *Myths of Sexuality: Representations of Women in Victorian Britain.* Oxford: Blackwell, 1988.

Nelson, Claudia. 'Sex and the Single Boy: Ideals of Manliness and Sexuality in Victorian Literature for Boys.' *Victorian Studies.* 32.4 (1989): 525–50.

——. *Boys Will Be Girls: The Feminine Ethic and British Children's Fiction, 185–71917* New Brunswick: Rutgers UP, 1991.

——. *Invisible Men: Fatherhood in Victorian Periodicals, 1850–1910.* Athens: U of Georgia P, 1995.

Newman, John Henry. *The Idea of a University.* Notre Dame: U of Notre Dame P, 1982.

Newman, Teresa and Ray Watkinson. *Ford Madox Brown and the Pre-Raphaelite Circle* London: Chatto & Windus, 1991.

Newsome, David. *Godliness and Good Learning.* London, Murray, 1961.

Noble, Jean Bobby. *Masculinities Without men?: Female Masculinity in Twentieth-Century Fictions* Vancouver: UBC P, 2003.

Oakley, Ann. *Woman's Work: The Housewife Past and Present.* New York: Pantheon Books, 1974.

Orwell, George. 'George Gissing.' *George Gissing: Critical Essays.* Jean-Pierre Michaux ed. London: Vision and Barnes and Noble, 1981: 195–203.

Onsby, John. 'Loose Men.' *Cornhill Magazine.* 39 (1879): 476–88.

Palmer, Phyllis. *Domesticity and Dirt: Housewives and Domestic Servants in the United States, 1920 – 1945.* Philadelphia: Temple UP, 1993.

Patmore, Coventry. *The Angel in the House.* London: John W. Parker, 1858.

Peck, John. 'Introduction.' *David Copperfield and Hard Times: New Casebooks.* London Macmillan, 1995. 1–30.

Pecheux, Michel. *Language, Semantics and Ideology.* New York: St. Martin's P, 1982.

Perkin, Harold. *The Rise of Professional Society: England Since 1880.* New York Routledge, 1989.

Poole, Adrian. *Gissing in Context.* Totowa, NJ: Rowman and Littlefield, 1975.

Poovey, Mary. *Uneven Developments: The Ideological Work of Gender in Mid-Victorian England.* London: Virago, 1989.

——. *Making a Social Body: British Cultural Formation 1830–1864* Chicago: U of Chicago P, 1995.

Purbrick, Louise. 'The Bourgeois Body: Civic Portraiture, Public Men and the Appearance of Class Power in Manchester, 1838–50.' *Gender, Civic Culture and Consumerism* Manchester: Manchester UP, 1999.

Prasch, Thomas. 'Photography and the Image of the London Poor.' *Victorian Urban Settings: Essays on the Nineteenth-Century City and its Contexts.* Debra N. Mancoff and D. J. Trela, eds. New York: Garland, 1996, 179–194.

Rabin, Lucy. *Ford Madox Brown and the Pre-Raphaelite History Picture.* New York Garland Press, 1978.

Rachwal, Tadeusz. *Labours of the Mind: Labour in the Culture of Production.* Frankfurt Peter Lang, 2001.

Redgrave, F. M. *Richard Redgrave: A Memoir Compiled from his Diary.* London: Cassell Company, 1891.

Richards, Thomas. *The Commodity Culture of Victorian England: Advertising a*

Shelley, Percy Bysshe. *Poetical Works*. Ed. Thomas Hutchinson. Oxford: Oxford UP, 1970.

Silverman, Kaja. *Male Subjectivity at the Margins*. New York: Routledge, 1992.

Sims, George Robert. *How the Poor Live*. London: Chatto, 1883.

Skoblow, Jeffrey. *Paradise Dislocated: Morris, Politics, Art*. Charlottesville: U of Virginia P, 1993.

Spear, Jeffrey L. *Dreams of an English Eden: Ruskin and his Tradition in Social Criticism*. New York: Columbia UP, 1984.

Spector, Stephen. 'Monsters of Metonymy: *Hard Times* and Knowing the Working Class.' *ELH* 51:2 (Summer, 1984): 36 –384.

Spengemann, William C. *The Forms of Autobiography: Episodes in the History of a Literary Genre*. New Haven: Yale UP, 1980.

Stallybrass, Peter and Allon White. *The Politics and Poetics of Transgression*. Ithaca: Cornell UP, 1986.

Stamp, Gavin. *The Changing Metropolis: Earliest Photographs of London, 1839 – 1879*. Harmondsworth: Penguin Books, 1984.

Stanley, Liz ed. *The Diaries of Hannah Cullwick, Victorian Maidservant*. New Brunswick, NJ: Rutgers UP, 1984.

Stearns, Peter N. *Be A Man! Males in Modern Society*. New York: Holmes & Meier, 1979.

Stocking, George. *Victorian Anthropology*. New York: Free Press, 1987.

Stoddart, Judith. *Ruskin's Culture Wars: Fors Clavigera and the Crisis of Victorian Liberalism*. Charlottesville: U of Virginia P, 1998.

Stoltenberg, John. *Refusing to be a Man: Essays on Sex and Justice*. Portland, OR: Breitenbush Books, 1989.

Street, Brian. 'British Popular Anthropology: Exhibiting and Photographing the Other.' in Elizabeth Edwards (ed.) *Anthropology and Photography 1860 –1920* New Haven: Yale UP, 1992.

Surtees, V. ed. *The Diary of Ford Madox Brown*. New Haven: Yale UP, 1981.

Sussman, Herbert. *Victorian Masculinities: Manhood and Masculine Poetics in Early Victorian Literature and Art*. Cambridge: Cambridge UP, 1995.

Swindells, Julia. *Victorian Writing and Working Women*. Minneapolis: U of Minnesota P, 1985.

Taylor, Frederick Winslow. *The Principles of Scientific Management*. New York: Norton, 1967.

Thompson, E. P. *The Making of the English Working Class*. Harmondsworth: Penguin Books, 1980.

——. 'Time, Work-Discipline and Industrial Capitalism' in *Customs in Common*. New York: New Press, 1991: 352–403.

Thompson, F. M. L. *The Rise of Respectable Society: a Social History of Victorian Britain, 1830–1900* Cambridge: Harvard UP, 1988.

Tosh, John. *A Man's Place: Masculinity and the Middle-Class Home in Victorian England*. New Haven: Yale UP, 1999.

Trevor, William. 'Middlemen.' Jean-Pierre Michaux, ed. *George Gissing: Critical Essays* 129–130. London: Vision & Barnes and Noble, 1981.

Treuherz, Julian. *Hard Times: Social Realism in Victorian Art*. London: Lund Humphreys, in association with the Manchester City Art Galleries, 1987.

Trodd, Colin. 'The Laboured Vision and the Realm of Value: Articulation of Identity in Ford Madox Brown's *Work.*' *Re-Framing the Pre-Raphaelites: Historical and Theoretical Essays*. Ellen Harding ed. Aldershot: Scolar Press, 1996: 61–80.

Ulrich, John M. *Signs of Their Times: History, Labor and the Body in Cobbett, Carlyle and Disraeli*. Athens, OH: Ohio UP, 2002.

Usherwood, Paul. 'William Bell Scott's *Iron and Coal*: Northern Readings.' *Pre-Raphaelites: Painters and Patrons in the North East*. Tyne and Wear Museum Services and Hindson Print: Newcastle upon Tyne, 1989: 39–56.

Vance, Norman. *Sinews of the Spirit: The Ideal of Christian Manliness in Victorian Literature and Religious Thought*. Cambridge: Cambridge UP, 1985.

Vanden Bossche, Chris. 'Cookery not Rookery: Family and Class in *David Copperfield.*' *Dickens Studies Annual* 15 (1986): 87–109.

Waters, Karen Volland. *The Perfect Gentleman: Masculine Control in Victorian Men's Fiction, 1870–1901*. New York: Peter Lang, 1997.

Weber, Max. *The Protestant Ethic and the Spirit of Capitalism*. Translated by Talcott Parsons. New York: Scribner, 1958.

White, William Hale. *The Autobiography of Mark Rutherford; Mark Rutherford's Deliverance*. New York: Garland, 1976.

Wiener, Martin J. *English Culture and the Decline of the Industrial Spirit 1850–1980*. Cambridge: Cambridge UP, 1981.

Weltman, Sharon Aronofsky. 'Female and Maelstrom: The Gender Vortex in Carlyle and Ruskin.' *Carlyle Studies Annual* 17 (1997): 91–99.

Wilde, Oscar. 'The Soul of Man Under Socialism.' *The Complete Works of Oscar Wilde Volume X*. Garden City, NY: Doubleday, Page, 1923: 1–68.

Williams, Raymond. *Culture and Society. 1780–1950*. London: Chatto & Windus, 1967 [1958].

——. *The Country and the City*. New York: Oxford UP, 1973.

——. *Marxism and Literature*. New York: Oxford UP, 1977.

Wolfreys, Julian and Ruth Robbins. eds. *Victorian Identities: Social and Cultural Formations in Nineteenth-Century Literature*. New York: St. Martin's, 1996.

Young, Arlene. *Culture, Class and Gender in the Victorian Novel: Gentlemen, Gents and Working Women*. New York: St. Martin's, 1999.

# Index

clerical work *see* labor, clerical
clerk *see* labor, clerical
Coetzee, J. M. 46
Cohen, Michele 46
Cohen, William A. 123
commodification 33–5, 145–6, 155–6
commodity fetishism 54, 140, 162
Connell, R. W. 2, 612, 18, 20, 111, 157
Cope, Charles West 61–2
Cross, Nigel 149
Crowe, Eyre 65
Cullwick, Hannah 14, 79, 81, 105–124
cultural capital 10, 101, 145, 152, 161
Culture, definition of 9–12
Curtis, Gerard 89, 91, 99
Curtis, Liz 29

Danahay, Martin A. 11–12, 20, 85, 104, 124
dandy 19, 45–6, 99
Danon, Ruth 14, 20, 85
David, Deirdre 41, 97
Davidoff, Leonore 77–8, 94, 106, 112, 122–3,
Davidson, Caroline 80, 86
Dawkins, Heather 113, 123
demasculinization 42, 80, 122, 141, 144, 153, 160–1
Dickens, Charles 14, 64, 67–86, 89, 94, 100, 123
digging *see* labor, digging
Dollimore, Jonathan 108, 123
Donkin, Richard 20, 35, 39
Donzelot, Jacques 83
Dowling, Andrew 41, 103, 143, 152, 155–6
Downs, David 129, 132
Drucker, Peter F. 142
Dupré, John 46

Dury, Richard 109, 123
duty, *see* labor, as duty

Edelstein, T. J. 52–3
Elias, Norbert 8
Engels, Friedrich 26, 33–42, 44, 46, 50, 141

feminism and masculinity studies 2, 18, 110
Ferry Hincksey 10, 32, 35, 91, 125, 127, 129–32, 134–38, 140,
fetish 105–8, 111–5, 121, 123, 148
fire as symbol of sexuality 67, 70–1, 84
flower seller 96–99
Foucault, Michel 40
Friedson, Eliot 102

Gagnier, Regenia 5, 18, 46
Gallagher, Caherine 65, 71, 116
Garber, Marjorie 123
Gardner, Judith Kegan 18
Gaskell, Elizabeth 8, 37, 56, 72, 85
gentleman 11, 15, 18–19, 28, 31–2, 87, 91–2, 96, 103, 145, 150, 152, 154, 158–9
Gikandi, Simon 46
Gill, Stephen 8, 19
Girouard, Mark 19
Gissing, George 7, 9, 24, 141, 143–162
Gleyse, Jacques 138, 141
God 7–8, 19, 21, 24–5, 27–8, 32–3, 39, 72, 88
Goode, John 143, 146, 155–6
Gospel of Work, the 23–47
governess 50–1, 54, 64, 68, 94, 96, 159
Gramsci, Antonio 6
Graver, Suzanne 74
Grossmith, George 147
Grosz, Elizabeth 124